FRENCH PAINTING

THE IMPRESSIONIST
PAINTERS

Library of Congress Catalog Card Number 60-12416

© PIERRE TISNÉ ÉDITEUR, PARIS, 1960

PRINTED IN FRANCE

MAURICE SERULLAZ

FRENCH PAINTING

THE IMPRESSIONIST PAINTERS

Translated by
W. J. STRACHAN

UNIVERSE BOOKS INC., NEW YORK
PIERRE TISNÉ, ÉDITEUR - PARIS

Impressionism
Origins and Definition

According to tradition the term Impressionism was invented by a minor journalist Louis Leroy. In an article in *Charivari*, dated April 25, 1874, he used the heading *Exhibition of the Impressionists* for his account of the combined exhibition of the Cooperative Society of Painters, Sculptors and Engravers which was held on the premises of the photographer Nadar, 35 Boulevard des Capucines, from April 15 to May 15, 1874. The picture by Claude Monet, described thus in the catalog : *Impression, Sunrise*, had suggested the term to him. Why this title ? Edmond Renoir, brother of the painter and responsible for the catalog, had criticized the titles Monet had given his paintings for their monotony. " Put impression ! " [1] was the painter's retort. Monet subsequently corroborated the fact that for a painting executed at Le Havre from his window evoking the sun in a misty light in which the ships' masts were enveloped he decided that " that couldn't pass for a view of Le Havre, " and, when asked for the title, replied : " Put Impression. " [2]

Louis Leroy employed the word " Impressionists " in his derision for painters who expressed themselves in blobs of color and appeared to neglect form for visual impression.

The fact is historically correct, but if we refer to the interesting descriptions provided by M. Louis Dimier [3] it was not, it seems, the first time that the term had been used to designate this new manner of painting.

" Everybody knows, " he writes, " the *Souvenirs* which Antonin Proust published on Manet in the *Revue Blanche*. They were printed in 1913 by the publishers Laurens, and it was in that form that I first met them. As the original articles bound up by a meticulous art lover have recently come into my hands, I have been able to study the original text, frequently modified in the volume by M. Barthélemy who published it, in conformity, he maintains, with notes provided by Proust himself. You can imagine my surprise and satisfaction on finding (page 925) the following passage which had been omitted from the volume : ' The expression *Impressionism* arose ' not as M. Bénédite has written, from a picture by Claude Monet

5

exhibited under the title *Impression*, but out of our discussions in the year 1858. '
A commentary follows which gives the definition of ' spontaneity ' to the word.
But that is not the point here.   I am not quoting Proust as evidence of the sense of
the term but of the date.   The meaning is the fruit of his reflections, the date that
of his memory.   By 1858 the terms Impression, Impressionist, were being used by
Manet and his friends to describe his way of painting. "

The reader will recall further that Corot used the word to define his conception
of painting.   " The beautiful in art is truth bathed in the *impression* we have received
when confronting nature... " [4]   And again, " ... we must never lose the first *impression*
which has moved us... " [5]

And in the course of a conversation with Robaut, May 9, 1870 [6], Corot remarked
" It is so good to see the sun.   There is something which never deserves our reproaches.   I adore its light; I have done everything I could to render it and communicate to others the *impression* of it that I myself have experienced... "

And did not Delacroix say, notes Baudelaire, " Since I consider the *impression* conveyed to the artist by nature as the most important thing to interpret,
should not the artist be forearmed with all the most rapid means for such an interpretation ? "

How are we to define impression?   It is " the effect produced to a greater
or lesser degree by the action of exterior objects on the organs of the senses. "   As
Bossuet [7] long ago asserted, " The perception of colors, sounds, good and unpleasant
smells, warmth, cold, hunger and thirst, pleasure and sorrow follows the effects of
the *impression* which perceptible objects make on our physical organs. "   And
again, " In every sensation there is a contact and a real and material *impression*
on our organs which comes either directly or originally from the object. "

And later Buffon discovers that " All the senses possess the power of preserving the *impressions* of exterior causes to a greater or lesser extent; but the *eye*
has this power more than the other senses. " [8]

As for *Impressionism* it is " the system of painting which consists in rendering in its pure simplicity the impression materially experienced, " the impressionist artist being " the painter who aims at representing objects according to
his personal impressions, without any concern for generally accepted rules. "

IMPRESSIONIST VISION : THE SUBJECT

IT is immediately obvious that impressionist painting is not intellectual; we are
a long way from Leonardo da Vinci's *la pittura è cosa mentale*.   The painter no longer
represents what his intelligence knows nor what his training has taught him
but what his marveling *vision* perceives as light in the flash of a moment.   It
was in fact light and its infinite variations which were to be the real subject of the
picture.   The Impressionists gave up painting religious, mythological, historical

and genre subjects and concerned themselves almost exclusively with landscape that sometimes contained figures, sometimes not. Painting abandoned narration for evocation.

Landscape painters were no longer content to open a window onto Nature, they were to paint exclusively " in the open air directly from life. " This method was not entirely novel, since Corot and Daubigny in particular had practiced it on occasion. But the Impressionists were to make it one of the principles of their art and quit studio painting altogether in favor of landscape. They completed the canvas they had begun on the original site, and the result was more in the nature of a sketch than a finished picture.

This direct and continuous contemplation of the subject throughout the execution of the picture allowed them to bring nature to life on the canvas. " The whole surface of the picture shines in the sun; the air circulates in it; light envelops, caresses, permeates the forms, penetrates everywhere, even among the shadows which it illuminates. " [9]

The favorite themes were to be the sea and its vast, changing horizons, the sky and its shifting clouds, the sun and its shimmering rays, the wind or breeze as it wrinkles the surface of the water, gently stirs the foliage and sends a quiver through the grass in the meadows. If the sea is their first great source of inspiration, since it is the liquid element that claims their particular attention, they are also attracted by the river with its mirrored reflections. Nevertheless they do not neglect the fields, gardens, houses, villages, nor the road that leads there—in short, the whole world of nature.

The town also exercises its fascination over them, Paris particularly. The street in which shadowy figures and carriages move like so many bright splashes of color; public gardens, the ponds and fountains in them; the Seine and the mirror of its muddy waters, its morning mists; the buildings which the light fashions at the caprice of the river's glistening reflections.

This predilection for the fugitive, the evanescent, was to induce the Impressionists to record the effects of smoke as it curls upwards and lightly dissolves in the air, or the fog, engulfing every object, robbing it, apparently, of all its substance, melting the forms of reality in order to create the poetry of the vague and mysterious.

They were fond, too, of painting after rain—reflections on shining roads, mirror-like pools, wet earth; the atmosphere which Claude Debussy was to recreate later in sound in his *Jardins sous la Pluie*.

Finally, snow and its whiteness colored with a nacreous iridescence captivate the hypersensitive retina of the impressionist eye.

Thirst for the transitory, the ephemeral, expressed in its subtlest terms was to lead these painters to treat certain subjects in " series. " Not content with expressing the most fleeting elements they endeavored to evoke the many transformations undergone by a particular place or building from one moment to the next, according to the time of day and as affected by the perpetually varied and shifting light. These series—a later development—were to be the fruits of a deliberate and systematic observation, an intellectual analysis. They have lost the spontaneity of earlier Impressionist works.

7

CLAUDE MONET — IMPRESSION, SUNRISE. 1872 (19 × 25 ") — MUSÉE MARMOTTAN, PARIS

HOW THE IMPRESSIONISTS
RENDERED THEIR VISION : TECHNIQUE

INSTEAD of representing forms as they exist in their defined and unchangeable structure, the Impressionists were to reveal them as they *appeared* to them at a given moment. Light with its complementary shadow does in fact eat into the true form of objects, the architecture of buildings, the configuration of the soil, and modifies colors according to its intensity.

Before it was a manner of painting, Impressionism was first and foremost a way of seeing. And it was that magic of light conveyed by the magic of color which became the sole preoccupation of these artists. They solved it by liberating themselves from previous formulas.

No more drawn contour clearly defining the individuality of each form and enclosing the latter within arbitrary lines intended to suggest volume.

No more modeling by values—another method of expressing the density of objects : luminous intensity in fact abolishes contours, dissolves forms in the atmosphere and makes them indistinct. Vibrant blobs of color alone are to bring to life on the canvas what the painter sees.

No more chiaroscuro with its violent contrasts which fail to render the subtleties that exist in reality, since light colors shadows—which are never black—and mingles its reflections with them.

No more perspective determined by strict composition according to the rules of geometry. Henceforward it is to be created almost entirely by the abolition of the traditional brown or raw sienna foreground and replaced by a pure and luminous tone, blue or green for example, and the gradation of tints, tones and touches of color from foreground to skyline.

Since the words " tint " and " tone " are employed interchangeably in general use, let us follow Paul Signac's clarification. He defines " tint " as the quality of a color (all the range of blues—cobalt, ultramarine, Prussian blue, etc.; greens—viridine, emerald green, Hookers green, etc.; reds—cadmium, vermilion, carmine, etc.) and " tone " as the degree of saturation or luminosity of a tint, progressively from dark to light. A primary or secondary color as it moves towards another, passes through a series of intermediary tints, and each one of these tints on its progress towards light or dark passes through a succession of tones.

Banished now is the oft-repeated cliché, " light robs tints of their color. " In reality it is darkness which robs them, reducing them all to one, namely black. Take away the source of light in fact and there are no colors. Light gives them life, but it also greatly modifies them according to its intensity. A white milestone in

ÉDOUARD MANET — BOULOGNE HARBOR. 1869 (32 × 40 ") — LOUVRE, PARIS

a strong light appears a deep ultramarine, a sheaf of corn may in certain lights become pink, blue-gray or deep violet. Particularly in Monet's paintings the green grass is sometimes pink, blue or violet. The Impressionists paint the colors they see, not those which they know belong to this or that object by definition.

They simplify their palette by excluding black, grays, browns, the earth-colors, ochres, and make exclusive use of pure colors—those associated with the spectrum such as yellows, orange, vermilions, lakes, cadmiums, reds, indigos, blues, intense greens such as emerald green and viridine.

In what way are they going to use these colors? They do not mix them on their palette but juxtapose them on the canvas. There is no doubt that it was their study of the phenomena of refraction in perpetually moving water which led them instinctively to that characteristic division of tones. The reflected forms are in point of fact broken and fragmented. In order to convey them, the area is first broken up into juxtaposed blobs of color; then it is broken up until it becomes a vibrating patchwork of innumerable dots. Water acts on the luminous reflection like a prism and breaks it up into its basic colors. The Impressionists therefore, except in their early works, paint it by means of a series of broken touches of pure color. A green reflection was rendered by dabs of blue and yellow, the *optical mixture* of which would recompose a green to the spectator's eye, that is, an optical mixture as opposed to a *mixture of pigments* or coloring matter carried out on the palette.

It is a technique that the Impressionists were not only to apply to what is reflected in water but to all the solid elements in the country landscape, each painted as if it were a reflection.

Their purely visual observations are in agreement with the scientific discoveries of Chevreul (1839), Helmholtz (1878), O.N. Rood (1881). Light is composed of the sum total of seven colors which make up the solar spectrum—violet, indigo, blue, green, yellow, orange, red (indigo being a shade of blue, there are in fact only six colors).

Three of these we call primary, basic or fundamental colors, namely blue, red and yellow. Three are secondary or mixed, that is green, violet and orange, which are mixtures of two primary colors and the complementary of the third. The mixture blue + yellow produces green, the complementary of red; the mixture blue + red produces violet, the complementary of yellow; the mixture red + yellow produces orange, the complementary of blue.

A very simple diagram which Eugène Delacroix had already used provides a very clear summary of this theory (see plate, inset p. 12).

Each color tends to suffuse the surrounding space with complementary color: a red area will be surrounded with a green aura—its complementary. The shadow, therefore, is always slightly tinged with the complementary—a red object will have its shadow tinged with green; a blue object with orange.

According to Chevreul's theory which the Neo-Impressionists faithfully followed, every color has a corresponding shadow. For a yellow-green for example it would be purplish and not red.

10

By the law of simultaneous contrast, formulated by Chevreul, two complementaries (green and red for instance) or two secondary complementaries (violet and green) are enhanced when juxtaposed and become brighter ; whereas these same colors mixed in pigment form cancel each other out and kill the color.

The complementary of each juxtaposed color is added to the other color. In the case of the two complementaries green and red, the green complementary of the red is added to the green and the red complementary of the green is likewise added to the red. In the case of two secondary complementaries, violet and green, for example, the red, complementary of the green, is added to the violet which becomes redder, and the yellow, complementary of the violet, will be added to the green which will become yellower. The violet and green which contain blue will appear less blue. In fact the intensity of the color shared by two colors is diminished when they are juxtaposed.

However, and this is one of their great qualities, the Impressionists were incapable of applying a theory, since the essential point of their art is to paint instinctively " as birds sing, " that is spontaneously and with all possible speed so as to render whatever is most fugitive in nature. They practically never followed out their theories in a logical fashion. If it has been said that Claude Monet " was only an eye, but great heavens, what an eye ! " it has also been said that Impressionism was a vast eye, capable of capturing the subtlest nuances and values but incapable of taking it a stage further and realizing the synthesis between that eye and the intellect. Its fervent masters do not work out logically or scientifically the effects they desired to evoke; they put down their blobs of color as rapidly as they perceived them. There was no methodical application of this kind of vision such as the Neo-Impressionists were to make of it later on. The Impressionists observe one but neglect another phenomenon in their pictures. Signac [10] pointed out this indifference to the scientific problems of color :

" Perhaps an example will show how deceptive undisciplined sensation can be. Imagine the Impressionist painting a landscape directly from nature; before him he has grass or green foliage, some parts of which are in the sun, some in shadow. In the green of the shadowed areas nearest the spaces of light, the painter's keen eye is aware of a sensation of red. Satisfied that he has noticed this coloration, the Impressionist hurriedly places a dab of red on his canvas. But in his eagerness to fix his sensation he hardly has time to control the accuracy of this red which, somewhat at the caprice of the brush, will be expressed as an orange-red, a vermilion, lake or even violet. Yet it was in fact a very definite red, subordinated to the color of the green and not just any red. If the Impressionist had been familiar with the law : *the shadow is always slightly tinted with the complementary of the light color*, it would have been as easy for him to put a touch of the exact red, purplish-red for a yellow-green, orange-red for a blue-green, as the red he happened to choose. "

Nevertheless we cannot entirely endorse Signac's opinion when he adds : " It is difficult to understand how scientific knowledge could have spoiled the artist's improvisation in this connection. On the contrary we see very clearly the advantages of a method which prevents such dissonances since, trivial though these may be, they no more enhance the beauty of a picture than faults of harmony that of a musical score. "

11

Did not Renoir say, " You stand in front of nature full of theories; nature knocks them all down. Theories don't make a good picture, they mostly serve to cover up deficiencies in the means of expression. " And also, " I am always bewildered when young painters approach me and question me about the aims of painting. Some explain to me the reasons which cause me to put red or blue on this or that spot on my canvas. Obviously we pursue a difficult and complicated profession, and I can appreciate all these anxieties. But all the same a touch of simplicity and candor is indispensable. "

Let us take two examples, two landscapes, one by Seurat, *Port-en-Bessin, Outer Harbor at High Tide* (The Impressionist Museum, Jeu de Paume, Paris); the other by Pissarro, *Woman in a Garden* (Jeu de Paume, Paris). The first was painted in 1888, the second in 1887, at the period when Pissarro took up with the Neo-Impressionists without applying their theories methodically. Pissarro's canvas appears infinitely more luminous and more colored, more " intense " than Seurat's; it gives an " impression " of life; one is aware of the vibration of the light, the glitter of the reflections and also of the warmth of the atmosphere. All the pantheistic instinct is there, the sensual side of " mother Earth. " Seurat's picture, on the other hand, is certainly a better composition; the harmony and rhythm are more in evidence; but everything is crystalized, frozen, everything belongs to the realm of the intellect, pure science, nothing is natural.

Signac makes this further point [11], " In one and the same Impressionist picture, one part will be illuminated by a red suffusion, another by a yellow, as if it could be two o'clock and five o'clock in the afternoon simultaneously. " But is not this fantasy one of the virtues of Impressionism ? Codified, it seems to lose any justification for its existence.

Nothing sums up Impressionist vision and technique more aptly than these lines of Jules Laforgue in his *Mélanges posthumes* of 1903, entitled *Critique d'Art —L'Impressionnisme.*

" Physiological origin of Impressionism.—Prejudice about drawing. Admitting that if the pictorial work emanates from the intellect and heart, it does so only through the medium of the eye and that the function of the eye is that of the ear in music, the Impressionist is a modernist painter who, endowed with an unusual sensibility of the eye, forgetting all the pictures that have accumulated during the centuries, forgetting the optical education of the art school (drawing, perspective, color problems) simply by living and using his eyes frankly and primitively among the luminous sights of nature in the open air, that is outside the studio with its 45° lighting, whether in the street, country, interiors, has succeeded in restoring a natural eye, in seeing naturally and painting naively what he sees. " (pp. 133-134).

" The Academic eye and the Impressionist eye.—Polyphony of colors.— In a landscape bathed in light in which the figures are modeled like tinted grisailles the academic painter will only see white light spread over the whole, whereas the Impressionist sees it suffusing everything not with dead white light but a thousand vibrant battles, rich prismatic decompositions. Where the academic eye merely sees the contour line enclosing the modeling, he sees the true, living lines, in which all geometric form is absent, built up of hundreds of irregular touches, which seen

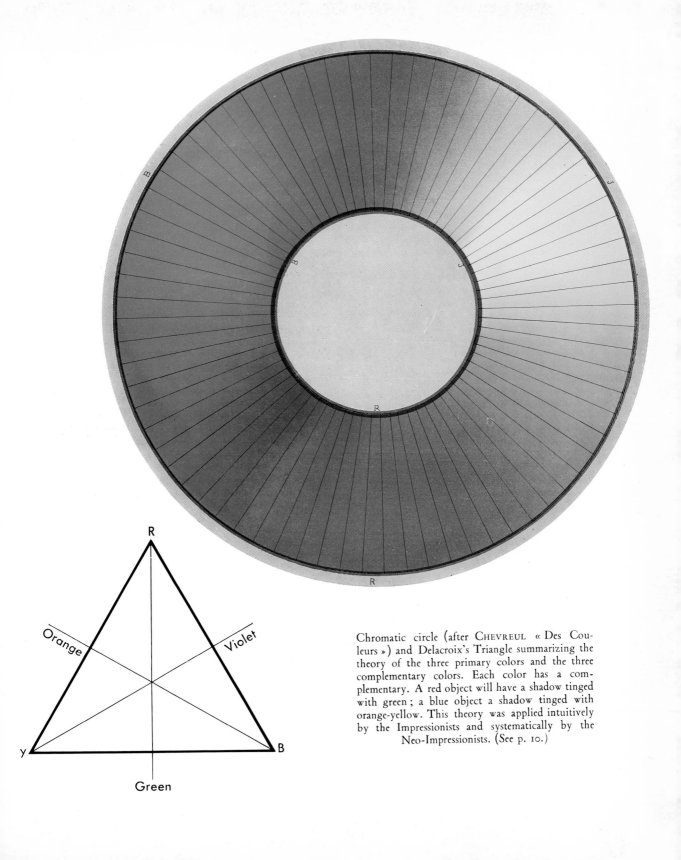

Chromatic circle (after CHEVREUL « Des Couleurs ») and Delacroix's Triangle summarizing the theory of the three primary colors and the three complementary colors. Each color has a complementary. A red object will have a shadow tinged with green; a blue object a shadow tinged with orange-yellow. This theory was applied intuitively by the Impressionists and systematically by the Neo-Impressionists. (See p. 10.)

VELAZQUEZ - LAS MENINAS - DETAIL - PRADO, MADRID

RENOIR - LA LOGE - DETAIL
COURTAULD COLLECTION, LONDON

RENOIR
AND
VELAZQUEZ

Photos Giraudon

CÉZANNE
AND
POUSSIN

CÉZANNE - LA MON-
TAGNE SAINTE - VIC-
TOIRE - COURTAULD
COLLECTION, LONDON

POUSSIN (ASCRIBED
TO) - THE FUNERAL
OF PHOCION - LOUVRE,
PARIS

Photos Giraudon

Broken touch : THE REGATTA AT ARGEN-TEUIL. 1873.

EVOLUTION OF THE

BRUSH STROKE

IN MONET

Commas of color : WOMAN WITH THE SUNSHADE. 1886.

Blended touch : HOUSES OF PARLIAMENT. 1904.

from a distance compose the life of the picture. Where the academic painter sees objects taking their place in their regular respective planes in accordance with a framework reducible to a pure theoretic drawing, the Impressionist sees perspective made up by the innumerable details of tone and touch, the various atmospheric states which are not fixed but in continual movement.

" In short, the Impressionist eye is the most advanced eye in human evolution, the one which up to the present has seized and represented the most complex known combinations of nuances.

" The Impressionist sees and renders nature as it is, that is to say, solely as a series of colored vibrations. No drawing, light, modeling, perspective, chiaroscuro— those childish classifications: all these are resolved in the real world in colored vibrations and should be rendered on the canvas solely in colored vibrations. " (pp. 136-137.)

PAINTING, LITERATURE AND MUSIC

T HE INTERPENETRATION of the arts seems from this point to be bound up with the interpenetration of the sensations experienced by the artist, whatever the realm to which he belongs : the poet or the musician " paints " what he feels and the painter " evokes " the poetry and music of things by means of light and color.

What a far cry to Cartesian classicism! The defense of knowledge is replaced by the defense of sensation. " I think, therefore I am " has now little attraction or meaning for creative artists; one can apply André Gide's " I feel, therefore I am " *(Les Nourritures terrestres,* 1897) to their exacerbated egoism. This exaggerated analysis of the fugitive moment in sensory contact with nature stimulates the exceptionally intense perception of the artists of this period in which the tempo of life is beginning to quicken. The age of reflection is past; each experienced phenomenon is immediately translated into " the impression of the moment, " in its evanescence. Let us note further that the painters forestalled the musicians and poets on this road.

Did not Baudelaire, the precursor, anticipate these " correspondances " *(Les Fleurs du Mal)* which were to spring to life in the poet's pen, the musician's fingers, the painter's brush ?

> *Vast as the night and like an effulgence,*
> *Perfumes, colors and sounds echo each other.*
> *Perfumes there are as fresh as a child's skin,*
> *As sweet as oboes, as green as the fields...*

René Huyghe, tackling these problems in an article entitled *Impressionism and the Thought of its time* [12], shows how literature and music obey the same imperatives; before the coming of the Symbolists had anyone ever been so enamored of wells and pools, delicate fountains dying in the basins? Melisand's ring is lost in the " depth of the waters " and " leaves behind only a circle of ripples on the surface " (" Was it by a fountain's edge that he found you ? ").

Henri de Régnier *(Les Médailles d'argile)* remembers, above all, things that have no weight or form.

> *The scent of the roses we have smelled,*
> *The water, the wind,*
> *The forest, the sea...*

Would it not almost appear that Verlaine was thinking of the music Gabriel Fauré was to compose for his poem when he wrote his *Art poétique* in 1884?

> *Music above all*
> *And prefer the irregular measure,*
> *Vaguer and more soluble in the air,*
> *With nothing posed or poised upon it...*
> *The Nuance is what we desire,*
> *Not color, just the nuance;*

Is not this subtlety of the nuance the characteristic of the Impressionist painters' vision? As for light, which is the very essence of painting at this time, this is what André Gide has to say about it, " What cheered me that day... Shall I write and will you understand me if I tell you that it was the simple rapture of light? I was sitting in this garden; I could not see the sun, but the air shone with a diffused light as if the blue of the sky was *liquified* and raining down. Yes, really and truly, there were *waves, eddies of light;* sparkles like raindrops on the moss; yes, indeed, you would have said that *the light flowed* down that great avenue, and golden foam hung on the tips of the branches in *those streaming rays.* " *(Les Nourritures terrestres.)*

It is however Marcel Proust more than anyone else who seems to personify Impressionism. In *Pleasures and Days* (1896), Study No. 1 entitled *Tuileries (Regrets, Reveries of the Past)* is sketched out like a canvas by Claude Monet who himself painted several " impressions " of the Tuileries : " In the Tuileries gardens this morning, the sun has slept by turns on each of the stone steps like a fair haired boy whose light slumber is immediately interrupted by a passing cloud... The breath of the charmed wind mingles the fresh smell of the lilac with the fragrance of the past... Iridescent in the sunlight and sighing with love, the fountains rise towards the sky... But the sky has darkened, it is going to rain. " These rapid changes in light and weather are precisely what the painters were trying to capture.

And further on, in Study No. XIX, entitled *Sea Breeze in the Country,* Proust again shows his affinities with Monet and his circle, " In the garden, in the little wood, over the countryside, the wind displays its mad and futile zest, dispersing bursts of sunshine, chasing them, and at the same time shaking in fury the branches in the copse where they had first alighted, and as far as the sparkling thicket where they now vibrate and shudder... This helter-skelter of wind and light makes this corner of Champagne resemble a landscape by the seaside. Having arrived at the top of this road which, burnt by light and buffeted by the wind, rises in full sun towards a empty sky, surely it is the sea that we are about to glimpse, white with sunshine and foam ?... "

14

Proust was to go further, since he identifies his character Elstir in the series of volumes entitled *Remembrance of Things Past* with Claude Monet, that is to say with the leader of the Impressionist School. " But I was able to discern that the charm in each one (of Elstir's works) consisted in a sort of metamorphosis of things represented, analogous to that which in poetry we call ' metaphor ' and that if God the Father had created things by naming them, it was by taking away their names and giving them another that Elstir recreated them... But it was of those rare moments when we see nature as it is, poetically, that Elstir's work was made. One of the most frequent metaphors in the seascapes that he had by him at the present moment was precisely that which, comparing the land to the sea, suppressed any line of demarcation between them. It was this comparison, tacitly and tirelessly repeated in a single canvas, that gave it its manifold and powerful unity... "

And Proust succeeded in defining the very essence of Impressionism... " Surfaces and volumes are in reality independent of the names of objects which our memory imposes on them when we have recognized them... Elstir endeavored to extract what he knew from what he had just felt. His effort had often been aimed at dissolving the sum total of reasoning that we call vision. "

Claude Debussy palpably practiced the same language in the realm of music. Emile Vuillermoz, defining his style, notes that he " rehabilitated the nobility of sensation... he abandoned the solid, respectable ground where emotions were concerned for the phantasmagoria of reflections, fluidities, shimmering iridescence, phosphorescence, quivering surfaces. "

The Academy's strictures when Debussy sent his composition *Le Printemps* from Rome in 1887 are well known. The composer was warned against " this vague impressionism which is one of the most dangerous enemies of truth in works of art. "

And among the reproaches leveled at the musician later we find elements of the criticisms formulated against the Impressionist painters, " lack of form, fluid, blurred, amorphous art. Monotony, formulas, techniques. No rhythm, strength, or human values. No melodic line... Impressionism—descriptive music in which precise form is entirely absent. "

Paul le Flem [13] analyzes musical impressionism thus, " This imprecise term above all is the name of a movement, a musical reaction inaugurated by Debussy, although this composer rejected this definition and held the term in horror. At the turn of the century people were looking for analogies between the blobs of color of the Impressionist painters and the fugitive nuances, sonorous audacities that Debussy unleashed. Musical Impressionism can be defined as a ' reaction against Wagnerism; break with Neo-Classicism and the traditional forms of pure music; absolute freedom with regard to classical tonality, even the negation of the latter... recognition of the supremacy of chords and greater freedom in their sequences; much more distant relationship between notions of consonance and dissonance; prestige of harmony and devaluation of contrapuntal composition; pursuit of pure sound, permissible as the composer's chief aim. ' Like painting in conflict with the Academic tradition, like Symbolism rejecting the Parnassians [13b], musical Impressionism preferred suggestion to expression and this art of suggestion, inimical to opacity, made transparency its aim. "

Debussy tried to " paint in music " what he saw as much as what he heard;

he made this note in the *Revue Blanche* (July 1, 1901), " It is more rewarding to see the dawn than to hear the *Pastoral Symphony*. You are floundering because all you know is music... "

All through his career the titles of his compositions suggest things that Claude Monet and his friends were eager to express in paint : *The Fountain* (after Baudelaire, 1890), *Clouds* (Nocturnes, 1898), *Sketches, Gardens in the Rain* (Estampes, 1903), *The Sea (From Dawn to Noon on the Sea, Waves at Play, Dialogue between the Wind and the Sea, 1905), Reflections in the Water* (Images, 1905-1907), *Steps on the Snow, What the West Wind Saw, Sails, The Wind over the Plain, Sounds and Perfumes rise in the Evening Air* (after Baudelaire), *The Submerged Cathedral* (Préludes, Book No. 1, 1910), *Mists, Dead Leaves, Heath, Ondine, Fireworks* (Préludes, Book No. 2, 1913), etc.

Let us add that when in 1894 Stéphane Mallarmé first heard Debussy's *Prélude à l'Après-midi d'un Faune*, before its public performance, he said to the composer, " I didn't expect anything like that! This music prolongs the emotion of my poem and situates its setting—*more intense than color.* "

Furthermore did not Gabriel Fauré often compose music that flows so smoothly that the rhythm is scarcely perceptible? Up to his death he remained faithful to that refined, delicate impressionism in which, as in Debussy, the sea, waves, clouds and winds are evoked with ineffable poetry; his *Horizon chimérique* (1922) on the poem of Jean de La Ville de Mirmont bears witness to this :

> *The sea is infinite and my dreams are mad...*
> *The sea sings in the sun as it pounds the cliffs.*
>
> . . . .
>
> *The supple waves have taught me other cadences*
> *Lovelier than the tired rhythm of human songs...*

And do we not find among his melodies titles such as *By the Water's Edge, The Walled Garden, Mirage,* whose aims are so close to those of the painters ?

THE IMPRESSIONIST AESTHETIC

IN THE HISTORY OF PAINTING

W E HAVE defined Impressionism as a period in the history of art that covers the second half of the nineteenth century in France but, as we consider it possible to state and prove, we can also see it as a constant in pictorial evolution, an aesthetic to be found in various periods and countries. Two main problems form the basis of this aesthetic—the problem of light, and that of technique.

The evocation of light, conceived in terms of values, is above all a subtle evocation of atmosphere and differs fundamentally, for example, from the contrasted luminism of Caravaggio and the *Tenebrosi.*

As for technique, it consists in expressing the visual impression of the painter in love with life and its animation in terms of blobs of color.

16

These two characteristics are not the exclusive attributes of the Impressionists. Well before them, certain masters, the most painterly among the great geniuses, pondered over these questions. We must look for them more especially among the Realists, for the Classical and Academic painters merely show hostility towards anything that is not composition, drawing, form, intellectualism and theory. This impressionist aesthetic—the single moment in the life of forms—is in point of fact a deviation of the baroque aesthetic, realist in spirit, or, to be more precise, is closely bound up with it. Like the baroque artists—and we use that term not merely with reference to those who belong to the baroque *period*—the " impressionist " artists from Giorgione to Claude Monet show little interest in graphic form; touch for them being structure, they prefer the painted form. They model by mass effect, suggested by light and color, and this vibrant form, seen from a distance, creates the illusion of the animation of life. Generally speaking, these painters practiced little or no drawing; they sketch directly on the canvas with the tip of the brush.

They are also like the baroque artists in their fondness for light and color for their own sake, for the sensory pleasure of the eye. Finally they resolve the problem of pictorial matter in the same way; they aim at beauty and richness of pigment which they apply to the canvas with considerable freedom. They do not paint rigidly like David in his neo-classical canvases and they reject smooth painting, glazing and areas of flat color. Their brush strokes are often discernible—Ingres referred to the " drunken brush "—and suggest rather than represent.

But there are several major differences between these somewhat distant precursors and the Impressionists proper. They have recourse to linear perspective; their shadows are not always transparent or colored, nor are they necessarily the complementaries of the light tones; those among their number who practice landscape painting never carry out the work directly in the open air and they employ a brown and dark foreground to act as a foil to the more colored and luminous distance; they do not banish blacks, grays, browns and the earth colors from their palette in favor of pure colors; their broad and not invariably broken touches do not consist of the innumerable small commas of color, juxtaposed or intermingled, of the pure Impressionist; and they rarely use the optical mixture of tones.

Venice

It was in Venice that this impressionist aesthetic was first manifested; Venice where, during the Renaissance, the golden haze of the atmosphere, the glow of the sun on the buildings, reflections of the sky in the water, variety of lighting effects on the lagoon are " impressions " frequently evoked by Giorgione, Titian, Veronese and Tintoretto. " It was however at Venice, the *heart* of color... " writes Constable, " that the landscape assumed a rank and decision of character... "

In the technical realm, predominance of color over form, search after harmonies of complementary tones—particularly reds and greens—rendering of reflections of light, free style in the application of color, rich pigmentation, with visible, not smooth touches, which give the sparkle of life—all impressionist characteristics. We could multiply examples : Giorgione's *Concert champêtre* which renders something new in painting, the sensation of open air, and the nudes of which, modelled in the light, were to inspire Manet's *Déjeuner sur l'herbe;* Titian's *The Entombment* in which the carmine robe, shimmering with light, anticipates the dress in the center of Renoir's *Moulin de la Galette;* Titian's last works in which the " faceted " forms vibrate in their luminosity like Manet's or Renoir's; Veronese's *The Marriage Feast at Cana*, in which the clear and sunny sky, variegated costumes—a pretext for investigations of color harmonies—have an undeniable affinity with Renoir's *Déjeuner des Canotiers (Rowers at Lunch);* finally some of Tintoretto's seascapes or certain of his background landscapes, brushed in with astonishing freedom in colored and shimmering blobs which convey the feeling of nature in its fugitive moods, after the Impressionist manner. We might add further, moving to the eighteenth century, that some of Francesco Guardi's *Views of the Lagoon in Venice* in which water and sky merge into a mirage of nacreous iridescence, a liquid atmosphere of exceptional limpidity, make us think in particular of Monet's *Vétheuil, Sunset.*

This love of light and color, this triumph of truthfulness and sensation are the marks of a new vision that could look forward to a prolonged development. The impressionist aesthetic was born and from this time on was destined to spread, living and renewed, through many schools of painting.

Spain

It is in Spain, the country of pure painting, that we encounter the next and decisive stage in its development, which was revealed in a striking fashion. El Greco, a disciple of Tintoretto, Velasquez and Goya were each to play an essential role in this pursuit of light as in this interpretation not only of the life of human beings but of the " silent life " of objects, animated with their own reflections.

M. Camon Aznar, in an address which he gave at Bordeaux in 1953 on *Spanish Impressionism* [14], particularly on El Greco, made this observation, " Embarking on this theme, I should make it clear that I shall not be referring to the nineteenth century school of painting but to the *technical constant* which runs through Spanish painting from El Greco to our own time. This impressionist technique cannot be linked up with any particular national group; it is a universal trend, a form of expression in painting which adopts its own distinctive modality in each country. It consists essentially in the fragmentation of brush strokes with the aim of momentarily arresting light and movement. " Further on, he continues, " This historic Impressionism could be called *instantism.* It is this way of seizing the luminous or dynamic moment, of leaving gaps between the brush strokes that is the main characteristic of Spanish Impressionism, which is not fundamentally concerned with open air, that is certain, nor with primary colors but makes a generous use of black... "

There is no doubt that El Greco was responsible for introducing a totally new and original technique, broken in its touches and bold in its lively and light tones, put down in the form of blobs that vibrate with luminosity.

The palpitating light which models the body of *Christ on the Cross* (Louvre; Zuloaga Museum, Zumaya) or the nude figures in the vision of the Apocalypse (Zuloaga Museum, Zumaya), has technical affinities with Cézanne, particularly in his *Bathers*. El Greco's *The Baptism of Christ* (Galleria Corsini, Rome), *St. John the Baptist and St. John the Evangelist* (Hospital of San Juan Bautista, Toledo) reveal El Greco's impressionist tendencies still more—spots of bright color, light impregnating and suffusing the figures, variegations anticipating their dissolution in a final ascending vortex, are to some extent precursors of the shimmering reflections, the fairy-like ballets of cloud and flowers in Claude Monet's *Water Lilies*. And the *Portrait of Covarrubias* (Louvre) with its juxtaposition of flecks of color, its pigment modelling in the light, evokes some of Renoir's portraits such as that of *Madame Charpentier*.

This vibrating " tachism, " this avant-garde art which so shocked the court of Philip II of Spain has led M. Camon Aznar to suppose that Lope de Vega was alluding to El Greco's painting in these lines from the " Merited Crown " :

> *Oh! picture by the skillful painter*
> *Which, seen close to, is a stain.*

The Spanish historian adds that the following fragment of a sermon preached in Seville is likewise an undoubted allusion to El Greco, " ... You will see him (the painter) as he paints the canvas, stepping back to judge the effect, unconvinced about the brush stroke which he applied close up until he can examine it from a distance... "

Velasquez, the painter of truth, was concerned with truthfulness, not mere semblance. With the aim of making his forms more effective as " suggestion, " therefore, he broke away from the somewhat academic procedures honored in his time, particularly the smooth finish. He exploited the colored, often broken, patches of paint which caught and refracted the light, thereby expressing the direct sensation beloved of the Impressionists.

The Spanish poet, Quevedo, a contemporary of the artist, has given us a description of his lively manner of painting [15].

In his portraits—those of *Queen Mariana of Austria, Philip IV* and the *Infanta Margarita in Pink* (all preserved in the Prado), the light " flickers " as much over the flesh as on the costumes and jewelry. The faces are not treated as contour but built up in innumerable little touches which create a living modeling. The artist has abandoned the Caravaggio methods of his early days with its violent chiaroscuro. The embroidery on the materials, braid, ribbons, jewelry is indicated by blobs of paint, often broken up. The artist then adds small, vibrating touches to produce the effect of light and create the perfect illusion of volume. By this time he has got very close to impressionist vision, so close, I think [16], that his work already contains in embryo certain canvases of Renoir such as *La Loge* of 1878 (Courtauld Collection, London) in which the rose of the bodice and that on the hair have their direct equivalent in the portrait of the little Infanta Margarita between *Las Meninas* (Maids of Honor; see inset p. 12) and show a close kinship with the bouquet in the hand of the *Infanta Margarita in Pink* (Renoir notes, furthermore, concerning the *Portrait of the Infanta Margarita* (Louvre), " the whole art of painting is in the little pink ribbon of the Infanta Margarita ! "), likewise *Madame*

Charpentier and her Children of the year 1878 (Metropolitan Museum, New York) in which in addition to technical affinity we discover identical details, the large dog, for example, of *Las Meninas*.

Finally we should mention one of the two landscapes which he painted of the gardens of the Villa Medici at Rome (*El Mediodia*, Prado) during his second journey to Italy in 1650. He creates a complete illusion of open-air atmosphere, by means of a continual play of vibrations of light among the leaves, on the ground and even on the figures. From this point of view it may be compared with many lively landscapes of Renoir's (*The Railway Bridge at Chatou*, 1881, Jeu de Paume, Paris), Pissarro's (*Coach at Louveciennes*, 1870, Jeu de Paume) or Claude Monet's (*The Quay at Argenteuil*, 1875, Jeu de Paume) for example.

Nor is Goya's work, particularly in the details of the clothes and jewelry and at times in the rendering of the flesh, without a certain almost impressionist treatment, that colored and gradated " tachism, " composed of values of gray, black and pink, which Edouard Manet and Renoir were to borrow so often. Thus in the *Frescoes of San Antonio de la Florida*, 1798 (above all in the studies of *Angels*) and in certain of his portraits such as *The Woman with the Fan* (1815-1817, Louvre) we find a hint of the method by which Renoir, at the end of his career, obtained the fleshy roundness of forms, modelling them entirely in juxtaposed touches of bright pink and without any contour.

The *Milkmaid of Bordeaux* (1827, Prado) is conjured up in an open-air atmosphere and some of the artist's last compositions are brushed in with swift, staccato strokes. We can agree with M. Sanchez Canton that Goya " anticipated Impressionism. "

Flanders

In Flanders, where artists are particularly attracted to a strictly objective art which leads them to interest themselves in every aspect, even the most realist, of life, it is curious to note that few painters show any inclination towards the impressionist aesthetic either in their sense of light or in their technique.

If Pieter Brueghel the Elder proves himself a great innovator in the realm of landscape painting as far as rendering the seasons and work in the fields is concerned, his strongest interest is in popular customs and manners, and although his naturalism is very pronounced it is not enough to justify our connecting him with the impressionist family, from which his use of an even, unvibrating light and somewhat traditional technique divides him.

Rubens, whose whole art is color and light, can obviously claim a place here although his technique lacks that flickering quality noticeable among the Spanish masters. Delacroix, who was so much influenced by his great Flemish predecessor, made several attempts to analyze the latter's manner, which offers analogies with that of the Impressionists.

" His *light* is composed of fresh, delicate tints, etc. In the shadows, on the other hand, very warm tints which are the normal constituent of the *reflection*, thus adding to the effect of the chiaroscuro. *In particular* he makes no use of *black* in them." [17]

"It is difficult to say what colors Titian and Rubens employed to make and keep their flesh tones so brilliant and especially the half-tones in which the transparency of blood under the skin is perceptible despite the element of gray that all half-tones contain. I am convinced, for my part, that they produced them by the use of the most brilliant colors... tones that Rubens obtained with pure, virtual colors such as bright greens, ultramarines, etc. " [18]

In the landscapes executed at the end of his career the artist gives an increasing importance to a light that is now golden, now pearly (*Landscape*, Louvre).

His nude studies in the *Landing of Marie de Médicis at Marseilles* (Louvre), among others, have those colored reflections, reddish, orange, sometimes green or blue-tinged in their shadows, that we are to discover later in Renoir's open-air nudes.

Holland

In seventeenth century Holland we see Franz Hals employing a technique of broken tones of amazing boldness. He applies the color with brush or palette knife in straight or oblique and extremely triturated touches which he uses much more than drawing to express form and volume and the substance of things seen in the light... *The Gypsy Woman* (Louvre) is one of the most typical examples of this technique which Manet was to take up in a number of his works. Towards the end of his career, in 1664, when he was 84, in *The Governors* and *The Sisters of the Almshouse* (Haarlem) he exploited broken tones and pure colors as the Impressionists were to do later.

A number of landscape painters were now to apply themselves to the problem of the open air and often succeeded in creating the illusion of it without venturing to paint directly from nature. Their landscapes were not invariably chosen for "subject" with an eye for the picturesque, but rather because of the particular atmosphere of a place, rapid changes of light, reflections in water, the movement of vast cloud-filled skies. These Dutch painters have had a profound influence on French landscape painters of the Barbizon School who form the link between them and the Impressionists.

Jacob Ruysdael was one of the first to set about capturing not only a season of the year or one day, but a particular hour or even a fleeting moment when an effect of sun or shadow suddenly transformed the natural scene. His Louvre landscapes, *The Interval of Sunshine, The Bush,* or the *View of Haarlem* in the Rijksmuseum, Amsterdam, are remarkable for their sense of space and the beauty of their shifting skies.

For what was to prove his masterpiece, *The Avenue, Middelharnis* (National Gallery, London) Hobbema chose no more complicated subject than a road moving away between two rows of trees beneath an infinity of sky into which the eye can escape unimpeded. After him, Corot, then Monet, Sisley, Pissarro, Renoir and many

21

other painters of the impressionist circle were to take up a similar theme on many occasions.

We should not here omit a too often neglected artist, Paul Potter, who was not merely an animal painter but proved himself an astonishing landscape painter and innovator, particularly in a canvas in the Mauritshuis, the Hague, *Het spiegel-ende Koetje (The Cow Reflected)*. Groups of naked boys, bathing, splashing or drying themselves in the sun in the middle distance were to find their equivalent in some canvases of the Impressionist period—Renoir's *Naked Boys Bathing*, Seurat's *Bathing at Asnières* and especially the *Summer Scene* or *The Bath* by Bazille (Fogg Art Museum, Cambridge, Mass.) in which there are striking analogies of conception.

Jan Van Goyen's chief concern was the representation of water—rivers and seashore (we shall see in due course that the appeal of the latter was responsible for the pre-impressionist movement of the School of Saint Siméon of about 1860) and the rendering of the subtlety and movement of reflections in a monochrome scale with a dominant gray, very different of course from Boudin's or Lépine's but with a kindred sensibility : *View of Dordrecht* (Louvre), *A Stiff Breeze* (National Gallery, London).

Vermeer, whose purely subjective approach runs counter to the impressionist aesthetic, has recourse however to some of its technical methods—his shadows are colored and transparent, and if he does obtain them by using the complementary tone, eschewing black or brown, he employs a modulation of local tone. For him color—which he sometimes applies in pure tones and a restricted key—is a means for delimiting the form. His cold, even light is still a long way from the luminous vibration of the Impressionists, but he sometimes applies scintillating touches like liquid drops which catch the light (*View of Delft*, Mauritshuis, the Hague; *The Milkmaid*, Rijksmuseum, Amsterdam).

England

The landscape is the most original contribution of English painting, and from the end of the eighteenth century (we must not forget that this School was then in its infancy) many painters were attracted by nature. But it was not until the first half of the nineteenth century that two men of genius, Constable and Turner —and we could add Bonington—exercised a direct and decisive influence on the development of the impressionist aesthetic on the eve of its full efflorescence in France.

Constable's innovation was not in the choice of subject but—and he was a pioneer in this—he insisted on the necessity of the *study made directly from nature* at one sitting. This artist's contribution may be defined as the pictorial rendering of the momentary impression in all its spontaneity, that is to say its most irreducible, most individual and most elusive element. As Constable himself asserted, what he aimed at in his pictures were " light, dews, breezes, bloom and freshness; not one of which has yet been perfected on the canvas of any painter in the world. " He anticipates the observations of the Impressionists, " ... no two days are alike, nor even two hours; neither were there ever two leaves of a tree alike since the creation of the world; and the genuine productions of art, like those of nature, are all distinct from each other. " He comes to the conclusion that " ... every truly original picture is a separate study, and governed by laws of its own; so that what is right in one, would be often entirely wrong if transferred to another. " Is not this an analysis " before the event " of a painting series by Claude Monet? Any site may be represented an indefinite number of times, it will never be altogether the same.

As a marine painter Constable succeeded in conveying the elusive moods of wind and atmosphere before the masters of the Saint Simeon School and before Claude Monet, particularly in *Weymouth Bay* (circa 1819, National Gallery, London) or *Harwich, Sea and Lighthouse* (circa 1820, Tate Gallery London); these spontaneous and subtle visions are very characteristic of the painter who wrote, " That landscape painter who does not make his skies a very material part of his composition, neglects to avail himself of one of his greatest aids... The sky is the source of light in nature, and governs everything. " The sky is " the key note, the standard of scale and the chief organ of sentiment. "

Constable wanted to represent—therein lay the novelty of his art—the most unexpected, fugitive, evanescent aspects, the brief moment in the flight of time. From December 21, 1822, for example, two small pictures painted between 1:30 and 4:00 in the afternoon and inspired by the movement of the clouds, *Looking South* (Sir Farquhar Buzzard Collection), anticipate Delacroix's and Boudin's pastel *Sky-studies*.

Through studying variations of light, he produces—as Corot likewise was to do—sketches vibrating with reflections, much more impressionist than the finished picture, for example those for *The Hay Wain* (1821, Victoria and Albert Museum) and for *Salisbury Cathedral seen from the Bishop's Garden* (1823, Private Collection, London). The latter with its delicate harmonies of browns and pearly blues provides us with a foretaste of what the art of Cézanne with its aim of rendering " le frisson de la durée " was to be.

It was nevertheless a finished picture, *The Hay Wain*, exhibited in Paris at the 1824 Salon, which was to mark a stage in Delacroix's work. After seeing it, Delacroix altered the sky and lighting in *The Massacres at Scio* (which he showed in the same Salon), impressed by the feeling of space that he discovered in the English painter. Fascinated too by the technical side, he was to note in his Journal, September 23, 1846 [19], " Constable says that the superiority of the green of his fields comes from the fact that it is made up of a host of different greens. The lack of intensity and animation in the greenness of the general run of landscape painters is accounted for by the uniform tone that they usually employ. What he states here concerning the green of the fields applies to all tones. " Delacroix's modelling by hatchings, and later on the juxtaposed comma-touches of the Impressionists, had their origin in this technique of Constable's.

Bonington's untimely death prevented him from realizing his full potentiality; his spontaneous art, his studies of atmosphere, his modelling in the pigment allow us to suppose that he could one day have played an important part in nineteenth century painting. His influence on Delacroix is undeniable, and in some of his works, particularly in a *Seascape* (Louvre), we are aware of the first fruits, in embryo, of Impressionism. In a letter of December 31, 1858 to Th. Silvestre [20], Delacroix states, " Turner and Constable are true reformers. They have got out of the rut of the old landscape painters. Our school which is now rich in talented men in this genre has greatly profited by their example." And much later, in 1902, Pissarro, recalling the stay he had in London with Monet in 1871, remarked to Dewhurst, " We are also seeing the art galleries. The water colors and paintings of Turner and Constable, the canvases by Old Crome have certainly had an influence on us... We were particularly struck by the landscape painters who shared our views concerning open air, light and passing effects, still more. "

Turner showed from the start a marked preference for seascapes and landscapes whose execution like the titles proclaim " Impressionism. " *Calais Pier* (1803) and above all *Sun Rising in the Mist* (1807) reveal the same preoccupations as Claude Monet's *Sunlight Effect* or *Impression*. *Morning Frost* (1813) is treated in a similar spirit to the various *Frost Effects* by Claude Monet, Sisley, Pissarro or Guillaumin, and *Yachts on the Solent* (1827, National Gallery, London) are the equivalent of *Regattas at Argenteuil* by Claude Monet or Renoir.

Between 1819, the date of his first journey to Italy, and about 1840, Turner gave free rein to his fondness for light, and for lively, dramatic colors, in canvases in which sea and sky are the dominant elements, melting in a fairy-like atmosphere. The critics' reactions were mostly hostile, and Hazlitt did not hesitate to talk of " very life-like paintings of nothing "; the French Impressionists were to be greeted later with a similar lack of understanding.

In his *Views of Venice*, which date from this period, Turner drenches city, lagoon and sky in an opalescent light from which all form is banished. Here again we cannot avoid the comparison with Monet. From 1840 to 1850, the painter's last creative period, Turner gave himself up to experiments, taken to their logical extreme, in the rendering of pictorial atmosphere—*Snow Storm* (1842), *Yacht Approaching the Coast, Rain, Steam and Speed* (1844) are remarkable from this point of view : the painter creates a diffuse, unreal universe where all the elements merge in a mysterious phantasmagoria.

Although in his vision of the world Turner is the painter who comes closest to the impressionist conception, he parts company when it comes to its realization. He still has recourse to dark foregrounds and shadows without color; he does not always use pure tones, and his technique does not show the extreme fragmentation of touch of the Impressionists. Finally, he reserved the open air for his sketches and painted his pictures in the studio. Pissarro notes in a letter of May 8, 1903, written to his son, " Turner and Constable, useful though they have been to us, have confirmed our impression that these painters did not understand the *analysis of shadows*, which in Turner is always a calculated effect, a hole. As for the division of tones, Turner confirms its value as a method but not its soundness. "

We cannot leave the English School without a word about one of its favorite media—the water color whose fluidity excels in rendering water, light filtering through clouds, transparency of atmosphere. The Society of Water Color Painters was founded in London in 1805; the present Institute of Water Color Painters goes back to 1830. Turner and Constable explored to the full all the resources offered by a medium that enabled them to capture fleeting effects in nature with rapidity and directness.

24

We must go back to the seventeenth century to discover the first signs of an impressionist aesthetic in France. The somewhat surprising thing is that it was in two of her greatest classical painters, Nicolas Poussin and Claude Gellée, called Lorraine, that these early manifestations occur, and it was on Roman soil that the first drawn or painted landscapes were worked out in which some of the elements characteristic of the vision and technique of the future Impressionists came to light. Both of them enjoyed drawing, usually with pen or brush and bister wash, sketches of the Roman Campagna in which they made concise notations of their first impressions, with a particular emphasis on the problems of the interpretation of light effects. Back in their studios they composed their pictures—in a more arbitrary fashion—from these studies. Their very different respective styles must however be examined separately.

Poussin is one of the masters of French Classicism; all the same an essentially baroque element is observable in his work, the part played by light in his paintings and his landscape drawings. Far from being dull and uniform as it is with the pure classics or academics, far from being violently contrasted in the Caravaggian manner, this light is vibrant in its reflections, transparent in its shadows. But Poussin is in love with rhythm and harmony; furthermore he combines the elements of duration, permanence, strictly classical construction with fugitive vibrations of light. And in this, bringing these two apparently contradictory aspects together in a single amazing synthesis more than two centuries before Cézanne, he anticipated that painter's art still more than the art of the pure Impressionists. His *Drawings of Trees* (Louvre) can be compared with Cézanne's *Tree Studies* or *Landscape Studies*. Some of his *Bacchanalia* offer analogies with the *Grandes Baigneuses* (Philadelphia Museum) of the Master of Aix, and his *Funérailles de Phocion* has a close kinship with the various *Montagne Sainte-Victoire* paintings (see plates inset page 12). It is interesting to note that Cézanne's view that " in painting there are two things, the eye and the brain " was wholly shared by Poussin, who in one of his letters writes the following characteristic passage :

" We must realize that there are two ways of seeing objects, the first consists of merely seeing them, the second in considering them attentively. Merely seeing is nothing else than receiving the form and resemblance of the thing perceived in the eye. But viewing an object critically means that, over and above the mere natural reception of the form in the eye, we are seeking the means towards knowing this same object properly with particular assiduity : thus we can say that the mere appearance is a natural operation and what I call the View is a function of the reason... "

Claude Gellée, called Lorraine, truly makes light the very principle of his art in which everything emanates from the sun, its reflections and shadows; he recreates that golden mist which sometimes drenches everything in nature and renders it evanescent; with more subtlety he strives to evoke that atmosphere, those unsubstantial layers of the " air " suggested by blue-gray " values " in his paintings, which convey the feeling of space without any need for linear perspective.

When by means of a simple bister wash he animates reflections of light on the ground or the leaves and renders the shimmering of water in these drawings, Claude Gellée proves himself an impressionist precursor. Eliminating the details, he organizes the forms and dissolves them in the mist and in this simplified synthesis he draws close to the artists of Japan and therefore by this fact to the Impressionists. His painted landscapes, in fact mostly seascapes, are only superficially conventional. We soon forget the foreground figures, mediocre enough in any case, and the historic, mythological or biblical themes are eliminated by the real subject, the sun and its pervading light.

Is not the whole of Claude Monet's Argenteuil period already implicit in Claude Gellée's innumerable *Seaports* with their glittering reflections on the water? (*Ulysses restores Chryseis to her Father; Harbor at Sunset; Cleopatra at Tarsus,* Louvre). Is not all the subtlety of the versions of *Rouen Cathedral* the result of memories of these palaces painted by Claude? And through the very divergent techniques of these two painters one is aware of this same instinctive and purely visual pursuit of the instantaneity of the sun's light.

From the very beginning of the eighteenth century we see Watteau fascinated by atmosphere and the play of light; but solely in the world of reverie and enchantment, not in that of observation of natural phenomena. Nature in point of fact does not interest Watteau; for him it is merely a pretext for the display of human beings, a frame, an unreal diversion in the open air. The sparkle that the painter is so anxious to render does not come from the sun but from artificial lighting like that on the stage. If waters, mountains and foliage melt into an evanescent phantasmagoria in the distances of his landscapes, they are there to convey what his imagination suggests and not what he sees. It is all very far removed from impressionist art, but there are certain resemblances : transparency and clearness of atmosphere, buoyancy of roseate and opalescent skies, a light that sometimes breaks up the forms, the poetry of evocation. We can from this point of view compare *The Embarkation for Cythera* (Louvre) with Renoir's *Road leading through Tall Grass* (Jeu de Paume) or with Pissarro's *Landscape at Chaponval*, likewise in the Impressionist Museum (Jeu de Paume).

In the middle of the century Chardin, who confirmed the fact that the artist does not paint exclusively with his brushes but also with his feelings, nevertheless remains one of the greatest virtuosi of French painting. This " artisan " of the painting craft developed the craftsman side right up to his death. Beginning as a traditionalist he made an increasing use of broad parallel strokes, applying with some boldness the theory of the echoes of tones and reflections, and thus obtaining an accent that conveys the impression of reality in a striking manner. He is a great believer in the reflection, more the " colored reflection " of objects as they affect each other than the luminous refraction of the sun in nature. Moreover he did not paint landscapes; his was the art of intimacy that loved to catch the innumerable vibrations of colors as they pass from one object to another.

26

Towards the end of his career he practiced the art of pastel painting, and in his own *Portraits* he modelled his face not by a contour line but by quivering modulations in the form of hatchings which convey the illusion of movement and vitality, the kind of hatchings we are to find later, different technically but identical in principle, in Delacroix's " floss-effects " and the comma-touches of the Impressionists.

What is more, when Chardin wanted to represent a purple plum, for example, instead of mixing blue and red on his palette and then painting with the resulting pigment—in the traditional manner—he discovered a new technique and applied a whole series of little blue and red touches directly on his canvas side by side. The spectator could stand back and carry out the optical mixture of tones which all the Impressionists and Neo-Impressionists were to practice later.

Chardin played a role of paramount importance as an innovator in painting technique, and along with Velasquez he constitutes one of the great links in impressionist aesthetics.

We must be careful in this rapid analysis not to forget the painter Joseph Vernet, still, I think, undeservedly neglected and who in two landscapes executed in Rome, *The Castle of Sant'Angelo* and particularly *The Ponte Rotto* (Louvre) is a direct link between Claude and Corot and anticipates the Impressionists. It is true that his technique, like Claude's, is somewhat traditional; but in *The Ponte Rotto*, above all, his way of " seeing " the landscape in the light and conveying reflections in water is unmistakably akin to that of Monet in his *Quarries at St. Denis* (Jeu de Paume).

Fragonard, working at the end of the eighteenth century, has technical affinities with the " Impressionist family " in his use of broad, rapid, broken, vibrant touches and his light effects. He is a colorist and is fond of heightening tints; he employs colored, often red shadows after the manner of Rubens. He is also a baroque artist and revels in the turbulence of life; his *Baigneuses* (Louvre), frolicking in the sunlight, are precursors of the many studies composed by Renoir on this theme.

François-Marius Granet (1775-1849), a painter from Aix-en-Provence who distinguished himself as a water colorist, studied the problems of light. His subtle experiments in rendering reflections and misty atmosphere give him a place among the promoters of impressionist vision.

The real father of Impressionism before Claude Monet, however, was Eugène Delacroix. " Everything in nature is reflection, " wrote this painter who also declared, " Trees must be modelled in a colored reflection like flesh [1]. " His subtlety of perception enabled him, like the Impressionists later, to catch the smallest variations of light, and he treated every object in terms of its shadow, half-tint, light and reflection. " The more I ponder, the more I discover how much this *reflected half-tint* is the principle which should dominate, since it is this that sets the true tone, the tone which constitutes the value, which ' tells ' in the object and gives it its animation. The light to which we are taught in the art schools to attach an equal importance and which is applied to the canvas at the same time as the half-tint and the shadow, is merely an ' accidental ' and nothing more. All real color is there. I mean the color that conveys the feeling of thickness and that of the radical difference which differentiates between one object and the next. '' [22] *The Education of the Virgin* (1852), Hara Collection, Japan) and *Jacob Wrestling with the Angel* (1857-1861, in the church of St. Sulpice, Paris) show how well Delacroix applied this theory.

The complexity of his vision led to an extreme diversity in his palette. The Impressionists, always on the lookout for intensity of color, discovered their champion in him when he wrote, " Gray is the enemy of all painting, " [23] with the corollary, " Banish all the earth colors. "

As they wanted to express open air lighting in all its intensity, the Impressionists differentiated what one might call " local color " from " light-color. " Here once again Delacroix anticipated them when he wrote, " We should reconcile color that comes from *color* and light that comes from *light*, " [24] which he explains elsewhere, " Overemphasis on light and breadth of planes leads to an absence of half-tints and hence to decoloration. " [25]

But for the Impressionists, shadow, " faithful complementary of its governor light, " is visually colored by cold or subsidiary tints—violets, blues or green tints—in relation to the luminous, warm or dominant tints—yellows, orange, reds. Once more, Delacroix has the first word when he notes, " At Saint Denis du Saint Sacrement I had to paint the lights with pure chrome yellow and the half-tints with Prussian blue. " And further, " mat orange for the flesh tones, the brightest violets for the passage from the shadow and golden-yellow reflections in the shadow which are set against the ground. "

Abandoning pigmentary mixture in favor of optical mixture, that is the use of pure colors put side by side, the Impressionists once more found this problem dealt with by Delacroix " tints of green and violet put down here and there at random, unmixed in the light part. " In order to obtain a retinal impression, the Impressionists exploited the broken touch. Delacroix is a precursor in this too, " The larger the picture, the broader should be the touch, that is self-evident, but one should avoid the physical mixing of the blobs of color; they mix naturally at a certain distance from the eye through the law of sympathetic association. In this way color gains more vigor and freshness. " Delacroix's own touch, sometimes hatched, sometimes applied in spots of color (*The Algerian Women*, 1834, Louvre) forestalls that of the Impressionists and also brought violent criticisms down on his head, " a hatched, incoherent touch " (C.-P. Landon), " a regular daub " (E. Delécluze). Hear him defending his method against smooth, cold " finished " painting, " In all the arts there are agreed and adopted methods of procedure, and one is but an imperfect connoisseur if one is unable to see through these betrayals of the mental process; the proof is that the ordinary man has a marked preference for the smoothest and least brush-marked pictures and prefers them for that precise reason... What should we say then about those masters who produce a hard contour line yet make no use of the touch?... There are no contours in nature any more than there are touches. We must always come back to the conventions in each art which constitute the language of the art in question.

" Many of these painters who assiduously avoid the touch with the excuse that it does not exist in nature exaggerate the contour, which does not exist in nature either.

" Many masters have kept the touch invisible in their painting under the illusion that they are thus approaching nature which also shows none. But the touch is like any other means that helps to convey thought in painting. A painting can doubtless be very beautiful without showing the touch, but it is puerile to imagine that we are getting any closer to nature thereby; we might just as well produce actual reliefs in color on the ground that objects stand out in real life. "

Delacroix's technique—methodical and reasoned—shows an affinity with that—purely instinctive—of the Impressionists which the poet Jules Laforgue defined thus, " the shimmer in a host of dancing sparkles which we find in the Impressionists, the wonderful discovery, anticipated by Delacroix, that painter so infuatuated with movement, who among the chilly Furies of Romanticism, not content with violent movement and unbridled colors, models in vibrant streaks of paint. "[26] As early as 1825, while in England, Delacroix had been captivated by the water color and its potentialities for conveying the mood of a landscape (*Sketchbook*, Louvre). But it was during his journey in North Africa, in 1832, that the magic of colors and the shimmering light that enhances forms and transforms nature was fully revealed to him (cp. his numerous *water colors* executed in Morocco and Algeria). This new vision, later, led him to very definitely pre-Impressionist works such as his *Etretat Water colors* (1835) or his painting *The Sea at Dieppe* (1852) which have a kinship with some of Monet's pictures.

But there is an essential difference of conception between the art of the leader of the French Romantic School and the Impressionists. As Delacroix himself states in the passage quoted above from his *Journal*, for him the touch " is like any other means that helps to convey *thought* in painting. " And Baudelaire in his account of the Universal Exhibition of 1855 notes, " You would say that this painting (by Delacroix), in the manner of magicians and mesmerizers, projects *his thought*. This strange phenomenon results from the colorist's power, the perfect concord of the tones and from the harmony (pre-established in the painter's brain) of color with the subject. One has the impression that this color—if I may be forgiven for such subterfuges of language to express extremely subtle ideas—*thinks* by itself, independently of the objects which it clothes. "

These two statements give us the key to what divides these two forms of art. In Impressionist painting no thought-content—merely an impression; a purely visual sensation, independent of the " work " of the mind. In Delacroix, an intellectual painting executed by a man, however, whose eye was as practiced as the impressionists' eye, though it never—or almost never—took precedence over the brain.

EUGÈNE BOUDIN — SAINT-VALÉRY-SUR-SOMME. 1890 (15 1/2 × 22 ") — PRIVATE COLLECTION, PARIS

Pre-Impressionism

ABOUT the year 1850 two very marked trends appeared in French painting —chiefly in landscape—thanks to two artists whose personalities were diametrically opposed, Corot and Courbet. Both were to exercise a decisive influence on the subsequent development of painting. To them must be added—their importance is less but far from negligible—the masters of the Barbizon School, particularly Daubigny, whose aesthetic principles approach those of Corot, and Diaz, who has more affinity with Courbet.

Corot

Beginning from his first journey to Italy (1825-1828) Corot painted his small pictures in the open air; his aim was primarily to convey light and in the second place to re-create local atmosphere. One of the most successful examples is his sketch for the *Narni Bridge* (Louvre) wholly composed of values and subtleties of tone, very different from the larger painting executed later in the studio. In this version the landscape has lost the lively and spontaneous side which is so admirable in the sketch. However, Corot remarked, " After my excursions I invite nature to come and spend a few days with me; it is then that my madness begins : brush in hand, I search for nuts in the woods of my studio; I hear the birds sing, the trees rustling in the wind, I see the streams and rivers flow past me, bearing the thousand reflections of earth and sky; the sun sets and rises in my studio. " [27]
All through his career Corot displays the same predilection for rhythm and harmony, which relates him to the great classical masters of the past; his search for the permanent runs counter to the search for the evanescent, beloved of the Impressionists. Indeed one day he made this remark to Pissarro who had called for advice, " The two things one should study are first form and then values. " But if the Impressionists are not concerned with form, they are, like Corot, with values. From the year 1850 his preoccupation with values, in works which become increasingly vaporous, is more marked. His *Souvenir de Mortefontaine* (1864), drenched in the silvery mist of dawn, was to have a direct influence on certain impres-

31

sionist canvases : Sisley's *Mists*, Monet's *Tower of London* among others. By the close of Corot's career we could point to more and more examples which already contained impressionist elements : *The Sèvres Road* (1855-1865) with light effects on the road which were to be seen again in Pissarro or the early Sisley and Monet; *The Bridge at Mantes* (1868-1870) with its reflections in the water that anticipate Monet's; *The Belfry at Douai* (1871) which has the sensibility of Sisley in its atmosphere; *Sens Cathedral* (1874), one of his last works in which the stained glass windows, vibrating with color—juxtaposed touches of blue, pink and red—are a prelude to the optical mixture of tones. Aiming to express the invisible layers of air, Corot at this time frequently veils the whole landscape in an infinite variety of grays and blue-grays, which captivated a group of artists working in the environs of Honfleur in Normandy about 1860 who compose the School of Saint Siméon, from the name of the farm in which they had established themselves. There is no denying the affinities between Corot's *Harbor of La Rochelle* (1851), some of Jongkind's seascapes, including the *Fishing Boat at Low Tide* (one of his last works), and Boudin's or Lépine's seaside paintings. Boudin, furthermore, acknowledges the paramount influence of Corot on himself and his friends, " The idea was, " he explained, after a stay in Paris, " that I should return three years later an artistic marvel; I returned more baffled than ever, attracted there by the celebrities of the time, going from Rousseau who fascinated us to Corot who was beginning to show us a new way... "

Antoine Chintreuil (1814-1873), a pupil of Corot's, extremely faithful to nature in his realism, anticipates Impressionism in his studies of atmosphere. Canvases such as *Space* or *Rain and Sunshine* (Louvre) are testimonies of experiments parallel to those of Turner in England.

Daubigny and Diaz

Daubigny likewise aimed at rendering the subtle values of atmosphere, and in order to capture them more accurately he worked from his boat-studio, the *Botin*, along the Oise and the Seine, in the open and in continuous contact with nature. He also sailed to the coast of Normandy off Villerville, near Honfleur. " Was it not in fact his purpose, " as Prosper Dorbec [28] quotes him, " to collect *impressions*, instead of depicting places and odd corners, and replace definite colors by modified and relative tones... "

Before embarking on Courbet, it should be said in passing that the influence exercised by Diaz (he too, incidentally, worked in Normandy at the farm of Saint Siméon kept by Mère Toutain) on the Impressionists, and chiefly on Renoir, is more modest and lay more especially in his " facet " technique for expressing the vibration of light.

Courbet

For Courbet, the man of 1848, the problem of light and particularly that of its intensity is one of the aspects of realism. He uses it to create the illusion of the open air and, let us add, with great success, although his landscapes were mostly carried out in the studio and he disapproved of painting directly from nature. Despite the democratic intentions of the subject, *The Stone Breakers* (Dresden Museum, destroyed 1945) painted in 1849, like the *Village Girls* of 1851 (Metropolitan Museum, New York) provides a pretext for evoking figures moving about in the light and open air. Théophile Silvestre enlightens us about his method of work... " After preparing his canvas according to the kind of picture, now with a brown ground for *The Wrestlers,* reminiscent of the blackest Riberas, now with a red for his *Village Girls* with its bright lawns and sky, he roughs out the figures in white chalk, fashions and re-fashions them completely as many as three times over, and makes great use of the palette knife with which he applies the color to the canvas with brutal frankness while the hairs of the brush hollow out tiny furrows in which the light is softened as in velvet.

" He moves by degrees from the strongest shadow to the brightest light and calls his final touch ' my dominant. ' ' Follow, ' he says, ' this comparison. ' We are shrouded in the dawn twilight; objects are hardly visible; the sun rises—the forms assume an outline; the sun rises—they are lit up and seen in their wholeness. I do in my pictures what the sun does in nature. "

One of his biographers, Georges Riat [30], notes that " the harmony of his pictures is the simple result of partial tones, juxtaposed; in this way he obtains the relief of objects, aerial depth, harmony of color, " and in this technique he sees an anticipation of Impressionist art.

Baudelaire, too, was perfectly aware of it when, analyzing the genius of Ingres and of Courbet, he noted, " But there is this difference : the heroic sacrifice made by M. Ingres in honor of tradition and the notion of Raphaelesque beauty, is made by M. Courbet *for the sake of exterior, positive, immediate nature.* "

The canvas of 1854, famous under the titles *The Encounter,* or *Bonjour, Monsieur Courbet* or *Wealth Encountering Genius* (Montpellier Museum), an abstraction made from the painter's socialist propaganda, is in truth merely a marvelous landscape, flooded with light which splashes the ground and figures with reflections : the " true " subject here is the sun, a crushing Provençal sun as it was revealed to Courbet during a journey to his friend Bruyas at Montpellier. From then on he attached an increasing importance to the factor of light, eager to render its dazzle and vibrations; his palette-knife impasto enabled him to obtain striking effects of brilliance and transience in warm and golden reflections. Thus his canvas *Les Demoiselles des bords de la Seine,* painted in 1856 (Petit Palais, Paris) is steeped in warmth and light. In the foreground, grass and flowers quiver in the luminous air, and behind them the river water gleams and shimmers under the sun's rays. Renoir was to be strongly influenced by it. With *The Haunt of the Deer* of 1866 (Louvre) Courbet resolved a further problem—that of the vibration of light broken by the foliage into countless flickerings that cleave to the rocks or play over tree trunks and water.

And if in Diderot's opinion " flickerings of light destroy harmony " it is none the less true that they open the way to seeing nature, to *plein-airisme* and the " impression " of mobility that now became the preoccupation of the Impressionist group. But Courbet's innovations were not limited to this; he was also a precursor in his interpretations of snow landscapes such as *A Hind driven on to a Snowdrift* of the Salon of 1867 or the *Poachers in the Snow,* circa 1867 (Besançon Museum). His subtle eye perceived certain rainbow effects and, unlike his predecessors who painted snow exclusively with blue-gray shadows, he employed varied tints, opalescent with much more luminous shadows. The Impressionists, taking this purely visual experiment to its logical extreme, did not hesitate, for their part, to represent snow diapered with light values of lilac, pink, yellow, green and orange tints as well as bluish ones.

Courbet, like Claude Monet and his friends, was finally much attracted by the sea. Doubtless it was the sensation of space and infinity—a profoundly realistic one—that he sought in it rather than that of perpetual change. In June 1859 we find him at Le Havre in the company of the painter Schanne. He also met there Eugène Boudin whose small seascapes, painted with great freedom, he had noticed in the window of a stationer's and framer's shop. Together with Boudin, Courbet and Schanne covered the whole district, especially Honfleur and its surroundings where they stayed at the now famous inn of Mère Toutain at the farm of Saint Siméon, marvelously situated, facing the Seine estuary.

Courbet executed several landscapes there, and particularly seascapes, which Zacharie Astruc discovered in his studio, fascinated as he was by " all the strange transformations of the sea, that liquid, tempestuous sky as deep and infinite as the other... all the poems of the sea joined together and expressed in a tone so simple, delicate, great, bold, perfect. " [31]

One morning Courbet, Schanne and Boudin met Baudelaire by the harbor, and Courbet praised Boudin's painting and the beauty of his skies to the illustrious poet and critic. Baudelaire then called on the painter and, when he returned to Paris, writing his account of the 1859 Salon, devoted to his pastels some enthusiastic lines, pointing out the necessity of retaining the spontaneity of the sketch in the finished picture, thus anticipating the pictorial conception of the Impressionists, the direct improvisation, free and direct, onto the canvas. " Yes, imagination avoids the landscape... Perhaps the artists who cultivate this genre distrust their memories too much and adopt an immediate method of copying perfectly suited to their mental laziness. If they had seen, as I have recently at M. Boudin's, who, may I add in passing, has exhibited an extremely good and dignified picture *(The Pardon of Sainte-Anne-la-Palud)*, several hundreds of pastel studies improvised in front of the sea and sky, they would understand what they do not seem able to understand at present, that is to say *the difference that divides a study from a picture*. But M. Boudin, who has every reason to be proud of his devotion to art, is very modest about showing his curious collection. He fully realizes that all this can turn into pictures only through the process of *poetic impression*, recalled at will; and he is too unpretentious to supply the ' notes ' for his pictures. Later, I have no doubt at all, he will reveal the prodigious miracles of air and water in his paintings. These amazing studies, so swiftly and faithfully noted down from those most inconstant and elusive elements in form and color, waves and clouds, always have the date, time of day and wind recorded in the margin; thus, for example : ' October 8, midday, wind north west. ' If you have ever had time to make the acquaintance of these meteorological beauties you would be able to verify the accuracy of M. Boudin's observations from your own recollections. You could put your hand over the description and guess the season, hour and wind. I am not exaggerating. I have seen for myself. Finally, all these fantastically shaped and luminous clouds, this storm-rent blackness, these gaping furnaces, these firmaments of black or violet satin, threadbare, rolled or tattered, these horizons in dark mourning or running with molten metal, all these depths, all these splendors mount to my brain like a heady drink or the eloquences of opium. And, most odd, not once, as I stood before these liquid or airy miracles, did I resent the absence of man. " [32]

Boudin's visits to Courbet were most instructive. In his notebooks of June 18, 1859 he remarks, " Courbet has already helped me to throw off some of my timidity. I shall attempt some large paintings, ambitious projects, more studied in tonality [33]. "

Courbet carried out many more seascapes at Trouville in the years 1865-1866, the period when he came across Boudin again and met Monet for the first time; the vastness of the open sea, sky and water in their grandiose isolation was what, as in the case of the Romantic artists, seemed to have captivated the artist about this time. The studies in which he noted down his immediate impressions were merely the starting point of works in which the superficial and momentary effect was progressively transformed into an ensemble of volumes, rounded forms, dense colors of opaque paint substance that convey the notion of permanence and the fundamental structure of the elements.

Such is the development we now observe in his seascapes, executed about 1869 at Etretat during his stay with the painter Narcisse Diaz and his sons, which reach their climax in the *Stormy Sea*, better known under the title *The Wave* (Salon of 1870, Louvre). And if we compare the famous *Cliffs at Etretat* (Salon of 1870, Louvre) with Monet's work, likewise in the Louvre, executed at almost the identical spot, we can observe the difference between the two masters. Monet is concerned only with the fugitive *impression* which he feels and desires to communicate. He suggests more than he puts down, and it is very understandable that contemporary critics reproached him with his lack of construction and the absence of drawing and real forms in his art.

Thus, despite all the profound differences between himself and them, Courbet led the next generation towards the solution of open-air painting; he who used to say to his pupils :
" Don't do what I do.
" Don't do what the others do.
" Don't do what Raphael did.
" Do what you *see*, what you want to do, what you *feel*. "

THE SCHOOL OF SAINT SIMÉON

W E have just seen that the Normandy region around the Seine estuary attracted many artists, and it was there that this new art, uniquely open-air, which gave rise to Impressionism, really developed. Sea-bathing had been fashionable for some years and the Duc de Morny had just launched Trouville and Deauville as resorts. The great center of attraction for the painters was Honfleur and its environs. Fascinated by the reflecting expanse of sea and sky, they settled at Mère Toutain's inn at the farm of Saint Siméon. So it was possible to refer to an Honfleur or even to a Saint Siméon School.

Here it is that in 1862 we find Boudin. Henceforward he was to spend the summers there, working in the district, specializing in seascapes and beach scenes. There, from life, in the open air he recorded the slightest changes of light atmosphere and could even suggest the sea breeze as it raised white horses, flapped a flag on the shore or bellied out a ship's sail in the offing. He notes down the fact that, " three brush strokes directly from life are better than two days' work at the easel. " Boudin's sensibility made him tend towards harmonies of very subtle gray values which Corot seems to have been the first to introduce and which were no more popular among contemporary landscape painters than they were to be later with the pure Impressionists. Boudin in fact confesses, " Gray-tone painting was out of favor at this time, particularly for sea paintings. Gudin sat in judgment; Isabey improved on the colors in nature; Le Poittevin and others who painted without models were all the rage. It was hardly the moment to introduce gray into pictures. They wouldn't have it at any price. One could only retire to one's province and wait for better days; and so I stayed where I was for almost fifteen years without returning to Paris. "

Boudin felt a permanent need to remain true to nature seen under its own light, and ceaselessly renewed his vision as he contemplated the swift changes in the seaside atmosphere. This is his note on Sunday December 12... " I went out this afternoon. It was a feast—I did well to extract some enjoyment from this wonderful day; it led me to all manner of conclusions about painting. How one is continually painting depressingly and without enough light! I must have made twenty fresh starts to capture this subtlety, this exquisite light which is playing all round me. How cool it all is; what a soft, faded, pinkish atmosphere. Objects are *drenched* in it. It is all light-values. The sea was wonderful; the sky was downy, like velvet, then it took on a yellow tinge; it became warm, then as the sun set, it suffused the scene with shades of purple. The earth and breakwaters assumed the same tones... "
" Objects are drenched. " Is not that a large, and by no means the least important aspect of Impressionism? And a little later, in a letter of April 3, 1866, Boudin states, " One should use tones in all their freshness and endeavor to give them brilliance. " Thus, his ideas by then were not far removed from those of Claude Monet whom he had initiated into open air painting in 1858. The latter recorded that if he had become a painter, he owed it to Boudin [34], " I confess, " Monet said to me, " that I was far from enthusiastic about doing the kind of painting that Boudin was doing. However, persuaded by him, I agreed to work with him in the open air; I bought a box of paints and off we went to Rouelles, though with no great conviction on my part. Boudin set up his easel and began to paint. I watched him with some apprehension, then more attentively and finally it was like the sudden tearing of a veil. I had understood, grasped what painting could be; through the mere example of this painter in love with his art and independence, my destiny as a painter had opened up. "

During 1862 Boudin befriended the Dutch painter Jongkind whom he had met at Trouville, where the latter had already spent a little time with Isabey who had introduced him to the district. Jongkind stayed at Le Havre and Sainte-Adresse, and during the summers of 1863, 1864 and 1865 he was to return regularly to Honfleur. It was from the contact between these two painters that what was called " Pre-Impressionism " first arose. Boudin was not slow to express a deep admiration for Jongkind, stating that, " It is Jongkind who opened the door through which he himself and all the Impressionists entered, " an opinion shared by Edouard Manet, who described Jongkind as the " Father of modern landscape, " and followed by the Goncourt brothers who in 1882 noted in their *Diary*, " All landscape painting of any value at the present time originates in this painter. "

And Signac himself relates that, returning from London in 1872 where they had been studying Turner... " Monet and Pissarro joined forces with Jongkind, then in full possession of his effective technique which enables him to interpret the most subtle and fugitive play of light. They observed the similarity between his method and Turner's; they realized all the profit they could derive from the purity of the one and the technique of the other... " [35] Actually Jongkind was both an astonishing innovator and a traditionalist. An innovator in his shimmering, vibrant water colors, executed in the open and inspired by his master Shelfhout; traditionalist in his studio painting with the memory of his great predecessors, Jacob Van Ruysdael, Van Goyen, Vermeer, present in his mind.

By 1862 Jongkind was already painting direct from nature water colors which were to have a decisive influence on the art of Monet and his circle. In August 1864 Monet wrote to Bazille after the latter had stayed at the farm of Saint Siméon, " There's quite a crowd of us at the moment... Boudin and Jongkind are here; we get on wonderfully together. I'm very sorry that you are not here, for there's a great deal one can learn in such company. "

In point of fact Monet owes a good deal to Jongkind; and if he is indebted to Courbet for his first pictorial experiments in the direction of realism and to Boudin for the art of outdoor painting, he first became aware of all the vibrant animation of nature in Jongkind's water colors. Jongkind had, indeed, a special technique for suggesting the instantaneousness of reflections : his brush " sweeps over " the paper in light " moving " touches with incomparable fluidity and transparency. And in his account of the Salon of 1863 Castagnary makes this remark in connection with him " ... For some time there has been no doubt about his highly expressive and original talent... those striking *Views of the Seine*, unforgettable once you have looked at them. I like this Jongkind; for me, he is an artist to his finger tips; he has a rare and true sensibility. With him, *everything is in the impression;* thought takes the hand along with it. He is scarcely concerned with technique at all, which means that you are not concerned with it either, as you face his paintings. Once the sketch or the picture is finished, you don't bother about the execution; it melts away before the power or charm of the effect. " [36] And later [37], " Jongkind's *Canal de Hollande*, with its fantastic appearance and its *quivers of light...* "

Now that he was part of the Impressionist *milieu*, although he was never an official member of the group nor did he ever exhibit with it, Jongkind continued to paint in Normandy, Paris, Holland, England. Sometimes his production became a commercial matter, and the artist underwent various crises of alcoholism and madness. In 1873 he retired to the Dauphiné and two years later took up residence at Côte-Saint-André near Grenoble. There he executed his best paintings and marvelous water colors, heightened with gouache, a technique which enabled him, like the rest of the Impressionists, to make snow and its opalescent reflections a frequent subject. He does not paint white, he " suggests it "; thinning his palette, he colors it with innumerable tints, and by means of a host of little touches conveys the most transient effects in nature. This painter of atmosphere set himself to fix his retinal impressions with a staggering freedom of technique, deliberately practicing the " unfinished " sketch under the stimulus of the immediate sensation.

JOHANN-BARTHOLD JONGKIND — THE ISÈRE. WATER COLOR. 1877 (11 × 15 3/4 ") — CABINET DES DESSINS, LOUVRE, PARIS

STANISLAS LÉPINE — THE SEINE AT IVRY. 1882 (23 × 44 1/2 ") — PRIVATE COLLECTION, PARIS

Lépine

In connection with the masters of the School of Saint Siméon who came under the influence of Corot, those artists who were more captivated with the subtleties of gray atmosphere than light and its intensity, we should mention Stanislas Lépine. Although he was born at Caen, of which he has left many views, he did more painting from the quays of the Seine in Paris than in Normandy. A pupil of Corot's, he fell under the latter's influence to such a point that some of his works are completely imbued with the spirit of the Master, his sensibility in light-values and in his variations on the " gray atmosphere " theme. Quieter, more " intimate " than Boudin's or Jongkind's, Lépine's art remains essentially poetic and vaporous. He first exhibited in 1859 and submitted paintings to the Salon with great regularity. Although outside the groups, he took part in the first Impressionist Exhibition of 1874.

It is strange to think that the development of Impressionism was partly carried out through the intermediary of painters experimenting with harmonies in gray, subtle values though in a fairly uniform key, and attracted by the misty atmosphere of the Northern beaches or the banks of the Seine ; whereas the Impressionists proper practically outlawed gray from their palettes, never recoiled before the boldest colors and had a predilection for bright light effects.

PAUL GUIGOU — THE BANKS OF LA JOUINE AUX MILLES. 1869 (11 × 18 ") — PRIVATE COLLECTION, PARIS

THE PROVENCE SCHOOL

HOWEVER, another group of artists, fascinated in this case by the intensity of light, limpidity of brilliant blue skies, violently contrasted shadows and the splendor of bright, clear colors opposed to deep and " colored " blacks, was to arise in sun-drenched Provence. They derived from Courbet and realism but at the same time prepared the way for Impressionism. Is it permissible to use the term Provençal School just for two masters, Guigou and Bazille? Certainly, for these artists had a very characteristic style. Their technique was to have a certain repercussion on that of the Impressionists proper with whom they joined forces when they stayed in Paris.

Nor should we forget that another Provençal painter, Adolphe Monticelli (1824-1886), similarly strongly influenced by Courbet and Diaz, though his part in the birth of Impressionism was small, was associated with the circle. His influence, exercised much later, was none the less considerable, particularly on Van Gogh who wrote to his brother in 1888, " My present studies are carried out in single squeezes from the tube. The touch is not divided up to any extent and the tones are often broken and, in a word, I find myself involuntarily using impasto in the Monticelli manner, " and, May 15, 1889, in the same vein, " There are times when I think I am really an extension of this man, only, I haven't produced his amorous color. "

Guigou

Théodore Duret records that Paul Guigou often accompanied him to the Café Guerbois where he got in touch with Pissarro. In an article on the Salon which appeared in the *Electeur Libre* [38] in 1870, the critic writes, " Paul Guigou began by painting landscapes which, because of their crude colors and violation of the conventional rules, at first frightened the public off. Since then, he has fortunately shed some part of the archaic roughness and exaggerated crudity of his initial work and has succeeded in producing landscapes in which the truth of tones and color-accent merge into a harmonious whole... His favorite subject is the bare and desolate landscape of Provence, and he compensates for the aridity of the scene by the sincerity with which he renders the coloration of water, rocks, mountains and the lively light which he projects over this country. "

The role played by Guigou in the development of Impressionism is insignificant compared with that of Boudin or Jongkind both of whose influence was truly decisive. But it was far from negligible, for Guigou is one of the indispensable links between Courbet's realism and the Impressionist vision; he had a share in the creation of clear, luminous painting; he was successful in evoking the burning intensity of the sun, and he painted with a full brush with somewhat rough pigment such as the Impressionists were to use on many occasions; he worked on subjects at Saint-Mammès and along the banks of the Loing before Sisley. One of the best examples of his work is *La Route de la Gineste près de Marseille* (Jeu de Paume) or *The Banks of la Jouine aux Milles* (Private Coll., Paris).

Bazille

From 1862, Bazille frequented Gleyre's studio where he met Monet, and began working out of doors at Easter 1863. He writes to his mother, " ... I have been spending a week at the little village of Chailly near Fontainebleau. I was with my friend Monet from Le Havre who is pretty good at landscape. He gave me some very helpful advice... "

At the beginning of 1864 he shared a studio with his friend Villa and wrote to his father. " ... The owner has let us have a bit of garden that contains a peach tree and some lilacs; it will be very nice for us in summer to paint figures in the sunlight there. "

We see then that Bazille was interested in the problem of painting figures out of doors and his experiments in this domain are parallel to those of Claude Monet who was to take him to Normandy in June 1864, " As soon as we arrived in Honfleur, " he writes, " we looked for landscape subjects. They were easy to find, for this country is paradise... We are putting up in Honfleur itself at a baker's who has let us have two small rooms. We have our meals at the farm of Saint Siméon, situated on the cliff a little below Honfleur... I get up every morning at five and paint all day long until eight in the evening. You mustn't expect me to bring good landscapes back; I am making progress, that is all I can say. It's all I ask; I hope to be satisfied with myself after three or four years painting." From that time on he devoted himself exclusively to his work and during the summer of 1864 he painted a figure in the open air, the portrait of his cousin Thérèse des Hours *(The Pink Dress)*, seated on the edge of the terrace at Méric, overlooking the village of Castelnau-le-Lez, golden in the setting sun (Jeu de Paume).

That same year, no doubt under the influence of Monet, he left Gleyre's studio. "What M. Gleyre is teaching me—the craft of painting—can be learned very well anywhere," he writes.

His friendship with Monet led him to help the latter in the execution of his large-scale painting, *Women in a Garden*, of 1867, for which he paid 2,500 francs in monthly installments of 50 francs. M. Gaston Poulain has in fact proved that this composition was inspired by photographs shown by Bazille to Monet of his sister-in-law and his three cousins in the Méric garden.

But Monet's work and Bazille's pictures were turned down that year by the Salon. Far from being discouraged by this setback, the latter derived a kind of pride from it and even began to think of a private exhibition in which some of the "independent" painters would form a group. In a letter announcing the news to his parents, he remarks, "... I am sharing this fate with all the best artists in the Salon this year... Courbet, Corot, Diaz, Daubigny and many others whom you may not know have promised to send pictures to us and strongly commend our idea. With these people and Monet, who is stronger than all of them, we are bound to succeed." But the scheme failed for lack of funds. It was to be taken up again in 1874 when these same artists under the collective title of "Anonymous Society of Painters, Sculptors, Engravers, etc." were to exhibit at the premises of the photographer Nadar. It was the first Impressionist Exhibition.

Bazille encouraged Monet to paint his *Women in a Garden* and was also himself attracted by the subject of figures in the open air. In 1867 he embarked on his masterpiece *La Famille Bazille*, called *La Réunion de Famille*, shown in the 1868 Salon under the title *La Famille X...* and repainted by the artist in 1869 (Jeu de Paume). Under the large chestnut tree on the Méric terrace, from left to right we see the painter himself, half-hidden by his uncle, M. des Hours; then, sitting on a bench, his mother and father, Mme and M. Gaston Bazille; standing behind them, Dr. Teulon and his wife (the artist's cousin, Pauline des Hours); seated by a table, Mme des Hours, Frédéric's maternal aunt with her daughter Thérèse; on the right, Marc Bazille and his wife (Suzanne Tissié); lastly, his youngest cousin, Camille des Hours.

This composition, apart from a few retouches, was, like Monet's *Women in a Garden*, painted entirely out of doors. Nevertheless the figures look ill at ease; they have the air of posing before the painter as before a photographer. It is nearer to the realism of Courbet or Manet than Claude Monet's free spontaneity. The latter treats his figures in the light more like silhouettes. We should however draw attention to the light effects on the ground, common to both artists, and proof of their insistence on the expression of shimmering reflections.

Now a more regular customer at the Café Guerbois where he met his Impressionist friends again, Bazille painted further open-air canvases between 1868 and 1870. *The View of the Village* (1868, Montpellier Museum) is permeated with the golden light of the Provençal atmosphere. Berthe Morisot, recounting her visit to the Salon, to her sister, Mme Pontillon, writes in a letter dated May 1, 1869, " The great Bazille has painted something that I consider very good—it is a little girl in a very light colored dress, in the shadow of a tree behind which you can see a village; there is a great deal of light and sunshine, *he is trying to do what we have so often attempted—to paint a figure in the open air;* this time he seems to me to have succeeded. "

But Bazille was keen to take his experiment a stage further. Before Renoir, Cézanne and Seurat, he proposed to paint nudes in the open air, bathing scenes. This enabled him to study, over and above the effect of intense luminosity on the landscape and the flickering light on the leaves, the reflections in water and their effect on flesh. His *Summer Scene* which we might also call *Bathing in the Lez* (1869, Fogg Art Museum, Cambridge, Mass.) is characteristic from this point of view. Bazille's historiographer, M. le Canon Sarraute, quotes one of the notes of the artist in his sketchbook, " For the bathers—remember to compare the value of the clear water properly with the grass in the sunlight. Factories in the sunlight in the background. "

In June 1870, shortly before his enlistment in the army and his premature death in the Franco-Prussian War, Bazille started a landscape by the banks of the Lez near the Naviteau mill; in a letter to his father in which he speaks of " this large landscape which is beginning to take shape " and which he left unfinished, he adds, " the heat is evaporating everything and reigns tranquil and alone. " Haven't we got in that last sentence the essential principle of the first impression of the artist and of that Impressionism which he anticipated, nay more than anticipated, truly inaugurated ?

FORMATION OF THE IMPRESSIONIST GROUP

The Académie Suisse and the Atelier Gleyre

WHILE OPEN air painting was developing in these two provincial centers, one in Normandy, the other in Provence, in Paris some artists were banding together who, passionately believing in their new pictorial conception, were to defy sarcasm and insult. Between 1857 and 1863 they formed two distinct groups, one at the *Académie Suisse*, the other in the studio of the artist Gleyre whose liberal teaching had appealed to these painters, reluctant as they were to submit to the discipline of the École des Beaux-Arts. The *Académie Suisse* and the *Atelier Gleyre* provided these bold young men—the future Impressionists—eager to work outside established principles, with a haven of peace where they could discuss at leisure, draw and paint freely and at a moderate cost.

The *Académie Suisse*, situated on the quai des Orfèvres, near Pont Saint-Michel, owed its name to the proprietor, a former model. In this unofficial academy they could work from life, on their own resources, without advice or correction. Both Courbet and Edouard Manet had attended it. Camille Pissarro, who had come from the Antilles in 1855, went there in 1857 and met the young Claude Monet, also present. Cézanne arrived there from Provence in 1861 at the age of twenty-two, and came under the influence of Pissarro. Guillaumin went there to draw in 1863 and formed a friendship with Pissarro and Cézanne.

Moreover, another group which was known as the *Groupe des Quatre* set itself up at the end of 1862 in the studio opened by Gleyre, a teacher at the École des Beaux-Arts. This unofficial studio, only indirectly connected with the Beaux-Arts and very unexacting, attracted those who showed a certain hostility to official and academic teaching. So it came about that Frédéric Bazille became the first pupil, in the autumn of 1862, followed in November of the same year by Claude Monet, then Auguste Renoir and finally Alfred Sisley.

But even in the first weeks a certain hostility was manifested between the professor—who did his criticisms on Mondays—and his four recalcitrant pupils. Later Monet tells that one day when he had copied the model too closely, Gleyre gave him the following advice, " ... Remember, young man, that when you are drawing from life, you must always think of the antique. Nature, my friend, is all very well as material for study, but it offers no interest. Style, you know, that's what matters ! " [39] And Renoir, who had also joined in 1862 and had tried to copy the model as faithfully as possible, had once heard Gleyre remark, after a rapid glance at his study, " I expect you paint for amusement ? " " Certainly I do, " replied Renoir, " and if it didn't amuse me, believe me, I shouldn't do it ! " [40]

A bond of sympathy was soon established between Monet and Renoir who were joined by Bazille and Sisley, though the two latter took their work there more seriously—Sisley in fact had even contemplated competing for the Prix de Rome. These four painters now formed a separate group.

Monet, who, thanks to his contact with Courbet, Boudin and Jongkind, already had some experience behind him, soon rebelled against his master, and gradually won his friends over to his libertarian doctrines. In 1863 he led them out of the studio (" Let's get out of this, " he said, " the place is unhealthy, the atmosphere's false ") to work in the Louvre after the old masters, and, even recommending open-air painting, took them off to the Forest of Fontainebleau. When by the beginning of 1864, Gleyre had to give up his school, the four friends were completely independent, and from that moment their friendship never relapsed.

Still through Monet, who, as we have seen, had also attended the *Académie Suisse*, by the year 1863 relations were established between the *Groupe des Quatre* and the *Trois* of the *Académie Suisse*. They were soon joined by Whistler, Fantin-Latour, Edma and Berthe Morisot, Manet, Degas and Odilon Redon. Some of them, for the sake of economy, shared a studio in common; Monet and Bazille for example, from January 15 to February 4, 1866, lived in the same studio—6, rue de Furstenberg, the house in which Eugène Delacroix had died.

44

BUT IT WAS Edouard Manet who, thanks to an exhibition of his work, followed by the Salon des Refusés episode, was to become the hero of the aesthetic revolution. From this time on, as leader of the avant-garde school, he was associated with the future Impressionists, and although he was not yet painting in their manner, to which he did not come round until between 1873 and 1874, it was he who watched over the destinies of the new tendencies.

The bolder spirits among the young artists turned to this man whose frank and daring technique and method of contrasting bright colors with velvety and colored blacks, whose realist subjects borrowed from modern life according to the aesthetic principles preached by Baudelaire, marked him out as an innovator.

Thus the exhibition of his works that Manet organized at the Galerie Martinet, 26, boulevard des Italiens, March-April 1863, had far-reaching effects. The artist exhibited fourteen canvases, including some that had been inspired by the variegated costumes and picturesque poses of a troupe of Spanish dancers who had performed at the Paris Hippodrome in 1861 and 1862. We should draw particular attention to *The Absinthe Drinker* (1859, Ny Carlsberg Glyptotek, Copenhagen), *Concert in the Tuileries Gardens* (1860, National Gallery, London)—an attempt if not at direct open-air painting, at least one that aimed at that effect—*The Old Musician* (1862, National Gallery of Art, Washington, Chester Dale Collection), *The Spanish Ballet* (1862, Phillips Collection, Washington) and above all the picture of the ballerina, *Lola de Valence*, begun in 1861 and finished in 1862 (Jeu de Paume). The latter, inspired by Goya, was shown to the public accompanied by Baudelaire's celebrated quatrain :

> *Entre tant de beautés que partout on peut voir,*
> *Je comprends bien, amis, que le désir balance,*
> *Mais on voit scintiller en Lola de Valence*
> *Le charme inattendu d'un bijou rose et noir* [40 b].

Both critics and public were furious. Even the most intelligent of the former saw in these paintings " a motley of red, blue, yellow and black which is the caricature of color and not color itself. " The young painters, on the other hand, especially the " four " from the *Atelier Gleyre*, were, as we have said, fascinated by this lively, colorful painting.

Nevertheless I must here express my astonishment at the widely held opinion that Edouard Manet was the originator of *peinture claire* [40 c]—that is, working from light to dark—objecting as I do to the term " light " when the truth is that Manet very often employed blacks, except during his later Impressionist period ; and Baudelaire and Renoir both noticed this, the former when he speaks of the "pink and black jewel" with reference to *Lola de Valence*, the latter when he remarks, " Manet was still much surer with his black and white than with the light colors. " We might observe, further, that artists before Manet used just as light and lively colors—Delacroix, for example, in his *Death of Sardanapalus* and *Algerian Women* particularly, Courbet in his portrait of the *Sénora Adela Guerrero*, a Spanish dancer (1851, Musée des Beaux-Arts, Brussels), which has a kinship with *Lola de Valence*, and in

45

his *Demoiselles des bords de la Seine*, with their dresses of bright, high-keyed colors, contrasted with the dark tones.

The severity of the Salon hanging committee aroused a reaction on the part of the critics and of public opinion. The Emperor Napoleon III then resolved to exhibit the rejected works *en bloc* in another part of the Palais de l'Industrie. Some of the artists, resenting this gesture, withdrew their pictures, but three hundred painters had the opportunity of showing about six hundred pictures to the public. The so-called Salon des Refusés opened on May 15, shortly after the official inauguration on May 1. Criticism was virulent and the public flocked to jeer or protest. Among the artists represented we should mention in particular Cals, Jongkind with three canvases, Pissarro with three landscapes, Whistler with a single work, Fantin-Latour, etc. But one name, Edouard Manet, and one of the three paintings he exhibited, *Le Bain* (No. 363 in the catalog) also called *La Partie carrée* and still better known as *Le Déjeuner sur l'herbe (The Picnic)*, produced the most vigorous reactions—indignation, protest, jeers for the most part but admiration, understanding and complete approval from a minority, grouped round Antonin Proust and Zacharie Astruc who boldly declared, " ... Manet's talent has an astonishingly authoritative side, an uncompromising, sober, energetic element accounted for by a temperament that is both reserved and rapturous and above all responsive to intense impressions. " [41]

The independent artists we have named looked upon Manet as the standard-bearer of the new tendencies in painting and from this time on associated him with their own experiments, although this painter vigorously denied that he was a revolutionary, believing himself on the contrary a traditionalist, since he owed his inspiration for this work which had been so violently decried to an engraving by Marc-Antoine Raimondi after a lost composition of Raphael as well as to Giorgione's famous *Concert champêtre* (Louvre).

Although this huge composition of Manet's was painted in his Batignolles studio it created to some extent the illusion of the open air. It is painted in very freely applied brush strokes and the term " light-keyed " was mentioned in its connection. In point of fact Manet, who had |considered Giorgione's *Concert champêtre* too dark, had stated, " I want to paint that over again, and do it in the transparency of the atmosphere. "

In my opinion, however, the work is far from being as light and luminous as people have made out, at any rate in comparison with the paintings of the future Impressionists. I will go further and say that it is not as light and luminous as many canvases painted by Courbet, whose *Demoiselles des bords de la Seine* of 1856 (Petit-Palais, Paris) perhaps conveys the sensation of open air more effectively. *Le Déjeuner sur l'herbe* is still far removed from that play of reflections, luminosity, intensity of truly light colors—black was banned from their palettes—of the Impressionists proper. In |spite of everything, the work is imbued with the tradition of the old masters; the attitudes, gestures and expressions of the figures—Eugène Manet, the painter's brother, Ferdinand Lennhoff, the Dutch sculptor who became his brother-in-law, and Victorine Meurend, Manet's favorite model between 1862 and 1874—are artificial and look posed; the light, cool and uniform, is indeed a studio light and not the vibrating shimmer of true open air.

At the time of the 1864 Salon when two of Manet's canvases were accepted, *Episode in a Bull-Fight* and *The Angels at the Tomb of Christ*, the caricaturist Bertail in the *Journal amusant* satirized the various influences which the painter had undergone so far : " Spanish toys done up with a Ribera *black* sauce by M. Manet y Courbetos y Zurbaran de las Batignolas. "

Shortly after, on the occasion of the opening of the 1865 Salon, a new scandal broke out. Manet's *Olympia*, which he had painted in 1863 from his model Victorine Meurend, was accepted. The composition of the picture was inspired by Titian's *Urbino Venus* (Uffizi, Florence), which he had copied in Italy in 1853, the spirit and technique by Goya's *Maja desnuda* (Prado, Madrid). Once more Manet aimed at being traditional and representing a kind of odalisque; but the Negress and cat, with their Baudelairian atmosphere, lent themselves to the worst constructions. The subject was regarded as a vindication of prostitution.

And although Baudelaire wrote Manet a letter of encouragement from Brussels and Émile Zola had the courage to state, " This canvas is truly the painter's flesh and blood; fate has marked it out for a place in the Louvre, " the critics pounced on the picture and its author. " What is this odalisque with the ignoble yellow belly representing Olympia; God knows where the model was picked up ! " exclaimed Jules Claretie in *L'Artiste*. " The Venus with the cat is merely a kind of female gorilla... Women about to become mothers... would do well to avoid this spectacle, " mocked Amédée Canteloube. " The crowd flocks in front of the overripe Olympia and the horrible *Ecce Homo* of M. Manet's as if they were at the Morgue, " wrote Paul de Saint-Victor in *La Presse*, and even Courbet exclaimed, " It's flat, it isn't modeled, it looks like the Queen of Spades coming out of a bath ! " [42]

Thus, wearied with it all, Manet fled the scandal and Paris the same year, 1865, and went to Spain to see on the spot those masters who were such a deep influence on him. It was there that he met Théodore Duret who became one of his most fervent champions and admirers and wrote to Fantin-Latour, " Velasquez is decidely *the* painter among painters. He did not astonish me, he enraptured me. " Strangely enough, Manet abandoned the technique and subjects of the Spanish masters after this brief stay and sought his inspiration in contemporary life. The year 1866 saw the rejection of two of his pictures from the Salon, *The Piper* and *The Tragic Actor* or *Portrait of Rouvière as Hamlet*.

Despite this exclusion of the artist from the Salon, controversy broke out following a series of articles by Emile Zola in *L'Evénement;* in his third article, devoted to Manet, he was daring enough to reiterate, " Manet's place is reserved for him as it is for Courbet in the Louvre and like that of any artist of a strong and original temperament. Our fathers jeered at Courbet and now we rave over him. We jeer at M. Manet and our sons will rave over these canvases. " Defying public opinion in this way Zola, yielding to the violent protests, had to resign without completing his series of articles. However, he resumed the battle in a long monograph devoted to Manet which appeared in the *Revue du Siècle*, February 1867, under the title *A New Way of Painting : M. Edouard Manet*.

The same year saw the rejection of many artists by the Salon; Renoir and Monet in particular were among the two thousand turned down. Manet, who had not submitted any paintings, was anxious to follow Courbet's example and hold a comprehensive show of his work at the International Industrial Exhibition of 1867. He therefore had a private hut erected, not far from Courbet's, by the very entrance gates of the Palais de l'Industrie, close to the Place de l'Alma, in order to display some fifty of his canvases with an introduction by Zacharie Astruc. Zola provided a separate edition of his previous articles with the title *Edouard Manet, a Critical and Biographical Study*. Despite this effort, Manet's exhibition only succeeded in becoming a public joke; this is how Antonin Proust describes it, " Husbands took their wives along to the Pont de l'Alma. It seemed that everybody had to go along and offer himself and his family this unique opportunity of splitting his sides. The whole Paris population of so-called painters met their friends at the Manet Exhibition. It became a chorus of guffawing fools... The press unanimously followed suit. "

The Café Guerbois

Because of all these happenings, Edouard Manet, in spite of himself, was regarded as the champion of an " avant-garde " art. Every new trend or revolutionary idea was associated with his name. It therefore seemed natural to the young embryonic Impressionists to seek the support of their elder brother, the more wonderful in their eyes the more he was discussed. So these artists who had hitherto met in small separate groups in Fantin-Latour's studio, rue des Beaux-Arts, or in Manet's at Batignolles, decided to meet at least once a week—on a Thursday—in a quieter café than the Café de Bade, boulevard des Italiens, frequented by Manet up to this time. Their choice fell on the Café Guerbois (now the brasserie Muller), grande-rue des Batignolles (later 59, avenue de Clichy) to air their plans and new ideas about art.

Thanks to their notoriety, first Manet, then Zola presided over these meetings, which were attended by writers and critics including Duranty, Théodore Duret, Zola's friend Paul Alexis, Zacharie Astruc the sculptor and poet, Edouard Maître, a musicologist of taste, the photographer Nadar, Constantin Guys, Alfred Stevens, Guillemet, the engraver Bracquemond, Fantin-Latour, Bazille accompanied by his friend Major Lejosne, Degas, Renoir, Monet, Sisley, Pissarro and Cézanne, the latter less sociable, more reticent than the others, afraid " they might get hold of him. "

The exact date of the first meetings at the Café Guerbois is not known. According to Tabarant and Théodore Duret, they went back to 1866; other witnesses suggest an earlier date; at any rate, it was between 1868 and 1870 that the new way of painting was gradually worked out after many discussions. Claude Monet later revealed the importance these meetings—at which arguments, sometimes violent, led to the real genesis of Impressionism—had for him and his friends.

The Japanese Influence

About this time, that is to say during the decade 1860-1870, a number of factors which marked a decisive turning point in Impressionism supplemented the part played by Delacroix (who had just died in his rue de Furstenberg studio, August 13, 1863), the important contribution made by Corot and Courbet, and lastly the vital ascendency of Edouard Manet. The first of these was the influence of the Japanese print.

Following the resumption of trade relations with Japan in 1854, the works of the Tokugawa period poured into Europe and awoke a lively curiosity; *Japonisme* immediately spread in connoisseur and artist circles; the engraver Brac-

48

quemond " discovered " Hokusai in 1856. Shortly after, in 1862, a shop " La Porte chinoise " was opened in Paris in the rue de Rivoli, where painters and writers had an opportunity of admiring the works of the Far East. Finally everybody flocked into the " Oriental Pavilion " at the *Exposition Universelle* of 1867, already referred to. So it was possible for an author in 1879 to state, " *Japonisme* is the craze of the moment and will become, I hope, the artistic cult of the future. " But a short while before, in 1878, the critic Ernest Chesneau, in an article on *Japan in Paris* [43] and its influence on the Impressionists, had concluded, " And they all discovered in it a confirmation of their personal way of seeing, feeling, understanding and interpreting nature. Hence, a redoubling of individual originality instead of a cowardly submission to Japanese art. "

If Utamaro's works did not have a great appeal to French painters, some of Hokusai's prints, the innumerable woodcuts of his imitators and successors and Hiroshige's landscapes enjoyed an immense prestige.

In his *Thirty-six Views of Fujiyama*, Hokusai created those series in which the atmosphere of one single site is conjured up in all its diversity and subtlety— a prelude to the numerous series of variations of a Claude Monet. Light plays as important a role in Hiroshige's landscapes as in the works of the Impressionists.

Whistler was one of the artists most influenced by the masters of the Japanese print, and his subjects, like his technique, were profoundly affected. Manet, on the other hand, owes less to them. The Japanese vogue is more in evidence in the décor than in the style of his canvases, the *Portrait of Zola* and *Nina de Callias*, called *The Lady with the Fans* (Jeu de Paume).

Claude Monet followed this fashion in his *Japanese Lady* or *Camille Monet in Fancy Dress* of 1876 (Private Collection, U.S.A.). He was moreover so fascinated by these prints that he covered the walls of his Giverny house with them. It was no doubt looking at them that gave him the idea of his " series " and caused him once and for all to reject forms in favor of the atmosphere which dissolves them into evanescent evocations.

Even Degas abandoned the Florentines and M. Ingres, captivated by the instantaneity of life and gesture that he discovered in Hokusai's Mangwa, and his pictorial disposition was completely revolutionized as a result. From now on he adopted the oblique viewpoint, traditional in the Far East, as in *Absinthe* (Jeu de Paume), and even returned to certain themes such as *Women at their Toilet*. We shall be seeing later that this *Japonisme* inspired Toulouse-Lautrec's extreme schematization and nicely calculated economy of gesture, and that Van Gogh at Arles in 1888 was haunted by it. Finally Gauguin and the Masters of Pont-Aven, like the Nabis later, were to borrow their flat tints and *cloisonnisme* or partitioning from these prints.

Photography

Furthermore, from the mid-nineteenth century onwards, following Niepce's and Daguerre's experiments, photographic technique was making great strides. People admired the skill and audacity of Nadar who had opened a studio and, in 1854, started publishing under the title of the *Panthéon Nadar* a striking gallery of contemporary celebrities, and in 1856 had successfully taken some very remarkable aerial photographs from the balloon of the Godard brothers. Up to about 1871 the snapshot was a rarity and was not really developed until 1875.

Photography opened up new vistas to artists; it enabled writers to describe a landscape accurately without leaving their desks; it showed painters natural details which sometimes escaped them and frequently revealed familiar scenes at a novel angle; it broke up movements, those of horses on a racecourse, for example. It offered therefore new possibilities of expression, and we see Degas turning to this mechanical aid, newly at his disposal, to perfect himself in the study of actions. He could now analyze them and in them was to discover original arrangements, mostly for his racecourse subjects. Extensive compositions, inspired by those produced by the camera lens, abound in his work. Bazille and Claude Monet also made use of the camera for some of their pictures; we have already had an example in *Women in a Garden* which Monet composed from photographs that Bazille showed him.

However, the new invention which, to begin with, was merely a practical aid to the artist, rapidly turned into a rival. " It persuades us to renounce the desire to describe whatever is capable of being mechanically recorded, " asserted Paul Valéry, who as far as literature was concerned, welcomed this competition for writers inclined to over-descriptive realism : ... " with the first advent of photography the descriptive *genre* began to invade the realm of letters. Finally Daguerre came [43a]. "

There was an attempt to make photography into a new art to which Baudelaire was hostile, and declaimed vehemently against it in his famous diatribe [44]: " Concerning painting and sculpture, the current creed of the great public, especially in France (and I challenge anyone to deny the truth of this) is as follows : ' ... I believe in nature and I believe only in nature (there are good reasons for that). I believe that art is, and can only be, the exact reproduction of nature (a timid and dissenting sect insists on the exclusion of distasteful objects such as a chamber pot or a skeleton). ' Thus, an industry which would give us a result identical to nature would be an *absolute* art. An avenging Deity has granted the prayers of this multitude. Daguerre was their Messiah. They then said to themselves, ' Since photography provides us with every guarantee of exactness we could wish for (the idiots really believe that !) art is photography... ' Poetry and progress are a pair of ambitious fellows who hate each other with an instinctive hatred, and when they meet on the same road, one has to give way to the other. If photography is to be allowed to take over some of the functions of art, it will totally supplant or corrupt it within a short space of time, thanks to the natural ally it will find in the stupidity of the masses. It is therefore imperative that it should return to its true duty which is to be the servant of the sciences and the arts and the very humble servant, like printing and stenography which have neither created nor suppressed literature. But if photography is allowed to encroach on the domain of the intangible and imaginary on everything that owes its value to the contribution made by man's soul, then woe upon us ! "

In point of fact the Impressionist painters found in photography a rival of their new vision of the world and were to try and seize in flight the fleeting moment, those brief and rapid movements which escape the limits of photographic snapshots and were to create half-discerned reality, a hitherto unsuspected world of fiction.

50

It was perhaps under the stimulus of photography that the painters of this time treated subjects taken from the " modernity " to which Baudelaire refers in connection with Constantin Guys [45], " Modernity is the transitory, the fugitive, the accidental, the half of art whose other half is the eternal, the immutable. Every old master has his own modernity; the majority of fine portraits which have come down to us from the past are wearing the clothes that belong to their period... We have not the right to scorn or ignore this transitory, fugitive element whose metamorphoses are so rapid... I have said that every period had its own bearing, glance, gesture... for almost the whole of our originality derives from the stamp which our own time imprints on our sensations. "

This " fugitive modernity " is expressed on the one hand in the scenes of Paris life, on the other in the evocation of human figures in the open air.

Manet and Degas, as Toulouse-Lautrec later, preferred fashionable scenes, whereas Monet, Sisley, Pissarro and Renoir enjoyed painting the more popular, direct life of the boulevards which led them, about the year 1869, to choose their subjects from boating scenes by the banks of the Seine or bathing places *(la Grenouillère)*, and finally, later on, the tavern gardens as in Renoir's *Moulin de la Galette* (1876) or *Luncheon of the Boating Party* (1881).

For the starting point we have to go back to about 1860-1861 and the *Concert in the Tuileries Gardens* by Manet (National Gallery, London), a real " open-air party " at which numerous personalities of the time are to be found. Degas, Manet, and later, Lautrec adored race-course scenes, another aspect of fashionable life in Paris; Degas' *Courses de Gentlemen, Avant le départ* (1862, Jeu de Paume) and Manet's *Courses à Longchamp* (1862, Art Institute, Chicago) are typical examples. Degas' work finally included an important series of racecourse scenes.

Manet painted a *View of the International Exhibition* (1867, Oslo) after admiring a canvas by Berthe Morisot, *Paris Seen from the Heights of the Trocadéro* (J.T. Ryerson, Chicago) in the Salon of that same year. Degas was embarking on his first studies inspired by the theatre, or the ballet, to be more precise, with that artificial lighting which differentiates him from the Impressionists, devotees of the pure open air—*Mademoiselle Fiocre in the Ballet, la Source* (1867-1868, Brooklyn Museum, New York) or the *Musicians in the Orchestra* (circa 1868-1869, Jeu de Paume).

Claude Monet, on the other hand, had a predilection for the open air and the gaily colored crowds in the light, in views seen from above such as *The Church of St. Germain l'Auxerrois* (Nationalgalerie, Berlin-Dahlem), *The Infanta's Garden* (1866, Dudley Peter Allen Memorial Museum of Art, Oberlin, Ohio), the *Quai du Louvre* (1866, City Museum, The Hague).

Renoir likewise embarked on this genre with the *Champs-Elysées* (1867, Private Collection, Zurich), the *Pont des Arts* (1868), *Skaters in the Bois de Boulogne* (1868-1869, Private Collection, Berne)—canvases which are still somewhat dryly painted but lead up to *The Bathing Place* (1868-1869, National Museum, Stockholm), the *View from the Pont-Neuf* (1872, Marshall Field Collection, New York), the *Grands Boulevards* (1875, Private Collection, U.S.A.) and *Umbrellas* (1882-1883, National Gallery, London).

Sisley exhibited two *Views of Paris* in the 1870 Salon; and Pissarro, but only

ALFRED SISLEY — THE SAINT MARTIN CANAL. 1870 (19 3/4 × 25 1/2 ") — LOUVRE, PARIS

beginning in 1893 towards the end of his career, was to paint a whole series of views of Paris, *Louvre Gardens, On a Gray Morning, La Place du Théâtre-Français* or the *Avenue de l'Opéra, in sunshine, on a winter morning.*

It was doubtless once more because of the influence of photography but certainly also through Courbet that the taste for painting figures in the open air developed.   We see them already in fact in his *Village Girls* (1851, Metropolitan Museum, New York), in *Bonjour, Monsieur Courbet* (1854, Montpellier Museum) and in *Les Demoiselles des bords de la Seine* (1856, Petit-Palais, Paris).

In less than five years we observe a series of masterpieces : Manet's *The Picnic* (1863, Jeu de Paume) and Monet's *The Picnic* (1865, sketch in the Museum, Moscow), his *Camille* (1866, Kunsthalle, Bremen), a year before *Lise with the Sunshade* (1867, Folkwang Museum, Essen) and *Diana* (1867, National Gallery of Art, Chester Dale Collection, Washington, D.C.) by Renoir; *Family Reunion* by Bazille (1867, Jeu de Paume), Monet's *Women in a Garden* (1867, Jeu de Paume), his *Portrait of the Writer Jacquemart* (1867, Kunsthaus, Zurich) and finally *The Sisley Household* by Renoir (1868, Wallraf-Richartz Museum, Cologne).

So far, however, Monet alone in this group really creates the illusion of open air atmosphere and the quivering reflections obtained by pools of bright colors—a

52

technique that alarmed the traditionalist Manet. But the movement towards the exploitation of light and colors pitched in a light key, towards that " puff of fresh air " which was the very essence of the new art, nevertheless is visible in such canvases as Renoir's *The Fishing Boat* (1867, Private Collection, Paris) and Claude Monet's *Argenteuil-sur-Seine* (1868, Art Institute, Chicago) and results—before the full blossoming of Impressionism (but is it not already all there ?)—in two versions of *La Grenouillère* (the *Bathing Place*) painted at the same spot by Renoir and Monet respectively and both decisive turning points in Impressionism. Renoir's version (National Museum, Stockholm) is permeated with an atmosphere in which tender shades of green and blue predominate; Claude Monet's (the Metropolitan Museum, New York) gleams with sunlight and is boldly executed in broad touches loaded with bright, iridescent colors.

CAMILLE PISSARRO — BOULEVARD DES ITALIENS, AFTERNOON. 1897 (29 × 36 1/2 ") — NIARCHOS COLLECTION

CLAUDE MONET — SUMMER. 1874 (22 1/2 × 31 1/2 ") — NATIONALGALERIE, BERLIN-DAHLEM

Impressionism

T HE Franco-Prussian War which witnessed a temporary dispersal of these French painters, marks a break in continuity. But by 1872 and 1873, a re-grouping was already taking place. Impressionism was now to embark on its full development which led to the *First Impressionist Exhibition* of 1874, its first public manifestation.

The decade 1870-1880 is by far its best period; it represents the high spot when, after the gropings, influences, experiments that mark its genesis, the new art comes into full fruition; when the artists—especially Claude Monet—look at nature, certainly, but see it through a kind of dazzle, fascinated by its infinite variations, and discover, as in a kaleidoscope, hitherto unknown colors, combinations of colors, harmonies, values of unparalleled refinement. No longer satisfied with approximations or memories, the painters now cease re-inventing an artificial nature. They contemplate, and this contemplation leads them to set down their manifold sensations or, to be more precise, their visual impressions; their eye receives an impression in the way a photographic plate does. The canvas records the instantaneous impact of their unpremeditated vision; there is no attempt at elaborate composition. Indeed the latter is sometimes quite arbitrary, and they paint intuitively, their hand, by a kind of automatism, merely being an instrument for applying the brush strokes. So far then, no formulas, no prescribed methods—those enemies of art! As Monet was to declare, " Pictures are not made with doctrines ! "

It was only later that, victims of their own mirages, these painters executed *planned, deliberate* works. By then they had ceased painting their own impressions; they were doing Impressionism, and as a critic wittily put it, " art ends where the *'ism* begins ! "

The celebrated " series " of a Monet, for instance, were merely a parody—artificially carried out—of the masterpieces which he himself had painted between 1870 and 1880.

The 1870 War caused, as we have mentioned, the dispersal of the Impressionists at the vital moment in their art. Some of them, Monet, Bazille and Degas in particular, enlisted, and Renoir did not evade his military obligations and was enrolled in the Tenth Light Cavalry and drafted to Bordeaux. Cézanne, on the other hand, took refuge at l'Estaque near Marseilles where he worked indefatigably at his landscape painting, in which the early dark manner was now giving way to a concern with lightness and luminosity; Pissarro and Monet, both socialists and therefore opposed to the régime, embarked for England and were in London during the autumn with Sisley who lived there at this time.

This reunion of the three artists in the English capital was doubly important for the destinies of painting. First and foremost it helped their contact with English masters, Constable and Turner in particular, and we have already seen the all-important role played by these two painters in the development of the Impressionist aesthetic.

At this period Monet painted landscapes of *Hyde Park* and several views of the Thames, including, *The Houses of Parliament* (1871, Hon. J. J. Astor Collection, London), and Pissarro several landscapes inspired by Constable and also *Penge Station, Upper Norwood* (1871, Courtauld Institute, London), directly influenced by Turner's famous *Rain, Steam and Speed.*

Furthermore, thanks to the intervention of Daubigny who was likewise in London, Monet and Pissarro got in touch with Paul Durand-Ruel. The latter had just opened a gallery at 168 New Bond Street, in which between the year 1870 and 1875 he was to organize several exhibitions of contemporary painting. He helped the two artists who were without other financial resources by purchasing some of their works. A strong friendship grew up between them, and Durand-Ruel was from this time on to be one of the chief promoters in Paris of the new school.

On his way back to France Monet passed through Holland where he rejoined Daubigny and painted a few canvases, including the *Landscape, Zaandam* (1871, Jeu de Paume), already impregnated with light and shimmering with reflections on the water. At the beginning of 1871 Pissarro returned to France and found his studio at Louveciennes completely ransacked by the Germans and all his canvases destroyed.

About the year 1872 these artists regrouped. Those belonging to the Gleyre Studio, now only three in number since the death of Bazille, were working in the Paris suburbs.

From this time on, Claude Monet became the undisputed leader of the new school and between 1872 and 1878 he made Argenteuil, where he now resided, with its regattas and rowboats, its main center. He even succeeded in bringing Edouard Manet around to his conception of painting done entirely in the open air. He also attracted Renoir, who lived in Paris but often came out to paint beside him, and Caillebotte. Sisley settled first at Voisins, then Marly where he painted a large number of views of local villages—his *Views of Louveciennes* for example—which have a close atmospheric affinity with Corot's.

At Pontoise Pissarro assumed the leadership of a similar movement with his two friends of the *Académie Suisse*, Guillaumin and Cézanne, who were often joined by Cordey and Vignon.

The Argenteuil group however, painted " as the birds sing "—to use Monet's phrase, without setting themselves any problems, in their healthy intoxication with light and color, whereas the Pontoise group carried out their experiments with a less intuitive bias.

56

The artists resolved to get themselves known by means of a joint exhibition. The Salons from which the majority of them were periodically rejected afforded them no opportunity of showing their talent, and Durand-Ruel's efforts to save them from poverty and bring them before the public were crowned with so little success that for the time being he was unable to back them. After considerable differences of opinion—some of the artists frowned on the scheme—it was decided in 1874 to found a Limited Company (cooperative) of painters, sculptors, engravers, etc.

From April 15 to May 15 they exhibited at 35, boulevard des Capucines at the corner of the rue Daunou, in the rooms which had just been vacated by their friend, the photographer Nadar.

Renoir's brother, Edmond, was responsible for printing the catalog, and although a committee was supposed to be in charge of the hanging, it was Auguste Renoir alone in point of fact who carried it out.

Thirty artists showed 165 works at this *First Impressionist Exhibition.* Cézanne was represented with three canvases, *La Maison du Pendu at Auvers-sur-Oise,* another Auvers landscape and his *Modern Olympia* (Nos. 42-44); Degas with ten paintings, pastels or drawings, the subjects being racecourses, laundresses and ballet dancers (Nos. 54-63); Guillaumin with three landscapes (Nos. 64-66); Monet with five canvases, including his famous *Impression, Sunrise, The Corn Poppies* and seven pastel studies (Nos. 95-103); Berthe Morisot with four paintings, including *The Cradle,* two pastels and three water colors (Nos. 104-112); Pissarro with five landscapes (Nos. 136-140); Renoir with six canvases, including *La Loge* and a *Danseuse,* plus a pastel (Nos. 141-147); finally Sisley with five landscapes (Nos. 161-165).

The other participants—some of whom were less criticized—were : Astruc, Attendu, Béliard, Boudin, Bracquemond, Brandon, Bureau, Cals, Colin, Debras, Latouche, Lepic, Lépine, Levert, Meyer, de Molins, Mulot-Durivage, de Nittis, A. Ottin, L.-A. Ottin, Robert and Rouart [46]. Although urged by his friends, particularly by Monet and Degas, Edouard Manet refused to take part.

The exhibition was open from 10.00 a.m. until 6.00 p.m. but also from 8.00 p.m. up to 10.00 p.m.—which was something new. The entrance fee was one franc and the catalog cost 50 centimes.

People crowded in from the start to make fun of it; jeers often alternated with insults, and the critics refused to take this now historic exhibition seriously. We saw at the beginning of this study that Louis Leroy summed up the general reaction in an article that appeared in *Charivari,* April 25, under the title *Exhibition of the Impressionists,* taken from Claude Monet's *Impression, Sunrise* painted at Le Havre in 1872 (Musée Marmottan, Paris).

The term " Impressionists, " used derisively, was from this time on to replace that of the " Intransigents " as they had hitherto been called.

Jules Claretie also vigorously entered into the attack on the group. " M. Manet " he writes [47], " belongs to those who claim that in painting one can and one should be satisfied with the *impression.* We have seen an exhibition of these ' impressionists ' in the Boulevard des Capucines at Nadar's. MM. Monet—a more intransigent Manet—Pissarro, Mlle Morisot, etc., appeared to be declaring war on beauty. "

However, amid the almost universal hue and cry, Philippe Burty, defending the new art in *La République Française,* April 16, 1874, declared, " ... The group which is the subject of discussion is pursuing with a very personal, very recognizable approach a common aim in art—in technique, the rendering of the broad light of the open air; in feeling, the vividness of the first reaction.   This aim is well worth discussing with our readers. "   This article was followed by a second, dated April 25, which was more analytical and eulogistic.

Nevertheless, since this exhibition did not have the financial success anticipated, the painters of the " Company " determined to hold a sale of their works at the Hôtel Drouot in order to raise some money.   It took place on March 24, 1875.   This caused an even greater scandal and was an almost complete fiasco.   The total profit resulting from the sale of seventy pictures was only 10,346 francs.   Duret and Caillebotte had done their best to run up the bidding, and a new patron, Victor Chocquet, a Customs and Excise Inspector, acquired one of Monet's *Views of Argenteuil;* he subsequently became one of the devoted admirers of the Impressionists, buying various works of theirs.

But the artists refused to be discouraged and in 1876 they decided to organize a second exhibition which took place during the month of April from 10.00 a.m. to 5.00 p.m. each day in the Galerie Durand-Ruel, 11, rue Le Peletier.   There were not a few defections, including in particular that of Cézanne, wearied and displeased by the bitter criticisms he had attracted at the previous exhibition.   Although this time there were only twenty participants, the ensemble of the works displayed—250 paintings, pastels, water colors, drawings and etchings—was much more important and more representative for each artist (no catalog numbers).

Degas was represented by twenty-four works, including *Portraits dans un Bureau (New Orleans),* better known today under the title *The Cotton Office at New Orleans* (Pau Museum); Claude Monet by eighteen paintings, almost exclusively of Argenteuil (several lent by the singer Faure), *The Bathing Place,* " *La Grenouillère* " and *Japonnerie;* Berthe Morisot by thirteen paintings, three water colors and three pastels; Pissarro by a dozen canvases; Renoir by fifteen; finally Sisley with eight landscapes.

These artists had been anxious to associate Frédéric Bazille, who died in 1870, with their exhibition, and he was represented by a portrait in oils and a pastel portrait.   Others who figured there were : Béliard, Beneau, Cals, Gustave Caillebotte (a newcomer who now joined the group), Desboutin, François, Legros, Levert, Lepic, J.-B. Millet (son of the Barbizon painter), L.-A. Ottin, Henri Rouart, Tillot.

If there were fewer visitors than at the First Exhibition, sarcastic comments, oral or in the columns of the press, were not lacking.   Albert Wolff's article which appeared in *Le Figaro* April 3, 1876, in its stupidity and lack of understanding, reflected and typified the almost universal opinion.   " There is a curse on the rue Le Peletier, " he wrote, " after the Opera fire, a fresh disaster has befallen this quarter. An exhibition has just opened at Durand-Ruel's which calls itself an exhibition of painting.   Allured by the banners that decorate the façade, the unsuspecting passer-by enters, and an appaling sight meets his horrified gaze—five or six lunatics, including one woman [49], a group of miserable victims of megalomania, have found a rendezvous in which to show their works.   Some people laugh their heads off in front of these things, but I am distressed.   These self-styled artists call themselves the ' Intransigents, the Impressionists '; they seize canvases, paints and brushes, hurl colors at random and appose their signature to the result.   At Ville-Evrard, deluded spirits pick up pebbles on the road in this way and imagine they have found

58

diamonds.   We have before us the terrible spectacle of human vanity, deranged to the point of madness.   Try to convey to M. Pissarro that trees are not violet, that the sky is not the color of fresh butter and that the things he paints are not to be seen in any country and that no mind can accept such aberrations !   You might as well waste your time trying to make one of Dr. Blanche's patients who thinks he's the Pope, believe that he inhabits the Batignolles quarter and not the Vatican ! Try to make M. Degas listen to reason; tell him that in art exist certain qualities called drawing, color, execution, intention, and he will laugh in your face and treat

AUGUSTE RENOIR — BAI-GNEUSE. 1885 (36 1/4 × 28 3/4")— STERLING AND FRAN-CINE CLARK ART INSTITUTE, WILLIAMSTOWN, MASS.

you as a reactionary. Try to explain to M. Renoir that a woman's torso is not a mass of decomposing flesh with green, mauve patches which denote complete putrefaction in a corpse! There is also, as in all groups of extremists, a woman; she is called Berthe Morizot *(sic)* and she makes interesting observation since in the midst of the excesses of a demented spirit, she maintains her feminine grace." However, these much maligned artists find a few sincere supporters. Armand Sylvestre in his account of the rue Le Peletier Exhibition in *L'Opinion*, April 2, 1876, concludes, "... These experiments are bound to find a place in the evolution of contemporary painting..."

Castagnary in his *Salons* seems to me to be judging the matter with lucidity, moderation and understanding when, in connection with the year 1876 (pp. 213-214), he comments, " Compelling a whole group of artists to refrain from submitting work to the Salon, the course taken by the painters who exhibited last month at Durand-Ruel's, is not a good thing either! What is generally expected of a Salon is that it should present French painting as a whole. Only to that extent can it have a meaning and be instructive. But with your system, such a result is impossible. Not only do your rejections prove that your choice could be improved but your methods exclude painters whose presence is indispensable. Thus what typifies the present Salon is an immense striving towards the light and truth to nature. The taste for techniques and tricks of the trade seems to have gone. All those things that remind us of the conventional, the artificial and the false are out of favor. We did not notice them before; now they shock us. I saw the dawn of this return to unaffected simplicity without realizing that its progress had been so rapid. This year, it has been striking and undisguised. Youth has thrown itself into it wholeheartedly, the public sides with the innovators. All eyes are on these pictures painted direct from life in which the sole aim has been to render the truth—people are ignoring paintings conceived and executed in the studio without the help of a model. Ah well! The Impressionists have played their part in the movement. Those who have visited Durand-Ruel's and seen those true and vibrating landscapes by MM. Claude Monet, Pissarro, Sisley, those subtle and lively portraits by M. Renoir or Mlle Morizot *(sic)*, those promising interiors by M. Caillebotte, the superb choreographic studies by M. Degas, cannot be in any doubt. For these painters the open air is a delectation, the choice of light tones and the banishment of bitumen a veritable act of faith. They should therefore be in the Salon where their presence would be a confirmation of the evolution accomplished and give it its full importance..."

Finally, the most penetrating study appeared that same year, 1876, in an extremely important pamphlet by Duranty, entitled *La Nouvelle Peinture* (apropos the group of artists exhibiting in the Durand-Ruel galleries). Eugène Fromentin having regretfully noted that in his opinion " open-air painting " was being given exaggerated importance, Duranty retorted with a piece of perspicacious pleading without ever making use of the term " impressionism." Analyzing the vision of these artists, he pointed out their qualities, " ... color, drawing and a series of viewpoints—all are original. In the matter of color they have made a true discovery whose origin we should vainly seek elsewhere... Their discovery consists in just this : they have recognized the fact that strong light *takes down* the tones, that sunlight reflected by objects tends through its brilliance to restore them to that luminous unity which turns the seven prismatic rays into one colorless brightness which is light. Progressing by a series of intuitions, they have gradually come to break up the solar light into its rays, its elements and recompose its unity by means of the general harmony of the iridescence which they spread on their canvases. From the point of view of refinement of vision, subtle penetration of color, the result is altogether extraordinary. The most learned physicist could find nothing wrong with their analyses of light...

" Yet in the middle of summer everybody must have passed through a hundred miles of landscape and noticed how hillside, meadow and field melt so to speak into one single luminous reflection that they receive from the sky and reflect back; for that is the law which causes the brilliance in nature; alongside the particular ray, blue, green or mixed, which each substance absorbs, and over and above this ray, it reflects the sum-total of all the rays and the color of the sky that covers the earth. Well, for the first time, painters have understood and reproduced these phenomena... "

Duranty ends this sensible and intelligent analysis by wishing these artists —whom he assures of his full confidence—patience and every success in their new way of painting.

From this time on, conscious of being understood and defended by an élite, the Impressionists fearlessly defied the public at large and retrogressive criticism and in 1877 opened a third exhibition, once more in April, in a vacated flat on the second floor of a block, 6, rue Le Peletier, since the Galerie Durand-Ruel was rented for a whole year.

Eighteen painters took part in the demonstration on this occasion. Some of the exhibitors of the previous years desisted, others, such as Cézanne and Guillaumin, returned; finally, there were some newcomers such as Lamy and Cordey, friends of Renoir, Maureau, a friend of Degas, and Piette introduced by Pissarro. Each artist was represented by an important selection; altogether there were more than two hundred and thirty works.

Caillebotte was represented by *Parquet-planers* among other works; Cézanne by sixteen items which included three water colors (Nos. 17 to 32); Degas by twenty-five oils or drawings (Nos. 37 to 61); Guillaumin by a dozen pictures (Nos. 62 to 73); Claude Monet by thirty (Nos. 90 to 119), including several views of *Gare St.-Lazare*—a series which he had just undertaken—and *The Turkeys;* Pissarro by twenty-two landscapes (Nos. 163 to 184); Renoir twenty-one canvases (Nos. 185 to 205), including *The Swing* and the *Bal du Moulin de la Galette* which Caillebotte already owned and was to bequeath later to the Louvre; finally Sisley showed seventeen landscapes (Nos. 211 to 227).

Others who participated were : Cals, Jacques-François (pseudonym of a woman painter), Levert, Berthe Morisot, Rouart and Tillot [50].

Once again these artists came up against lack of understanding on the part of critics and public; this, despite the fact that Chocquet made great efforts to defend his friends and Georges Rivière, at Renoir's instigation, published a modest journal, *L'Impressionniste, journal d'art*, some numbers of which appeared during the time of the exhibition. Shortly after its closing, the group once more decided on an

auction sale which took place on May 28, but Berthe Morisot and Monet withdrew. The results again proved more than disappointing—they were disastrous.

It was at this juncture that two newcomers, a young American, Mary Cassatt, introduced by Degas, and a stockbroker, Paul Gauguin, introduced by Pissarro, joined the group, whose meetings, long held at the Café Guerbois, began to take place from a date that it is difficult to ascertain exactly, but about 1875, in the more peaceful atmosphere of the Nouvelle-Athènes, a café in the Place Pigalle.

In the spring of the year 1878 Théodore Duret published his famous booklet *Les Peintres Impressionnistes* which, re-issued and enlarged, became the standard work on these artists. He was the first writer to insist on the traditional basis of these painters, whose art was linked to the past through Corot, Courbet and Manet, by also showing their debt to the masters of the Japanese print, and prepared monographs on the five whom he considered the true masters of the movement—Claude Monet, Sisley, Pissarro, Renoir and Berthe Morisot. He omitted Edouard Manet who, despite his decisive influence at the start, could not, he thought, be included in this School.

But his courageous effort proved fruitless; these painters hardly sold anything and each in turn fell a victim to poverty. Several of them even contemplated abandoning painting for some other calling which would at least allow them to eat and provide food for their wives and children.

It was then that Edouard Manet came to Monet's rescue by lending him a sum of a thousand francs on his paintings which enabled Monet to go and set up to paint in Vétheuil.

With a tenacity that compels our admiration today, these artists, despite the previous setbacks, contemplated a fourth exhibition. It took place from April 10 to May 11, 1879, at 28, avenue de l'Opéra; but the label " *Impressionist* " was replaced by that of " *Independant.* "

For various reasons Cézanne, Berthe Morisot, Renoir and Sisley refused to show there. We find the names of fifteen artists in the catalog to which must be added that of Gauguin who sent in a piece of sculpture at the last moment. Degas was represented by twenty-five works (Nos. 57 to 81); Monet with twenty-nine, including several *Views of Vétheuil* (Nos. 138 to 166); Pissarro with thirty-eight (Nos. 167 to 204). There were in addition to Bracquemond, Caillebotte, Cals, Piette (who had just died), Rouart and Tillot, several newcomers—Mme Bracquemond, Mary Cassatt, Forain, Lebourg, Henry Somm and Zandomeneghi [51].

The exhibition still enjoyed only a limited success, although the receipts showed a slight improvement.

At the same time as Cézanne and Sisley had been rejected in the Salon, Renoir's *Portrait of Jeanne Samary* and *Madame Charpentier with her two Children* were accepted; the artist was noticed by the public and even praised by the critics.

Except through the medium of the official Salon, it seemed difficult to arrive. Monet, who was resolved to gain entrance, decided in 1880 to submit two canvases to the hanging committee. One, *The Break-up of the Ice at Vétheuil*, was turned down, while the more traditional *The Seine at Lavacourt* was accepted. Degas showed Monet his violent disapproval of his action. A crisis then developed in the group as the result of the defection of Monet, Renoir, Sisley and Cézanne who were in no mood to jeopardize their first modest success by remaining associated with the anarchistic gang of Independents and Impressionists.

The Fifth Exhibition organized by the group therefore could not have the importance of the preceding ones. It was held from the 1st to the 30th of April 1880, at 10, rue des Pyramides. There were eighteen participators; but of the original

" old guard " the only ones remaining were Degas with a dozen works (Nos. 33 to 44); Guillaumin with twenty-two (Nos. 63 to 84); Berthe Morisot with fifteen (Nos. 113 to 127) and Pissarro, as loyal as ever to his ideas and now the leader of the group, with eleven paintings and five frames of etchings (Nos. 128 to 143).

On this occasion Gauguin was represented by eight works, including a marble bust (Nos. 55 to 62). Others represented were Caillebotte, Mary Cassatt, Lebourg and Mme Bracquemond, Bracquemond, Forain, Levert, Raffaëlli, Rouart, Tillot, Eugène Vidal, Vignon and Zandomeneghi [52]. This demonstration was received with a certain amount of indifference. It is a far cry from the violent scenes of the beginnings !

Internal dissension was marked still further. Monet broke away from his friends more and more and organized a one-man exhibition of his works at *La Vie Moderne* in June of that year, 1880. He replied to a journalist that he still wanted to remain an Impressionist, but, he added, " ... I very rarely see my male and female colleagues these days... "

Furthermore Zola, under the fallacious pretext of defending his friends, published in the *Voltaire* between June 18 and 22, a series of articles on *Naturalism in the Salon*, abandoning the cause he had hitherto defended. " They're all precursors, " he said, " the man of genius is not yet born ! "

The year 1880 marks in fact the decline of Impressionism, the pictorial conception of which was changing completely. Up to this time Monet and his friends had realized their " sensations, " their purely visual " impressions " in all their spontaneity, with a technique appropriate to that lightning " vision " and from which, it seems, all deliberation is absent. From now on their aim was to transform this fugitive impression into " Impressionism "; they were to follow out a process; their art was to turn into a formula. In spite of their dissensions, a School was set up with all the doctrines, theories and system that that implied. They began to ponder, and from that moment thought dominated impression at the expense of sensibility.

Finally, that period was to witness the progressive dispersal of the artists; the Paris region was no longer to be their chosen haunt. Sisley settled near Moret on the Loing in 1879; attracted by the sun, Renoir went to Algiers and Italy in 1881 and then joined Cézanne at l'Estaque near Marseilles. He was to persuade Monet to paint on the Côte d'Azur in 1883 and after, and he himself finally retired to Cagnes in 1899. Claude Monet also retired but in his case it was to Giverny in Eure (Normandy), in 1883, and Pissarro betook himself to Eragny in the same department. As for Cézanne he visited Provence with increasing frequency before finally settling there, near Montagne Sainte-Victoire.

Despite these differences and this separation, Degas and Pissarro resolved to organize a Sixth Exhibition. Caillebotte, who was hostile to the scheme this time, kept aloof. Nevertheless, in spite of the defections, the exhibition opened on April 2 and continued to May 1, 1881, once more at 35, boulevard des Capucines, in an annex of the Ateliers Nadar, but only thirteen painters were represented.

Degas limited himself to eight works, including a wax statuette (Nos. 12 to 19); Guillaumin showed sixteen (Nos. 40 to 55); Berthe Morisot seven; Pissarro alone sent

64

a larger assortment—twenty-eight paintings, pastels or gouaches (Nos. 63 to 90). Mary Cassatt took part, as did Gauguin, with ten paintings or sculptures (Nos. 30 to 39). They were joined by Forain, Raffaëlli, Rouart, Tillot, Eugène Vidal, Vignon and Zandomeneghi [53].

The exhibitors did not profess identical opinions and formed two distinct groups; on the one hand the most Impressionist—Berthe Morisot, Guillaumin, Gauguin and Vignon under the leadership of Pissarro; on the other, the most traditional, Mary Cassatt, Forain, Raffaëlli, Rouart, Tillot, Vidal and Zandomeneghi under that of Degas.

Finally those who took no part in the exhibition and sent to the Salon instead— Cézanne, Claude Monet, Renoir and Sisley—composed a separate group.

However, thanks to the intervention of Durand-Ruel, whose business was beginning to pick up and who bought a considerable number of works from several of these painters about this time, the basic group of the beginnings more or less reorganized themselves, excluding those who did not really belong to the impressionist tendency. Apart from these, Cézanne and, this time, Degas—the latter annoyed about the non-participation of Raffaëlli and his friends—refused to join.

Nine painters showed a sum-total of two hundred and three works. The Seventh Exhibition of the *Artistes Indépendants* (Degas' term was retained) opened on March 1, 1882, at 251, rue Saint-Honoré, in premises let by Durand-Ruel, and lasted the whole month. The extremely homogeneous collection included seventeen works by Caillebotte (Nos. 1 to 17); thirteen by Gauguin (Nos. 18 to 30); twenty-six by Guillaumin—thirteen paintings and thirteen pastels (Nos. 31 to 56); thirty-five by Claude Monet (Nos. 57 to 91); nine by Berthe Morisot (Nos. 92 to 100); thirty-six by Pissarro (Nos. 101 to 136); twenty-five by Renoir (Nos. 137 to 161), including a *Déjeuner à Bougival* (No. 140), now famous as the *Luncheon of the Boating Party;* twenty-seven by Sisley (Nos. 162 to 188); finally fifteen by Vignon (Nos. 189 to 203) [54]. The exhibition was a success with the critics and even as far as the sale of pictures was concerned.

Nevertheless, Durand-Ruel rejected the idea of a further collective exhibition for 1883. But, on the other hand, he arranged a series of individual exhibitions in premises specially prepared at 9, boulevard de la Madeleine, from January to July where Boudin, Monet, Renoir, Pissarro and Sisley were successively shown.

The world of art suffered a great loss with the death of Edouard Manet, April 30, 1883. An important retrospective exhibition of his work was organized in January 1884 by Antonin Proust on the premises of the École Nationale des Beaux-Arts; it aroused a certain amount of interest, and the subsequent auction sale held on the 4th and 5th of February produced unexpected results; the total realized amounted to 116,637 francs !

But Durand-Ruel, involved in further financial difficulties, was obliged to cut down the help he had been giving the impressionist artists. Some of them, therefore, as impecunious as ever, turned to other picture dealers. The outstanding example is that of Monet who made up his mind to show at the Fourth International Exhibition of Painting in the new and luxurious gallery which Georges Petit had

EDGAR DEGAS — LA COIFFURE. 1892-1895 (45×57 1/2 ") — NATIONAL GALLERY, LONDON

just opened at 8, rue de Sèze. Reasonably successful there, Monet organized a new one-man show at the *Vie Moderne* and took part, this time with Renoir, in the Fifth International Exhibition at Georges Petit's. Finally in 1887, as his prestige increased, he was elected to the committee and invited his friends to the Sixth International Exhibition, still held in the rue de Sèze, to which Berthe Morisot, Pissarro, Raffelli, Renoir, Rodin, Sisley and Whistler contributed paintings.

However, in the spring of 1886 Durand-Ruel set sail for New York with an important collection of his protégés' works.

The eighth (and last) Impressionist Exhibition took place from May 15th to June 15th in rooms above the restaurant *Maison Dorée*, No. 1, rue Lafiftte, at the corner of the Boulevard des Italiens. Seventeen artists participated. Degas with fifteen studies and pastels, and in particular his celebrated *Scenes of nudes of women bathing, washing, drying, rubbing down, combing their hair or having it combed* (Nos. 14 to 28); Berthe Morisot with fourteen (Nos. 82 to 94 *bis*); Camille Pissaro with twenty (Nos. 95 to 113). Round them were grouped Mme Bracquemond, Mary Cassatt, Forain, Gauguin, with nineteen works (Nos. 42 to 60); Lucien Pissarro (Camille's son), Odilon Redon, introduced by Degas, Rouart, Schuffenecker, a friend of Gauguin's, Seurat, likewise introduced by Degas, with nine paintings or drawings in-

66

cluding *A Sunday Afternoon at the Grande Jatte* which was to create a sensation (Nos. 175 to 183); Signac also introduced by Degas, Tillot, Vignon and Zandomeneghi. [55]

Various tendencies were represented; side by side with Impressionism (Guillaumin and Berthe Morisot), was born a new form of art, Divisionism or Neo-Impressionism (Seurat, Signac and Camille Pissarro, the latter moving over for a time to this new manner), and the first fruits of Symbolism (Gauguin and Odilon Redon) appeared. This incongruous collection disconcerted critics and public not a little.

In the meantime Durand-Ruel returned from New York where the reception accorded to " his painters " had surpassed his expectations. The exhibition had been opened on April 10, 1886, at the American Art Gallery, Madison Square, under the title " Works in Oil and Pastel by the Impressionists of Paris "; it represented a certain eclecticism, since Boudin and Lépine, Manet, Degas and Forain could be seen side by side with Monet, Sisley, Pissarro, Renoir, Berthe Morisot, Guillaumin, Caillebotte and finally Neo-Impressionists such as Seurat and Signac.

Without being a triumph, the result was encouraging, and so, on May 25th, the exhibition was transferred to the National Academy of Design where the reputation of French masters was decided at that time. The critic of *Art Age* extolled Degas and Renoir and added that Monet's, Sisley's and Pissarro's landscapes were of " ... an incomparable beauty "; his opposite number in *The Critic* even went so far as to state, " New York has never seen a more interesting exhibition than this. " A number of art lovers, endowed with a fresher eye and fewer academic prejudices than their French counterparts at that time, bought their pictures.

Their real success occurred once more abroad, for that same year the Society of the XX, founded in Brussels by Octave Maus, invited Monet, Renoir and Pissarro to contribute to its first exhibition.

In the years that followed the success of the Impressionists increased : thanks to the efforts of Durand-Ruel and Georges Petit, people were beginning to like and buy their paintings. Official circles however continued the battle and showed their hostility on two separate occasions.

In 1890, when Claude Monet conceived the idea of organizing a subscription to acquire Manet's *Olympia* to present it to the Louvre, the directors refused and would admit the work only on condition that it should be exhibited—provisionally again—in the Musée du Luxembourg, a long period in purgatory being required before its promotion to the Louvre. Shortly afterwards, in 1894, a regular scandal broke out following the death of Caillebotte who had bequeathed his collection of Impressionist paintings, consisting of sixty-seven pictures and two of Millet's water colors, to the Musée du Luxembourg.

After accepting this legacy, the officials, confronted with the intolerance of Gérôme and some of his friends who went so far as to resign from the Academy of the Fine Arts, felt obliged to give proof of their conciliatory spirit by accepting the gift only in part : two Manets out of four, eight Monets out of sixteen, two Cézannes out of five, six Renoirs out of eight, the seven Degas, six Sisleys out of nine, seven Pissarros only out of eighteen and finally the two Millet water colors—a total of forty of the sixty-nine offered !

But this was the last rebuff. After the year 1900, the success of the Impressionists was definitely established. Their consecration is proved by the manifold works which now begin to be published about them, by the affection in which they are held by an ever-increasing public and even, alas, by present-day speculation in the works of artists who almost all their lives suffered from the direst poverty. Nowadays their signature alone—sometimes forged—is enough to result in astronomical prices and often inappropriate eulogies at which they doubtless would have been the first to show surprise. Let us quote the example of Renoir who, in 1904, was given a blank check for his *Portrait* by Misia, the wife of the extremely wealthy banker Alfred Edward Sert and filled it in for a modest 10,000 francs. " I was really furious, " wrote Misia in her *Memoirs*. " It is a very high price, Misia, " said the painter solemnly, " *no canvas by any living painter is worth more.* "

But Renoir was a true artist, that is to say a craftsman (he says so himself) whose genius had nothing in common with the sense of commercial speculation possessed by some of our contemporary " artists. "

CLAUDE MONET

THE man who was considered to be the leader of the Impressionist movement, the man to whom Ruskin's phrase, " He came and unsealed the doors of light, " could be applied, was Claude Monet.

With a strict observation of nature in the open air as his starting point, this wonderful magician created a pure, luminous fairyland. He saw in an exceptional way. Far from being satisfied with what we call " studied vision " or " mental vision, " Monet, right from his early beginnings with Boudin on the shores of Normandy, was captivated by the mirage of light and atmosphere which his eye grasped with astonishing rapidity, and his hand was able to render immediately on the canvas with the same instantaneity.

However, carried away by his lyricism, in which harmony of color became a means of expression in itself at the expense of form, he reached a stage of neglecting the latter for what envelops it, to such an extent, that he sometimes achieved a kind of abstraction in which everything is dissolved in atmosphere. Sometimes too, alas, his exacerbated eye no longer looks, or looks without seeing, and the artist, in his famous " series " *Thaws, Haystacks, Poplars, Cathedrals* and *Nymphéas* (Water Lilies), allowed himself to yield to his interior visions. It is then that his art is dictated by the " will "—he *wants* a blue, purple, pink or green harmony *a priori* before looking to see whether it is in fact really blue, purple, pink or green. In this way, natural inspiration, that is " based on nature, " is replaced by a series of " systematized " sensations whose very principle runs counter to the Impressionist spirit.

Although he was born in Paris on November 15, 1840, the same day as his sculptor friend Rodin, Monet spent a large part of his childhood at Le Havre, and it was doubtless in this seaport that, like Raoul Dufy later, he formed his taste for seascapes and was, so to speak, marked by the sign of water. Sailors' eyes have in them the combined image of the sea and the sky, the reflection of the infinite. Claude Monet seems to belong to that family; his retina, abnormally impressionable, collected the luminous and colored vibrations and, through the intermediary of the brush reflected them onto the canvas in colors, now bright, now gradated, founded on pure prismatic elements. "He looked at Nature," writes Octave Mirbeau [56], "in which the treasure of the genie that the breath of man has not awakened, still slumbers; he dwelt in it, dazzled as he was by the inexhaustible magic of her changing shapes, her unheard orchestras, and he allowed his imagination to stray and wander in the magic dreamland of light that invests all living things and animates every dead thing with the charming life of colors. He would have no other master..."

We should not forget however that Monet, like most painters and particularly those of his generation, began with a dark period, though not black, since the latter was always excluded from his palette. And if in reference to him at this time, as to Manet, we talk about light color, it is only in relation to other painters who were still using bitumen and "earth-colors."

Furthermore, as we have seen, although Monet began to paint in the open air, in the company of Boudin, from 1858, he remained under the influence of Courbet and Diaz in his seascapes and canvases executed in the Forest of Fontainebleau for more than ten years.

The year 1866 marks a turning point in the development of his style. In the previous spring he had embarked on his huge composition *Déjeuner sur l'herbe* (sketch in Moscow Museum) which he hoped to exhibit in the Salon of 1866 (was it, as M. Germain Bazin conjectures, as a challenge to Manet?) and in which he was engaged in resolving the delicate problem of the reflections of light on trees, the ground, clothes, objects and even faces in the open air by means of large spots and flat areas of bright colors that sometimes differed from the color of the object itself. The work, rolled up, damaged by humidity, was cut up by the artist, who retained only a section from the middle and another from the left-hand side and sent another painting *Camille* (Kunsthalle, Bremen) to the Salon.

During that same year he executed several views of Paris "to experiment with effects of light and color"; then from the Louvre balcony he painted *The Infanta's Garden at the Louvre* (Oberlin, U.S.A.) and *The Palace of the Louvre with the Church of St. Germain l'Auxerrois* (Stedelijk Museum, The Hague). These two canvases were acquired by the dealer Latouche. Daumier who saw the first of these in his shop remarked indignantly, "Aren't you going to remove this horror from your window?"

With his eye on the Salon of 1867 Monet undertook another large composition, *The Women in the Garden* (Jeu de Paume); but it was rejected, and for lack of anywhere better, the painter had it displayed in a window in the rue Auber. Manet, who came to see it, exclaimed, "Ah! So that's what they call open air. Open air! Does open air exist? Did the Old Masters do open air?"

The work still shows traces of Courbet but it is treated with an extremely bold technique for the time; the various elements that compose it are merely sketched in with vibrating touches which do indeed convey, in their shimmering, the sensation of light in its intensity and reflections.

The Beach at Sainte-Adresse (Art Institute, Chicago) is also to a slight extent inspired by Courbet's—or Delacroix's—seascapes, whereas *Terrace near Le Havre* (Rev. T. Pitcairn Coll., Bryn Athyn, Pa.) shows an amazingly novel

CLAUDE MONET — WOMEN IN A GARDEN. 1866-1867 (100 × 78 1/4 ") — DETAIL — LOUVRE, PARIS

approach. You can breathe the air off the sea; the wind flaps the flags, bellies out the sails, dissolves the smoke from the cargo boats in the distance and wrinkles the sea in innumerable ripples; the sun suffuses the scene with a veritable fire, brightens the colors of the flowers. The artist even manages to suggest—and this is the miracle—the buzz of the insects and the murmur of the waves. A kindred atmosphere is to be found in his *Hôtel des " Roches noires " à Trouville*, dated 1870 (J. Laroche Collection, Paris). It was in 1868 that Claude Monet wrote in a letter to Bazille, " What I do will at least have the merit of not being like anybody else's work because it will merely be *the impression of what I have experienced myself alone.* "

We have already seen the importance, for its rendering of the iridescent reflections on water, of his painting *La Grenouillère* (1869, Metropolitan Museum, New York).

From 1872, the starting point of his Argenteuil period, up to 1878, Monet was at the zenith of his powers. He was shaking off the influences of other artists and beginning to find his own style. This, which was very individual, forms the culminating point of his Impressionism and of the whole Impressionist movement; the artist had not yet fallen into the method and formula which, in my view, were to bring about his decline. He neglected compositions with figures in them to devote himself almost exclusively to landscape. His famous *Impression, Sunrise* (Musée Marmottan, Paris) in which everything is drenched in a kind of dust-haze of light belongs to the year 1872, likewise *Carrières-Saint-Denis* (Jeu de Paume), a sunlit masterpiece in which the artist has created the illusion of the lazy current of the Seine and the density of the water in a marvelous way; and again the *Boats sailing at Argenteuil* (Jeu de Paume) in which Monet contrives to capture the brilliant light in all the purity of its tones and paints the reflections in the water in large broken touches which convey their shimmering and continually changing aspect. From this time on ,masterpiece succeeds masterpiece. In 1873 came *The Corn Poppies* (Jeu de Paume), a canvas painted at Argenteuil in which the artist so successfully evokes the specific atmosphere of the place, house, month and hour; in which the tall flowering grasses have tonalities of extreme refinement—delicate green, mauve, pink, gray—and wave gently in a light breeze; in which the poppies, tatters of color that suggest their fragility, seem eager to shed their petals. His canvas entitled *Rough Sea at Etretat* (1873, Jeu de Paume) is a triumph of pure Impressionism but, if we analyze it, we become aware of a certain lack of construction—a reproach frequently brought against the artist.

Whether it is the *Railway*, the *Sailing Boats*, the *Pool* or others of the Argenteuil views, they all represent the climax of Monet's Impressionism in a most striking way. The light effects, reflections on the lapping water and their myriad dancing gleams, that puff of cool air in the midst of the heat have all been effortlessly captured by the painter's subtle brush during this period, of which *The Bridge at Argenteuil* (1874, Jeu de Paume) is one of the masterpieces. In his enthusiasm Monet even persuaded Manet to come and visit him and work similarly in the open air at Argenteuil. One of the paintings the latter did there was *Monet in his Floating Studio* (1874, Neue Staatsgalerie, Munich), a boat that Monet had had constructed, following the example of Daubigny and his famous " Botin, " and on which he spent long hours capturing the " effects of light from one twilight to the next. "

CLAUDE MONET — GARE SAINT-LAZARE. 1877 (29 1/2 × 39 1/2 ″) — LOUVRE, PARIS

These atmospheric variations were to appear likewise in his *Views of the Tuileries*, about 1876-1877 (two of them are in the Jeu de Paume); at the Third Impressionist Exhibition in 1877 he showed three of them (Nos. 95, 105 and 119) in which the sun's haze reabsorbs the forms in a magic of quivering gold reflections.

It was during this six-year period that Monet had the idea of a series dealing with a single theme seen in various lights, a series that he undertook in 1877 with his numerous views of *Gare St. Lazare*. Seven of these he showed at the Third Impressionist Exhibition of 1877 (Nos. 97, 98, 100, 102, 116, 117 and 118). I do not think that it was the speed of that recent invention, the railway, that intrigued Monet and his friends as it had Turner shortly before. It had only been the fantastic side of the meteor hurled into space through the unruly elements that appealed to the latter. Monet, on the contrary, painted trains at a halt or dawdling along. What fascinated him was the peculiar atmosphere created by the smoke of the engines as it dissolved in the air in spiral curls and melted into the clouds in a vaporous iridescence.

72

In 1878 Monet began to be attracted by the village of Vétheuil, near Argenteuil, and was to reside there until October of the year 1881. During this so-called Vétheuil period, the artist was absorbed in the study of the constant variations of atmospheric phenomena : the sun and rain, the wind, snow and frost. *The Church at Vétheuil, Snow-effect* (winter 1878-1879, Jeu de Paume) evokes a Prelude of Claude Debussy's—*Des Pas sur la Neige.* The musicality of Monet's painting is the equivalent of the color in the music. The particularly severe winter of 1880 inspired his series of *The Thaw on the Seine at Vétheuil* which he worked on up to about the year 1893, rendering the pearl-like iridescence of reflections on the snow in an inimitable fashion. But his art was beginning to be less spontaneous; the artist was

CLAUDE MONET — ROUEN CATHE-
DRAL IN FULL SUNLIGHT. 1894 (42
1/2 × 28 3/4 ") — LOUVRE, PARIS

analyzing his impressions, taking away that immediacy in which their value lay, and as a result of these experiments he tended to set up a logical process in his sensations, to organize them; happily he had not yet adopted a process and an invariable formula for realizing what he wanted rather than what he saw. It is an intermediary period between pure vision and " mental " vision.

In April 1883 Monet left Poissy where he had been installed since October 1881 to live in Giverny in Normandy, where he was to remain up to the end of his life. In December he set off for the, Côte d'Azur with Renoir and alternated between France and Italy. His works of this period were often painted in strong colors. In the autumn of 1886 Monet spent some time at Belle-Isle-en-Mer where his inborn passion for the sea was rekindled. " He can be said, " writes Octave Mirbeau, enthusiastically, " to have truly invented the sea, for he is the only painter to have understood it in this way and conveyed its changing aspects, vast rhythms, movement, its infinite and endlessly renewed reflections, its salty tang. "

A painter of water, Monet was also continually returning to the river, which he loved to portray in all its various aspects. It was this that inspired him to visit the musician-poet Maurice Rollinat by the Creuse at Fresselines, in the company of Gustave Geffroy in 1889. During that same year he held an exhibition at Georges Petit's with his friend Rodin, in the introduction to which Octave Mirbeau makes the following important observation,... " Art disappears, so to speak, is effaced... Henceforward we are in the presence of living nature, conquered and subdued by this miraculous painter. And in this recreated nature with its cosmic mechanism,

CLAUDE MONET — THE WATER LILIES. 1900 (35 × 39 1/2 " — LOUVRE, PARIS

this life submitted to the laws of planetary movements, fantasy with its warm breath of love and its fits of exuberance beats its wings, sings and rejoices... "

By this time the painter had his followers; he was accepted and enjoyed some success. Then arose the terrible dilemma in which so many other artists have found themselves, not excepting Corot.

Every great artist starts with a period when influences and experiment combine and he is working toward a style of his own; such a period is usually followed by another which we may call one of " fulfillment " during which the painter, having finally adopted his pictorial form, creates a personal idiom in which he can give rein to complete expression. It is at this point that the problem arises: the greatest painters continue to develop by a process of renewal, whereas others—not devoid of genius moreover and Corot and Monet are among them—take refuge in their style which, in spite of them, degenerates into a process, a formula and sometimes, worst of all, into theory. Then we see repetition, saturation; the spirit of systematization which impoverishes art follows and replaces the creative impulse.

Monet's painting between 1889 and 1890 provides a typical example : we see him, victim of an idea, undertaking his systematic series, different in their conception from his first " free " series that were executed without any preconceived notion. He now *decided* to take a subject of varying appearance though lacking any intrinsic interest, *Haystacks*, for example, and to paint varying impressions in different pictures, with the intention of *proving* that one and the same site is continually transformed according to the variation of light.

First come *The Haystacks*, fifteen in number, exhibited in 1891 at Durand-Ruel's where they were sold in three days at prices varying between 3,000 and 4,000 francs; next *The Poplar Trees on the Epte*, shown in the same gallery in 1892. If, in these, the very rustle of the leaves is evoked in its suggestive musicality, the dissolution of the forms in the shimmering light is, alas, also accentuated.

Monet's boldness in this domain now knew no bounds, and in 1893 he tackled a new and important series of forty canvases depicting the west front of *Rouen Cathedral*. It was a risky subject, for building has a clearly defined form. Monet's aim was to prove that variations in the play of light transform this architectural structure; intense light and its complement, colored shadow, eat and devour the real forms and contours, and as a result of their disintegrating action conjure up unreal visions. He resorted to a technique of encrusted effects, a kind of confused magma in which flecked and criss-cross touches are worked in depth; the painter seems to have triturated the paint substance as if he were reproducing the actual material of the carved and eroded stonework in cement daubs.

According to the time of day, this or that part of the building was effaced to the advantage of another which assumed full importance. The colors are complementary :yellow and reddish violet, blue and orange; sometimes iridescent or dull and gray when it is cloudy or as the day closes. But we can understand the bewilderment of some of his contemporaries, looking closely at the canvas and seeing mere " palette scrapings "; it is, in point of fact, necessary to stand back a little way before you can see the cathedral bathed in light take shape and soar upwards.

On his visits to London in 1900 and 1901 Monet seemed more affected by Turner's influence than on his first journey. Now it is all fog and mist out of which *The Houses of Parliament*, *Waterloo Bridge*, *Charing Cross Bridge* emerge nebulous and full of mystery. However the colors, often discordant, now strident, now pale, are aimed at creating effect, and the marvelous has lapsed into bad taste. The series was exhibited at Durand-Ruel's in 1904. Then, four years later the painter went to Venice, the paradise of magic and reflection. But there again, the old master could not resist the temptation to re-create " his Venice, " one that was frequently nearer Ziem's than Corot's or Marquet's. These canvases were shown at Bernheim Jeune's in 1912. And Octave Mirbeau notes in his introduction, " ... It is strangely moving that Claude Monet who renewed painting in the nineteenth century succeeded in renewing himself. The color is applied in broad waves. The canvas is no longer pitted from repeated attacks. The hand seems content to follow the light. It renounces the effort to capture it. It slides over the canvas as the light slid over the objects themselves... "

Intoxicated by his new discoveries, the old painter imagined he could conjure up the mystery of the mirages in which he delighted. He retired to his estate at Giverny where, finding inspiration in the lily ponds of his grounds, he painted his last series, the *Nymphéas,* to which he largely owes his fame. Several monumental examples of these were placed after his death in two specially prepared rooms in the Orangerie. His friend Georges Clemenceau held these *Nymphéas* in high esteem.

Up to his death in 1926 Monet, like some magician, struggled to re-create his universe. Under the illusion that he was re-inventing the real which he had discovered so miraculously, he now merely plunged into a fantasy of his own, engulfed in a contrived and theatrical art in which décor replaced nature and stage lighting the real light of day. Now and again however he produced a lyrical work in which the forms, more and more elusive, disintegrate but are still charged with poetry.

For my part, I thoroughly endorse Charles Péguy's opinion as expressed in *Clio.* " Granted that a celebrated painter painted these famous water lilies twenty-seven and thirty-five times, when did he paint them best ? Which versions were most successful ? One's logical impulse would be to say, the *last,* because he knew more... But I, on the contrary, say the *first,* because he knew less... "

Monet's genius, in my opinion, lacked the power that is indispensable for resisting the danger of knowledge. Incapable of establishing a synthesis between eye and brain, he gave the latter ascendancy over the former. But, unlike Cézanne for example, he was unable to organize his sensations and finally painted compositions which, far removed from his wonderful masterpieces, were nothing more than abstractions.

In short, his art and with it the whole of Impressionism, found itself in an impasse. Cézanne had anticipated this when he reacted and wanted " to make of Impressionism a solid and lasting thing, like the art of the Museums. "

ALFRED SISLEY

ALTHOUGH the most timid of the Impressionist group in pictorial conception, Alfred Sisley was the least fortunate; he spent practically the whole of his life in poverty and he was hardly recognized until after his death, deprived even of the tardy success of Monet or Renoir.

He worked, especially in his early days, in the tradition of Courbet and Corot, sharing the latter's refined sensibility and his aversion to bright colors, preferring pastel tonalities, atmospheric subtleties. His art sometimes possesses a slightly effeminate side, reminiscent of that of Berthe Morisot.

His favorite subjects were views of small villages, especially in the Ile-de-France department—Louveciennes, Voisins, Marly, Meudon and Moret-sur-Loing, where he retired and whose peaceful charm he successfully evoked. His predilection for streets lined with shops and frequently leading up to a modest church (particularly *La Place d'Argenteuil*, 1872, Jeu de Paume, or *A Street in Moret-sur-Loing*) show his close affinity with Corot (I have in mind *The Belfry at Douai*, 1871, the Louvre); it links up with Maurice Utrillo who was later, in his views of Montmartre, to revel in similar subjects. He belongs then to that very French tradition whose characteristics are delicacy, nuances, values and poetry. His ambition is more limited than that of his friends; for him the impressionist technique is merely a convenient medium, put at his disposal, more for rendering his feelings in paint than conveying new visions or hitherto unexpressed sensations.

His *View of the Saint Martin Canal*, dated 1870 (Jeu de Paume) presents a certain analogy with the art of Boudin and Jongkind; that atmosphere with its gradations of gray, everything based on the color values, puts him in the line of the masters of Saint Siméon, who were themselves Corot's heirs. *The Highway, seen from the Road to Sèvres* (1873, Jeu de Paume) is inspired by Corot's on the same subject but its technique is impressionist. *Flood at Port-Marly* (1876, Jeu de Paume) is an extreme example of the fascination for water which he shared with Claude Monet and the majority of his friends.

The Seine at Suresnes (1877, Jeu de Paume) is one of his paintings that bear the most evidence of the new tendencies; the wind sets the foreground grasses quivering, wrinkles the surface of the water into countless ripples; the trees of the hillside sway in the light breeze; heavy clouds sweep past in the sky above... However, if the lower part of the picture is admirably painted, there is too much impasto in the clouds, and the curdled paint-matter makes the whole thing too heavy; a greater fluidity would have more aptly conveyed their mobility and the picture would then have been one of Sisley's masterpieces. Thus, the technical side—which Renoir or Cézanne emphasized so much—could lead to unfortunate results in painters who sometimes paid it insufficient attention.

Snow, like water, was, as we have seen, a favorite subject at that time. And it appealed particularly to the refined sensibility of Sisley. *Snow at Louveciennes* (1878, Jeu de Paume) is an unqualified success. This new school had derived its taste for winter landscapes from Courbet. The latter, as in the case of his seascapes, applied the paint vigorously with his palette knife, " constructing " his landscape with no attempt to render its iridescent reflections. Sisley, on the other hand, saw everything in terms of delicate nuances; he suggests more than he actually puts down and is aware of the poetic and fairy-like atmosphere of that vast white mirage which is not really white but imperceptibly tinted with hundreds of evanescent tones and which a mere nothing can smirch.

Sisley went to live near Moret-sur-Loing in 1879, then three years later in Moret itself. The banks of the Loing were now to be his favorite haunt; his manner changed, and, like Monet's, became more and more vaporous; the universe dissolves into one of outward appearances; everything is melted, drowned, flooded in tonalities of pink, lilac and faded ochre.   Such art, lacking in virility, is merely the reflection of a reflection.   Among the best examples of this period, his *View of Saint-Mammès* (1885, Jeu de Paume) is conceived like certain Boudins or Jongkinds; sky and water merge into a phantasmagoric vision.   His *Loing Canal* (1892, Jeu de Paume) with its pink lilac, blue and ochre tones is by no means free of insipidity.

Yet Sisley's art nearly always possesses a perceptible charm.   We can apply to it Paul Valéry's observations on Berthe Morisot, " Impressionism introduces a philosophic life of vision; an Impressionist is a contemplator whose meditation is

ALFRED SISLEY — SNOW AT LOUVECIENNES. 1878 (24 × 19 3/4 ") — LOUVRE, PARIS

retinal; he is aware of the creative function of his eye and raises sensation to the heights of revelation. And what, indeed, could be more miraculous? If the word 'mysterious' has any sense at all, I can conceive of no more appropriate application of it than to describe this fundamental quality of 'sensibility.'"

CAMILLE PISSARRO

As opposed to the other Impressionists who gave their attention particularly to water, river or sea, and sky, Camille Pissarro, like Millet before him, was strongly attracted by the earth. Nature as he represents it is bound up with the life of man, that is to say, the peasant; above all it is rustic. It is in fact no longer nature but the land. Occasionally he paints the landscape for its own sake, like his friends, and inspired by the way he sees it, but it is a rare event among the general body of his work which is devoted to French hamlets, village life, orchards, kitchen gardens and meadows where flocks are tended by a shepherd or shepherdess.

79

The sunlit slope on which the vine is cultivated, the enclosure where not flowers, but vegetables and fruit trees are grown, the soil, plowed, sown, productive, usually occupies two thirds or three quarters of the canvas. The earth dominates, triumphs. A rural painter, Pissarro looks at the fields and sky not only with his painter's eye and poet's imagination but with all the peasant's anxieties. The weather has its importance for him as it has for the latter, and the sun, wind and rain are not merely pure " impressions " but essential elements to be reckoned with. This attachment to the country leads him to represent the peasant in a familiar setting in the midst of his labor.

Sensitive to the beauty of the soil, Pissarro studies its structure to extract all the poetry out of it. In this way, he defines its forms, planes and architecture more than either Monet or Sisley. Nature as a creator of evanescent magic is lost on him. His aim is not to express the open air but life in the open air; and he evokes not so much the light as the warmth of the sun and its beneficence to the fertile earth, likewise that of the life-giving rain.

It was in the year 1855 that Camille Pissarro left the Antilles and came to Paris to give himself up to painting. He became a pupil of Anton Melbye and also enjoyed the advice of Corot. Two years later he made the acquaintance of Claude Monet at the *Académie Suisse*. He remained very much influenced by Corot and was accepted for the first time in the Salon of 1859, where he was to exhibit regularly up to 1870 (except in 1861 and 1863). He was represented by three canvases at the *Salon des Refusés* and was noticed by Castagnary.

Between 1866 and 1867 he painted many views of Pontoise in which the Hermitage slopes are a dominant feature ; the *Hillside at Jallais, Pontoise* is the best of these (Metropolitan Museum of Art, New York).

Deriving from both Corot and Courbet, he had an eye for simplified planes and he constructed by means of contrasts of light and shade; he applied his paint thickly, sometimes with the palette knife, and attracted Cézanne by his feeling for the architecture of natural forms and solid paint substance—*ce frisson de la durée* of which the latter was already beginning to be aware.

Pissarro lived in Louveciennes from 1868 until the Franco-Prussian War, gradually developing from his early realist technique towards Impressionism. *The Road between Versailles and Louveciennes* and *The Coach at Louveciennes* (1870, Jeu de Paume) both bear evidence of this transformation. Sunshine alternating with showers, innumerable rapid reflections of light are here incomparably rendered. He had successfully conveyed the misty atmosphere and the smell of damp earth; it echoes Debussy's *Jardins sous la Pluie* and certain passages of Proust. A further point : Pissarro in these two works treats the road theme which his friends liked so much and to which he frequently returned, as in *Entrance to the Village of Voisins* (1872, Jeu de Paume) which is in the tradition of a Hobbema (*Avenue at Middelharnis*, National Gallery, London) or a Corot (*The Sèvres Road*, Louvre). The road has a spatial significance, but it also represents country life; it is the way in and out of the village; it hints at the poetry of the place before you really enter.

In London where he spent some time during the war of 1870, Pissarro found more to interest him in Constable than in Turner, and his canvases *Environs of Sydenham Hill* or *Dulwich College, London* (1871, David Eccles Collection, London) reveal this relationship, especially in the technique. *Penge Station at Upper Norwood* (1871, Private Collection, Berlin), however, would seem to have borrowed its subject from Turner's *Rain, Steam and Speed* which we have already mentioned.

Back in France again, Pissarro returned to Louveciennes, but in 1872 he settled in Pontoise where he was to remain until 1884; during this time he initiated Cézanne into the impressionist technique and they often worked together, joined by another painter, Vignon. He now stopped sending to the Salon and was the only artist to contribute to each of the eight Impressionist exhibitions.

Pissarro's best works most certainly date from this so-called Pontoise period, the equivalent of the Argenteuil period for Claude Monet (1872 to about 1881), whose influence, in nature's perpetual movement and the continual vibrations of the reflections, we can detect, and still more Cézanne's—the initiated becoming the initiator—in the greater emphasis on plane and form and feeling towards construction; also Millet's in the rustic subjects and occasional lapses into the anecdotal. Continual financial difficulties, for he was in a state of almost complete penury, forced Pissarro to resort to bread-and-butter jobs : painting fans, executing engravings, gouaches, water colors, pastels and drawings in colored crayons, items that were more salable.

Among his paintings *The Harvest at Montfoucault* (1876, Jeu de Paume) is particularly worthy of mention. It was done in Mayenne on the estate of his friend, the painter Ludovic Piette, the subject being one often treated by the master and one which provided the opportunity of introducing some peasant figures—whose quick movements are suggested—in a country setting. One of his most celebrated canvases, *The Red Roofs* (1877, Jeu de Paume) was certainly painted in the Pontoise district. The sky line is placed very high, for the artist's particular interest was in the tilled soil, fruit trees rising out of the ground and, not least, the houses—which he constructs very solidly—of this unpretentious hamlet. His feeling for structure in no way prevents him from conveying the shimmering of light in juxtaposed and vibrant brush strokes. It is very revealing to compare this work with Cézanne's *La Maison du Pendu at Auvers*, painted in 1873 (Jeu de Paume). The style of composition is very close in the two artists, likewise technique, and the spirit is identical. However, although Cézanne's work is four years earlier in date, Pissarro most certainly initiated the Master of Aix in the Impressionist vision and manner while they were living and working together in Pontoise.

Another subtle masterpiece of this same year 1877 also merits our consideration, his *Orchard in Pontoise, Quai de Pothuis* (Jeu de Paume) of which Lionello Venturi has written, " I do not know if any other picture exists which conveys the delight, freshness, joy in rebirth inherent in Spring better than this ". This piece of orchard is dominated by the hillsides of the Hermitage, and it is interesting to note that Cézanne, who often worked side by side with Pissarro at this time, painted a picture at the same spot, *The Ravine Footpath, Seen from the Hermitage*. Pissarro was fascinated by the delicate tints of that ephemeral fruit blossom and rendered it with all the subtlety of the new art. Van Gogh, as we know, was later to be similarly attracted by trees in blossom.

Another flawless masterpiece is the *Landscape at Chaponval* (1880, Jeu de

CAMILLE PISSARRO — THE LOUVECIENNES ROAD. 1870 (17 3/4 × 21 1/4 ") — LOUVRE, PARIS

Paume)—between Pontoise and Auvers-sur-Oise—with its sunlit hillside sheltering a modest village while, in the foreground, a peasant woman tends her cow grazing amongst grass that is stirred by a gentle breeze.

By means of these patterns of subtle hatchings and a series of juxtaposed brush strokes, the artist creates the feeling of the open air in an inimitable way and successfully evokes the atmosphere of this smiling and typically French region. This time it is he who is under the influence of Cézanne; the work is composed, the structure of the ground and houses is carefully studied.

About 1881, without completely turning his back on Impressionism, but becoming aware of its dangers, Pissarro entered a period which was even more dominated by the spirit of synthesis and construction. After a stay at Rouen, he left Pontoise in 1884 and set up at Eragny, near Gisors, in the department of Eure. His

82

CAMILLE PISSARRO — LANDSCAPE AT CHAPONVAL. 1880 (21 1/4 × 25 1/2 ") — LOUVRE, PARIS

reflections on pictorial problems now caused him to turn his attention to a group of artists who were attempting to work out a theory and a coherent system on scientific bases. Pissarro was converted and from 1886 gave his allegiance to the new movement, Neo-Impressionism, which practiced Divisionism and Pointillism.

It was the year of the eighth and last Impressionist Exhibition, to which Pissarro, on this occasion, contributed pictures painted in accordance with the new aesthetic of Seurat and Signac, next to whose work they hung. In his critique, Félix Fénéon made this observation, " Pissarro, who has changed his manner, brings a spirit of severe mathematical analysis and the authority of his name to bear on Neo-Impressionism. He has begun to break up his tones systematically. "

And up to 1888 Pissarro was full of enthusiasm for this new manner of painting. Yet, at least in my own opinion, he was not a pure Neo-Impressionist, and if he practiced Divisionism, he did so less strictly than Seurat or Signac. His brush strokes, close though they are to Pointillism, do not really consist of " points " but of commas, the legacy of the original Impressionists. A study of the works of this period, particularly the *Woman in an Orchard* or *Spring Sunshine in the Meadow at Eragny* (1887, Louvre) shows us in point of fact that he is a long way from Seurat or Signac. The former picture gives an impression of brilliant light that rarely occurs in the works of those two artists; the colors are infinitely more intense and more luminous; everything vibrates, gleams, shimmers with light, whereas in Seurat's landscapes, particularly, everything seems static and frozen in accordance with well-established rules.

In Neo-Impressionism Pissarro discovered a means which allowed him to base his vision on solid and scientific principles, absent from Impressionism, without relinquishing that spontaneity which was its charm, and the pursuit of the immediate which was its chief quality. *Apple Gathering at Eragny* (1888, Max Epstein Collection, Chicago) or *Women Harvesting* (1889, Private Coll.) are still very typical of his new style which was to extend as late as about 1890.

Refusing to replace Seurat as leader of the Neo-Impressionist movement on the death of the latter in 1891, Pissarro went back to the Impressionist " sensation, " at the same time moving more and more in the direction of lyricism and violence of color—sometimes with doubtful taste, as in certain of his *Landscapes at Eragny*. He also painted many scenes of country life, work in the fields and at the market, in oils, pastel, gouache, water color or colored crayons. In 1892 Durand-Ruel arranged a full scale retrospective exhibition of his work which set the seal on his fame. The man who became " The Master of Eragny " had at last left the world of poverty and misunderstanding behind him.

In 1893 he embarked on a series of bird's-eye views of Paris in the vicinity of Gare St. Lazare *(Rue St. Lazare, Place St. Lazare, Cour du Havre)* in which he depicts the bustling crowd in various lights, in colored blobs. In 1896 at Rouen he took up a new theme, *Bridges*, seen in the mist, in sunshine or rain, indulging, like Monet, in the systematic study of variations on one subject. In 1897 we have the views of the Grands Boulevards, and in particular *Boulevard Montmartre*, all painted from the same spot in the Hôtel de Russie, a veritable series with practically no change in the composition, but the tonalities and " impressions " varying according to hour, day and season. The *Place de la Comédie-Française*, the series painted from the Hôtel du Louvre, followed in 1898, and in 1899 from a site at 204, rue de Rivoli, he continued a theme which Monet had previously treated, *Views of the Tuileries Gardens*.

Finally Pissarro, who from the end of the year 1900 lived at 28, place Dauphine, went on painting *The Louvre and the Seine seen from the Pont-Neuf* up to his death, and even in 1903 added a series of the *Pont-Royal* and another of the *Quai Malaquais* in which his sensations and impressions are painted more and more to formula. He had previously painted some oils of *Rouen Cathedral* (1898) and of the *Church of Saint Jacques at Dieppe* (1901) and he ended his career with some views of the *Pont du Havre* and *Orchards in Blossom at Eragny* before his death, November 13, 1903.

His son Lucien Pissarro, who exhibited with him at the eighth and last Impressionist Exhibition in 1886, was to continue his manner.

84

For my part, I have always repudiated the charge of being a revolutionary, I have always held and still hold that I am merely continuing the work that others have done much better than I." In these words Renoir defined his position. Steeped in tradition, he is one of the links in the chain not only of French but also European painting, for, despite his attachment to French masters of the eighteenth century, the aesthetic of the great Venetians, of Rubens and Velazquez was very much part of him. The man who could claim such illustrious ancestry was distrustful of verbal definitions and his art is exclusively the painter's. This wonderful craftsman said so himself when he headed the treatise on Cennini with these words, " Painting, like carpentry or iron work, is a *craft* and, as such, subject to the same rules. " And all through his life, Renoir endeavored to perfect his craftsmanship, never satisfied and always wanting to improve. He realized that Impressionism, for all its pictorial qualities, had the limitations that arise from absence of form and lack of drawing and that it was turning into a facile technique, a convenient formula. Hence, in 1881, as the result of his journey in Italy and his return to the study of Ingres' line, he did not hesitate to transform his style and, about 1883, to draw and reconstruct his forms which had sometimes begun to be formless. Here again, we may quote him, " I have only been myself, " he said to Vollard, " when I have managed to throw off Impressionism and return to the teaching of the Museums. " Note his humility. " About 1883 occurred a kind of break in my work. I had taken Impressionism as far as I could and made the discovery that I could neither paint nor draw. In short, I was in an impasse ! "

No one in the Impressionist circle thought more about the École des Beaux-Arts and Salon officialdom and was more *bourgeois* than he; nor was any one of them more modest. The fiercest and most unjust criticisms failed to rouse him. He possessed the common sense, serenity, self-sufficiency, goodness, love of his calling and poetry of a Chardin or a Corot. And despite all the accusations that his nudes in the open air looked like " decomposing flesh, " no art is more instinct with health and the joy of living than Renoir's, a joy that he expresses, like Dufy in that same period, in his exuberant and guileless painting. This artist endowed with an exceptionally fertile creative inspiration, retained throughout his life the soul of a child.

At the age of thirteen, Auguste Renoir became a painter's apprentice in a china factory, hoping ultimately to be taken on at Sèvres. To this early training he owed his predilection for flowing and transparent colors, related to the glazing process, omnipresent in his painting. Then he painted fans with motifs taken from Watteau, Lancret, Boucher and other eighteenth century artists, from whom he derived his preoccupation with women and their charms and the *fêtes galantes* which recur continually in his work.

Later he studied simultaneously at the École des Beaux-Arts and Gleyre's studio. During this period (1862-1864) and up to the War of 1870 Renoir found his inspiration in his great precursors—Delacroix, Courbet and Diaz. The latter, in particular, exercised a paramount influence on his early work, helping him to jettison blacks and bitumens and—before Monet—to paint in a high key.

In his nudes or figure compositions, recollections of Courbet can be seen even in the technique : the paint substance is applied *impasto* with a palette knife (*Diana*, refused at the Salon of 1867, National Gallery, Washington, D.C.; *Lise with a Sunshade*, accepted at the 1868 Salon, Folkwang Museum, Essen; *Sisley and his Wife*, 1868, Wallraf-Richartz Museum, Cologne; or finally, the *Bather with the Griffon Terrier*, 1870 Salon). His landscapes of this period—views of Paris and its environs —already reveal Impressionist tendencies and *La Grenouillère* (1868-1869, National Museum, Stockholm), very close to Monet's version, is the best example.

Back from the Franco-Prussian War, Renoir once more gave himself up wholeheartedly to his painting, and between 1872 and 1883, under Monet's influence, he adopted the Impressionist technique and applied it and the rendering of the human form in the open air as well as to pure landscape. His method at that time was extremely varied; sometimes the paint surface was smooth and fluid, sometimes thick and encrusted. He either merged his brush strokes into each other or divided them off sharply. It depended on the subject and his conception of it. We have evidence of this variety in his Paris views of that time : *The Pont-Neuf* (1872, Marshall Field Coll., New York) or *Paris Boulevards* (1875, Private Coll., U.S.A.); the former is of a tighter Impressionism, so to speak, with its more pronounced forms and in the dominants of blues and gray-blues, subtle values that he had inherited from Corot and the masters of the Saint-Siméon School; the latter is vaporous, suffused with a golden haze that drenches both human forms and buildings.

It was at this time that Renoir was noticed by Durand-Ruel who was now to watch his interests. Renoir expresses his gratitude in these words, " An event took place in my existence in 1873; I met Durand-Ruel, the leading picture dealer, the only one who, for many years, had faith in me. " Next, Renoir painted in company with Monet at Argenteuil and he too allowed himself to be captivated by the iridescent sheen of rippling water (*The Seine at Argenteuil*, 1873-1874, Art Museum, Portland, Oregon).

The year 1874 saw one of his most flawless masterpieces, *La Loge* (Courtauld Institute, London) for which Edmond Renoir, his brother, and Nini, a model from Montmartre, posed. If his choice of the theatre as a subject shows Renoir as a man belonging to his time, he belongs no less to that Impressionist aesthetic which we have already endeavored to define. His close affinity with Velazquez, before-mentioned, is here in evidence (see inset p. 12).

But the open air reappears in his canvases; *Nude Woman in the Sunlight*, circa 1875-1876, Jeu de Paume) was the source of his many subsequent studies of nudes and women bathing that reveal a vigorous pantheism and dynamic exuberance. Contemporaries and the ineffable Albert Wolff of *Le Figaro* saw in them " a mass of decomposing flesh with green and purple blotches such as indicate a state of complete putrefaction in a corpse... " But faced with this work worthy of Rubens, people realized the fatuity of such remarks.

In my opinion, there is no better summary of Impressionism than the landscape entitled, *Path Rising through Tall Grass* (painted according to some, circa 1874, and to others a little later, circa 1876-1878). For the true Impressionist, as we have said, a picture had no subject. This is certainly the present case; the artist has chosen a landscape in the environs of Paris that could scarcely be more banal; practically no sky (a feature cherished by the School), no houses, no trees (these miserable, stunted bushes do not deserve the name), no human figures (they are disappearing into the tall grass), nothing—or rather just some grass, a few umbellifers and wild poppies. With such material Renoir probably produced the greatest masterpiece in the history of landscape, purely by means of color, light, atmosphere, the subtle values of tints and tones, and above all by the infinite poetry which he has succeeded in putting into it, inspired by " impression " alone.

As in the case of Degas, though in a very different way, Paris life now inspired Renoir for almost the rest of his career, since he was above all—a trait he shares with Rubens—the painter of dynamic, vigorous, gay not to say turbulent life. He loved young people, their vociferous and healthy effervescence, as he loved woman and love itself, and stooped tenderly over children.

Here are some of the masterpieces of this period of 1875-1876 : *Mother and Children out Walking* (former Durand-Ruel Coll.); *Chez la Modiste* (Fogg Art Museum, Cambridge, U.S.A.), a theme equally cherished by Degas; *Mademoiselle Durand-Ruel* (Private Coll.); *Girl Reading* (Jeu de Paume) with her youthful face bathed in light and quivering with life. In 1875 he made the acquaintance of Monsieur Chocquet whose *Portrait* he painted the following year (Private Coll. U.S.A.) with a completely Impressionist technique. Between 1875 and 1877 he painted that unparalleled masterpiece *The Lady with the Veil* (Jeu de Paume), in which the femininity of his model who is turning away her head is equaled only by her grace and distinction.

This taste for outdoor scenes inspired him to paint *The Arbor* in 1876 (Museum of Modern Art, Moscow), *The Swing* (Jeu de Paume)—both shimmering with colored and luminous reflections in which pinks and blues predominate—and finally his immortal *Moulin de la Galette* (Jeu de Paume), a symbol of the " glorious years " and a veritable manifesto of Impressionism. Balls, country taverns and scenes of popular life—Renoir's models were very often his comrades or their friends, dressmakers and milliners, florists, Parisian midinettes with their natural charm—were never more attractively depicted. And in this again Renoir falls in line with the purest tradition : his canvas has close affinities with Rubens' *La Kermesse* (Louvre) in which we see a whole exuberant crowd truly reveling in the joy of living.

Renoir is also in the tradition of French painters of *Fêtes galantes* from Watteau to Fragonard, to whom we are indebted for representations of those amorous conversations, those furtive exchanges of glance or kiss of which the *Embarkation for the Island of Cythera* (Louvre) is rightly one of the most celebrated. Like those eighteenth century masters, Renoir has a predilection for pink and bluish tonalities for costume, and their reflection in the open-air light falls on a soil of bright rose and the blue-tinged shadows.

Finally we come to *La Première Sortie* (1876, Tate Gallery, London) and *La Sortie du Conservatoire* (1877, Barnes Foundation, Merion, U.S.A.) which give us a picture of the student milieu of the period.

At this time Renoir made contact with the publisher Georges Charpentier who commissioned him to do portraits of his wife and children. Renoir began by painting *Mademoiselle Charpentier in Blue* (circa 1876, Private Coll.), then the fine portrait of *Madame Georges Charpentier* (circa 1877, Jeu de Paume). There is so much vivacity in her glance, so much wit in her mocking lips that we seem to see her moving about in the midst of her friends. She kept a salon which was attended by men of letters, artists, actors and politicians, from Flaubert to Gambetta, from Carolus Duran to Degas and Renoir.

The following year the painter carried out the large group portrait—*Madame Charpentier and her Children* (1878, Metropolitan Museum, New York) which he showed later in the 1879 Salon. Here the attitudes and expressions are more conventional; the figures have adopted a more self-conscious pose. However, the presence of the large dog near the little girls once more reminds us of the Velazquez of *Las Meninas,* as does likewise the intensity of life expressed in its full humanity. In this same Salon of 1879 he exhibited the *Full-length Portrait of the actress Jeanne Samary* (Museum of Modern Art, Moscow), less Impressionist in technique and somewhat theatrical as far as the pose is concerned. Renoir's love of chilhood then inspired him to paint two little jugglers at the *Cirque Fernando* (1879, Art Institute, Chicago). It is significant that Renoir, unlike Lautrec who often treated this circus subject which served as a pretext for studies of rhythms and attitudes, in this case chose children, two little girls, exquisite in their youthful grace, purely for the joy of painting their portraits. Again, in 1879-1880 we have the *Portrait of Mlle Irène Cahen d'Anvers* (Private Coll.), *La Première Sortie* (Courtauld Institute, London) *Au Concert, dans la loge* (Private Coll., U.S.A.) or *Place Pigalle* (Courtauld Institute, London), a scene of Parisian life whose unconventional composition, nearer that of Degas or Lautrec, we find surprising in Renoir.

During the summers of 1879 and 1880, Renoir worked in the open air on the banks of the Seine at Chatou and Croissy. His canvas *Oarsmen at Chatou* (National Gallery of Art, Washington) is typically Impressionist with shimmering and iridescent reflections on the water, a bright light animating both figures and nature.

He also spent some time in Normandy and painted some seascapes, though he was less attracted by this genre than either the masters of the Saint-Siméon School or Monet. At Berneval he executed a large composition *The Mussel-Fisher* (Durand-Ruel Coll., Paris) and he also did some painting at Wargement, the château of his friend Paul Bérard. One of the most successful paintings of this period is the picture painted at Mère Fournaise's at Croissy, the *Luncheon of the Boating Party* (1881, Phillips Collection, Washington D.C.) which he exhibited at the seventh Impressionist Exhibition of 1882. In it the artist has brought to life all the gay ambience—not without some vulgarity—of the pleasure gardens by the Seine during those carefree years at the end of the century. On the left, playing with the dog, we recognize Aline Charigot who was to become Mme Renoir, and on the right, astride the chair and wearing a vest, Caillebotte. We have already found this materialism, rendered in all its colorful splendor in Veronese *(The Marriage Feast at Cana),* in Rubens *(La Kermesse)* and in Fragonard *(La Fête à Saint-Cloud).*

In spring 1881, Renoir undertook a journey extending over some weeks in Algeria and came back in March 1882 to recover from an attack of pneumonia. He brought some sunlit landscapes back with him, *The Ravine of the Wild Woman,* the *Banana Plantation* (Jeu de Paume) and also some exuberant canvases pitched in high tones such as *Arab Feast at Algiers, the Kasba* (Jeu de Paume). Eager to enlarge his vision, the artist also betook himself to Italy. He was captivated by the golden light, so peculiar to Venice, by the water and sky, the reflections, and he dashed off some lively canvases (*St. Mark's Square*, Minneapolis, Institute of Art).   In Florence and Rome he was still more attracted by the galleries and the study of the old masters, particularly Raphael.   He visited Naples, Pompeii and Palermo where he painted the *Portrait of Wagner*.   Back in France, he worked by the side of Cézanne at l'Estaque near Marseilles and there executed some landscapes (notably that in the Boston Museum) in which his art expressing " the shudder of reflections " contrasts with the more constructed, more symbolic art of Cézanne who, using the same

AUGUSTE RENOIR — LA PRE-
MIÈRE SORTIE. 1876 (25 1/2 ×
19 3/4 ") — COURTAULD FUND,
TATE GALLERY, LONDON

AUGUSTE RENOIR — ST. MARK'S SQUARE. 1881 (24 3/4 × 32 1/4 ") — INSTITUTE OF ART, MINNEAPOLIS

themes, is concerned with " *le frisson de la durée* " in a geometric equilibrium that was already reacting against Impressionism.

The theme of the dance which fascinated Degas and Lautrec also appealed to Renoir, as we have already seen in his canvas *Dancing at the Moulin de la Galette*. In 1883 it inspired three new compositions : *Dance at Bougival* (Museum of Fine Arts, Boston) treated in an unmistakably Impressionist manner (akin to *The Luncheon of the Boating Party*), *Dance in the Country* and *Dance in the Town*, two large vertical panels which were conceived, on the contrary, in a decorative spirit and, from the point of view of technique, more traditionally.

During that summer Renoir went to Guernsey and painted some iridescent landscapes, extremely free in handling and typically Impressionist. It was however from this period onwards that the artist was to abandon this manner and return to the teaching of the great masters of the past and the study of M. Ingres; his stay in Italy had doubtless contributed to this sudden transformation of his style. He realized the value of drawing, the important part played by line defining the forms, as exemplified in Raphael, the Florentines and Ingres. And since, as he put it, he had gone " to the end of Impressionism, " he understood the need to develop the latter so as to avoid becoming repetitive or foundering in the formless. This crisis

90

AUGUSTE RENOIR — LE MOULIN DE
LA GALETTE. 1876 (30 3/4 × 53 1/2")
— DETAIL — LOUVRE, PARIS

covered the years from 1883-1884 to about 1890. During this period, which has been dubbed " severe " or " Ingresque, " he enclosed his forms tightly in sinuous lines, an unusual method for him, and purposely employed weak colors—ochres in particular—but sometimes inharmonious and somewhat harsh in their relationships; his technique became dry, glazed.

A picture that marks the transition, *Umbrellas* (1883, National Gallery, London) still shows the technique he was anxious to abandon—in the right-hand section, for example, with the two little girls—in favor of more closely defined contours and a drier style—the left-hand group.

His *Grandes Baigneuses* (1883-1884, Tyson Coll., Philadelphia), inspired by a bas-relief by Girardon at Versailles, is typical of his new manner. Stylization of forms, contours defined by a cursive line, a striving for harmony and rhythm in the composition, less spontaneity and ease, less subtlety and fewer nuances in the color,

AUGUSTE RENOIR — THE JUDGMENT OF PARIS. 1908 (31 3/4 × 40 ") — PRIVATE COLLECTION, U.S.A.

brush strokes more detached and applied in flat areas, paint substance thinner—such are now his guiding principles, as exemplified in the *Après-midi des enfants à Wargemont* (1884, Berlin). I should also mention *La Natte* (Private Coll., Switzerland) for which it is said Suzanne Valadon posed—a deliberate painting, with strong emphases and an almost Teutonic dryness of technique.

Other bathers, very Ingres-like, other portraits, including *The Daughters of Catulle Mendès at the Piano*, are landmarks in this experimental period when Renoir was trying to find a way out of the Impressionist impasse.

Abandoning this linear style, alien to his temperament, about 1890, Renoir did not merely return to the Impressionism of his early period. That which follows, referred to as " pearly, " is, after all, a period of synthesis. A synthesis between a certain Impressionism in treatment and an increasing preoccupation with form, no longer linear but expressed in terms of values; the color is " contained " and the reflections are pearly—hence the term used to describe this phase. Renoir at this time partly rejected so-called " modern " subjects and concentrated on portraits and nudes (*Baigneuse brune*, Clark Art Institute, Williamstown, U.S.A.; *Baigneuse endormie*, 1897, Oscar Reinhart Coll., Winterthur, etc.).

He often worked at Essoyes, and his fondness for children inspired his many portraits, undertaken between 1895 and 1900, of his second son Jean, a rounded, chubby-cheeked baby, on the lap of Gabrielle, his servant, a model whom he immortalized in many canvases (*Gabrielle with the Rose*, Jeu de Paume, etc). Successive fits of rheumatism caused Renoir to retire to Cagnes in the Midi where he was to end his career in the villa " Les Collettes " and where, during this period of about 1903 to 1919, his art, bearing the stamp of an exuberant pantheism, reached full fruition. For if he worships a nature that streams with sunshine and is saturated in light, it is, more often than not, in order to display these feminine bodies, voluptuously posed, whose undulating curves are intimately linked with the rhythms of the earth. We are now conscious of the influence of his friend, the sculptor Maillol, particularly in *The Judgment of Paris* (1908, Private Coll., U.S.A.).

This succession of women bathers and nudes in the open air (Museum of São Paulo, Vienna Museum, etc.) culminated in his large painting of *Baigneuses* or *Nymphes* (circa 1914, Jeu de Paume), dubbed " Bibendum " or " Michelin tires " by a disconcerted critic who doubtless intended to emphasize by this witticism the unusual elasticity of the two bodies whose heavy yet flexible mass bears witness to the artist's genius for recreating volume in its weight of flesh.

The dominant reds (color of blood, color of life) in this final phase of the painter's career, do not indicate a systematic need but rather a sensitive mode of expression. " A painter's palette means nothing, " he used to say, " it is his eye that does everything. "

Renoir's art is above all one of sincerity, authenticity, love, health and life. This marvelous craftsman was always in rebellion against pseudo-theories and pseudo-tendencies. " Don't ask me whether painting ought to be objective or subjective, I confess that I don't care a damn ! "

Renoir remained subject to nature and hostile to any formulas throughout his life. " You arrive in front of nature with theories, " he said, " nature knocks them all down. " And again this admirable assertion, " Theories don't make a good picture : more often than not they merely cover up the inadequacy of the means of expression... " What a lesson for many painters !

BERTHE MORISOT

A N engaging woman painter is bound up with the Impressionist movement: Berthe Morisot. In company with her friends she defied sarcasm and insult and, refusing to be discouraged, persisted in the open-air method, employing the light, free touch which is her particular charm and participating in seven of the eight Impressionist Exhibitions. Paul Valéry, who was related to her, wrote the following paragraph which completely characterizes her achievement [58]:

" But Berthe Morisot's peculiarity was, on the contrary, that she *lived her painting* and *painted her life*, as if this exchange of action for observation, of light for creative sensuality were a necessary and natural function bound up with her physiological make-up. She took up, dropped and picked up her brush again exactly in the way a thought comes into one's mind, vanishes and then recurs. This faculty endows her work with the very special charm of a close, almost indissoluble relationship between an artist's ideal and the intimacy of an existence. Girl, wife, mother; at every stage her sketches and pictures follow the course of her life, and keep very close to it. I am tempted to say that the ensemble of her work suggests what the Diary of a woman would be like if her means of expression were color and drawing. "

She first came under the influence of Corot, with whom she painted about 1860 and her meeting with whom affected her whole life (*Lorient Harbor*, painted in 1869).

Next Jongkind induced her and her sister Edma to paint water colors and interested her more and more in landscape.

In 1864 the two sisters exhibited at the Salon, where their contribution roused considerable attention. Berthe Morisot who met Manet in 1868, as well as becoming one of his models (she posed for *The Balcony*), became his pupil and was from that time bound up with the Impressionists. However, she continued to exhibit at the Salons of 1872 and 1873, the pastel portrait of her sister *Edma Pontillon* being particularly noteworthy, before taking part in the first Impressionist Exhibition of 1874 at Nadar's.

Shortly before, in 1873, she had painted two works, still somewhat traditionalist, in which the subtlety of the values is very noticeable, and reminiscences of Corot, and hints of Manet blend happily with her own feminine sensibility—*The Butterfly Chase* (Jeu de Paume) and her masterpiece *The Cradle* (Jeu de Paume) in which we see her sister tenderly contemplating her baby under the transparent veils of the cradle. Only a woman—and a woman of great talent—could imbue a subject which sails dangerously near the sentimental and the ordinary with such exquisite freshness, love and poetry.

There is nothing effeminate about her fresh and subtle color, although her light touch suggests rather than defines the forms. " She finishes off her canvases with light brush-strokes as if she was plucking off the petals of flowers ", wrote Théodore Duret. Thus she found in the art of the Impressionists the form of expression she was looking for and the one perfectly suited to her painting.

Painting now indoor-scenes of feminine intimacy or family life, now open-air landscapes, frequently enlivened with figures of children or young women, she captures a fugitive effect of light as she does that of an attitude. *Young Woman*

94

BERTHE MORISOT — EUGÈNE MANET AND HIS DAUGHTER. 1883 (28 3/4 × 36 1/4 ")
ROUART COLLECTION, PARIS

sewing in a garden (1881, Pau Museum); *Eugène Manet and his daughter (1883*, Private Coll., Paris).

Her studies of *Femmes à leur toilette* have nothing in common with those of Degas. The latter obtains the whole of his effect by harmony and rhythm of gesture in a purely classical spirit and not without an occasional touch of cruelty, whereas Berthe Morisot narrates with simplicity the life of a woman caught in the poetry of the fleeting moment.

After 1890, Berthe Morisot often stayed at Mézy, near Meulan, where she worked alongside Renoir who had, since about 1886, exercised a great influence over her, as we can see, for example, in *The Cherry-tree* (1891, Private Coll., Paris).

An important exhibition of her works, to the number of 43, took place at the Galerie Boussod-Valadon in May 1892 and set the seal on a talent that is so eminently French—all poetry and sensibility.

" This existence with all its bravura ", writes Mallarmé who was her friend, " was to continue care-free, after victory and homage ".

ARMAND GUILLAUMIN

I am incapable, Guillaumin was in the habit of saying, of applying a single brush-stroke except ' from life. ' I will go further and add that, to a real artist, any other course is impossible. " Does that mean that he was more " impressionist " than his friends ? I do not think so. He was, above all, sincere and direct, copying what he saw — or what he imagined he saw — allowing very little scope to interpretation, fancy or imagination. His painting was, as Marcel Pays wrote, " the confidence of a genuine emotion confronting nature. "

However, one must make certain reservations about Guillaumin's art. He was not always able to select impeccable color harmonies. In his excitement when in direct contact with nature, he seems overwhelmed by the dazzle of the multiplicity of colors, and the abundance of all the prismatic tones even in his skies sometimes lends a touch of banality to his works. He does not appear however to have been able to discriminate sufficiently between iridescence and polychromy.

His artistic apprenticeship was spent in Paris at the *Académie Suisse* where he worked with Pissarro and Cézanne and formed a friendship with the latter. But he found it impossible to live by his painting. Thus under the necessity of earning a living, the only time when he could paint his views of Paris—the quays chiefly—and of the suburbs was Sundays. He took part in the first Impressionist Exhibition of 1874 and exhibited intermittently with the group up to 1886.

Apart from oil painting he also practiced pastel painting, a medium which enabled him to make use of a great variety of colors.

Among the paintings of his Parisian period, *Barges on the Seine at Bercy* (1871, Jeu de Paume) is among the best. It was praised by Cézanne who later etched a version of it while staying with Dr. Gachet. *La Place Valhubert* (Louvre) and *Le Port de Charenton* (1878, Louvre) also merit attention.

Having gained a considerable sum of money, he left his employment and devoted himself to full-time painting, making journeys to Saint-Palais-sur-Mer, then the Mediterranean coast where he painted the *Agay landscapes* (Private Coll.) very intense in color, dazzled as he was by the bright sunlight of the Côte d'Azur. In 1904 he went off to Holland, near Zaandam, where he painted many landscapes none of which achieve the sensitivity of the canvases by Monet who had likewise worked in that region.

At this stage Guillaumin retired to Crozant in the Creuse where he continued to paint until his death. " It is possible, " he said, " that a landscape as beautiful as that of Crozant exists, but that there is a more beautiful one I cannot believe. "

He became passionately attached to this picturesque country which he celebrated most of all at Crozant and Fresselines where a poet, bucolic like himself and no less enthusiastic about the Marche landscape near Berry, Maurice Rollinat had his home. The wild aspect of this country side delighted Guillaumin and he steeped himself in it, painting it in every season, every month, every hour of the day. He had a particular liking for frost effects on winter or autumn days, with purple heather, russet bracken, red cherry trees and golden foliage. He paints reflections in the water of the Creuse or the Sédelle, one of its tributaries, in a manner beloved of the Impressionists.

His best paintings of that region are *The Ruins of the Château de Crozant* (Private Coll.), *Le Moulin de la Folie* (Private Coll.), *The Creuse at Crozant* (Private Coll.), *White Frost at Crozant* (Private Coll.), etc., in which the dominating nuances of mauve, orange and pink are sometimes of exquisite subtlety while, at other times, an excess of polychromy results in over-artificiality.

ALBERT LEBOURG

THERE was little hint in Albert Lebourg's early work of his later adherence to Impressionism. Employed in an architect's office in Rouen, he took up painting and in 1872 went to Algiers where he became a professor in the School of Drawing in the Academy of Fine Arts. He then embarked, on his own initiative and without as yet any knowledge of the Impressionist artists, on high-toned colors, encouraged (*c.* 1875) by the Lyons painter Seignemartin who was residing in Algiers at that time. And it is worth noting that he painted several studies from the same subject, *The Admiralty* (1875), *Arab Fountain* (1876), *Moorish Café* (1877), opening the way to the "series" idea of the Impressionists. It was not until

ALBERT LEBOURG — BY THE SEINE AT CROISSET (18 × 33 1/2 ") — PETIT-PALAIS, PARIS

1877 that Lebourg went to Paris and discovered the new painting. At first he was somewhat surprised by an art so close to his own in its light tonalities but so different in its loose application of color from his own more traditional tightness. Nevertheless he participated in two of the group exhibitions in 1879 and 1880. But subsequently his training conditioned him to exhibit at the *Artistes français* and *Salon de la Nationale*. His favorite subjects were the banks and quays of the Seine in Paris and Rouen, and with the exception of a few journeys, particularly those to Auvergne in 1884 and Holland in 1895 and 1897, he alternated between Paris and Rouen, finally retiring to the latter.

His essentially personal procedure is markedly different from those of the Impressionists; fairly fluid, the paint substance covers the whole canvas, and innumerable, slightly broken small touches form small surfaces of juxtaposed light tones and give an impression of fading out, of mist and fog, conveying the atmosphere of Rouen and that region in a marvelous manner.

Evoking the iridescence rather than the vibrations of Impressionism in his own version of that movement, Lebourg created a delicately poetic, if rarely imitated idiom. The Petit-Palais in Paris and Rouen Museum possess many works of this master, *Views of Notre Dame, Quai St. Michel Paris*, the *Port of Rouen* or the *Quays of Rouen*, in dominating lilacs and blue-grays that suggest the atmosphere in which everything in nature is bathed.

GUSTAVE CAILLEBOTTE

ONE might have expected Gustave Caillebotte's training, which began at the École des Beaux-Arts *(Ateliers Bonnat)* in 1873, to lead him into official Academism. However, he soon abandoned that teaching and had only to meet the Impressionists to be completely converted to their way of painting. His most famous canvas *The Parquet-planers* (1875, Jeu de Paume), banal enough to his contemporaries, marks his development towards a luminous yet realistic idiom in which shimmering reflections play no small part. Expected to exhibit with his new friends, he participated—notably with this picture — in the second Impressionist Exhibition. Although he took part in the majority of the subsequent exhibitions of the group, helping and encouraging less fortunate companions, he nevertheless remained both in subject and treatment more traditionalist than they. He found his models in the everyday life around him, painting them in their normal activities with great fidelity. Huysmans recognized in him... " one of the most exact and original painters of his time. " His canvas *The House Painters*, painted in 1876, belongs to the same realist vein; the artist observes working-class settings in a new spirit. Between 1875 and 1880, roughly speaking, his painting, though light in tone, is still relatively dark in comparison with other Impressionists' work. Interiors alternate with outdoor scenes. The canvas *Portraits in the Country* (Bayeux Museum) is still reminiscent of Monet's *Women in a Garden* or the work of Bazille. Between 1877 and 1878 he painted *Boating Scenes* close in spirit if not technique to *Views of la Grenouillère* or *Rowers* by Monet and Renoir. Like the

98

Impressionists he was fascinated by scenes in Paris. He showed the *Pont de l'Europe* and *Rainy Weather* (Private Coll.) in the 1877 Exhibition, thus underlining his recent tendencies—bird's eye views, original and even daring composition as in his *Street Refuge, Boulevard Haussmann* (1880, Private Coll.).

The year 1882 marks a transformation in Caillebotte's art. He made his last appearance in the Impressionist Exhibitions, and if he continued to treat the same kind of subject, he showed a preference for still life and scenes on the coast of Normandy. Under Monet's influence his studies of water—sea or river—became more vibrant, lighter, and from 1882, much later than Monet and Renoir, he painted an important series of *Views of the Seine at Argenteuil*, of which *Sailboats at Argenteuil* (c. 1888, Jeu de Paume), remains one of the best.

As Mlle Marie Berhaut notes in the catalog she has devoted to him, " The title of 'champion of the Impressionists' has stuck to the name of Gustave Caillebotte. With exemplary tact he continually came to their rescue. " His generous intervention often saved them from poverty. " After the 1877 Exhibition, " reports Georges Rivière, " some new collectors materialized. Except for Caillebotte, they were not patrons, for it cost them only a few crowns, rarely more, to acquire genuine masterpieces. " And he adds : " He admired the talent of the Impressionists and paid more generously for their works than for any of the others that made up his celebrated collection. "

At the time of his last will and testament in 1883, it consisted of sixty-seven Impressionist oils which, at Caillebotte's decease (in 1894) were to be transferred to the Louvre. We have already seen the scandal caused by the entry of this collection into the national museums.

MARY CASSATT

IT is not surprising that Mary Cassatt who, despite her academic training, had an innate predilection for a lighter palette, should have moved into the Impressionist camp. She left the U.S.A. for Europe in 1868 and after first working with Chaplin and studying the old masters, particularly Correggio in Parma and Rubens in the Prado and Antwerp, she made friends with Degas who introduced her to the circle of the " independent painters " with whom she henceforward identified herself. She participated in the fourth Impressionist Exhibition of 1879 and continued to exhibit with them to the end, in 1882.

A certain originality, even sometimes boldness—which interested Degas—and which she doubtless owed to the masters of the Japanese prints, is manifest in her compositions; of these *La Loge* (shown at the fourth Impressionist Exhibition of 1879, is the most striking, and we should also mention *At the Opera* (c. 1880, Museum of Fine Arts, Boston, U.S.A.).

But all through her career her favorite theme was the very feminine one of maternity (*Mother and Child*, Jeu de Paume). Degas who had advised her and admired her gifts, showed a touch of irritation at this *leit-motiv* which tended to restrict her scope, and exclaimed one day : " Look, the Child Jesus with his nurse ! " Indeed, this pink, chubby cheeked baby with his over-pretty flesh tones, healthy and well-washed, often resembles an advertisement for a soap or for a body builder.   One prefers her portraits of young women in a garden (*Woman Reading* or *Woman Sewing*, Jeu de Paume) or those of little girls (*Girl sitting in a Park* or *Little Girl sitting in an Armchair*, pastel), works of exquisite subtlety.   Mary Cassatt excelled in pastel technique and proved herself a sensitive colorist.   It was through her acquisition of the works of her friends and her efforts to make them known that Impressionism first won favor in America.

Although his art is linked up with the Barbizon School tradition, Cals associated himself with the Impressionist group and even took part in its first four exhibitions.

He began as an engraver, entered the École des Beaux-Arts and, doubtless through the instrumentality of Jongkind, was introduced to the circle of innovators at the age of about sixty.   He settled in Honfleur in 1873 and frequented the Saint-Siméon farm in its later days.   His canvases of that period though in a lighter key are not characterized by outstanding luminosity (*Sunset at Honfleur*, 1873, Jeu de Paume, and *Lunch at Honfleur, Côte de Grâce*, 1875, Jeu de Paume).   His landscapes with their somewhat dark greens are still very close to those of Daubigny, and his flickering brushs trokes, like the latter's, lack the vibrating quality of pure Impressionism.

" ... Doing true Art, that is rendering what one feels at one's own risk and peril.   Art without this proviso is not Art, " he has said.   He was to apply these principles to his realistic and sincere work, and, in no way an innovator, he nevertheless associated himself with those who were revolutionizing painting, " desirous of serving... the principle of freedom in Art. "

Henri Rouart, who was an engineer, manifested a taste for painting early in life and began by following Millet's precepts.   An enlightened amateur, he joined the Impressionists and took part in some of their exhibitions, fascinated as he was by these new open-air tendencies.   His landscapes *(The Terrace*, c. 1880, Jeu de Paume, for example), technically less daring than those of the Impressionists, reveal a certain sensibility of eye before nature and the reflections of the light.   However, problems of the reabsorption of forms under the sun's rays were not among those that Rouart tackled.   He was an assiduous exponent of water color, a medium that provided scope for rapid notations and a greater freedom of execution.

Among the minor masters of impressionist tendency, we should mention the following : Cordey, whose landscapes, executed with a very hachured technique, are vibrant but somewhat dry; the Ottins, father and son, more conformist; Piette, whose idiom, inspired by rustic scenes, recalls that of his friend Pissarro; Tillot, still fairly traditionalist; Vignon, who worked in the Pontoise district with Pissarro and Cézanne and whose *terre à terre* idiom owes much to both these artists; lastly Zandomeneghi and de Nittis, two Italians, portraitists and landscape painters, whom Degas introduced into the Impressionist circle.

100

CONVERTS TO
IMPRESSIONISM

EDOUARD MANET

IMPRESSIONISM, the new way of painting—and seeing—attracted a considerable number of artists despite the violent attacks to which it was subjected. It converted in particular three great geniuses of widely divergent approaches, Edouard Manet, Degas and, later, Toulouse-Lautrec.

We have already seen that Manet has often been thought of, wrongly in my view, as the promoter of the Impressionist movement. In spite of himself he raised the banner of revolt, and the term *Indépendant*, which the Impressionists arrogated to themselves when they started, fits him much better. For a long time he refused to paint exclusively in the open air and never showed in the exhibitions of the group. Essential differences separate him from the latter : he always retained black, white and gray, colors (if such they may be called) completely banished from the Impressionists' palette, and his brush strokes though broken were never transformed into innumerable, tiny commas; finally, Manet rarely tackled pure landscape. A realist and painter of modern life, he usually animated it with some human figure.

His impressionism was progressive. First some " essays "—*Bordeaux Harbor* (c. 1870-1871, Private Coll., Berlin; Jeu de Paume), then *The Game of Croquet, Paris*, painted in 1873 in Alfred Stevens' garden, rue des Martyrs (Städelsches Kunstinstitut, Frankfurt am Main) and especially *The Railroad* (1873, Private Coll., New York), painted in a garden in the rue de Rome, which reveal his new tendencies.

However, about 1874, while painting at Argenteuil and yielding to Claude Monet's urgings, Manet was finally converted to painting in the open air, in light and above all, more luminous colors; in a word to a more vibrant handling of paint even if it was never wholly that of the Impressionists. Was it an indication of his curiosity and a mere desire to renew his subjects ? Was it a kind of weariness of realism, that is of one sort of realism ? Was it a whole-hearted support of the principles that Claude Monet so enthusiastically defended ? It is difficult to determine the real reasons. Perhaps the painter of the *Olympia* saw a means of developing his style, a " youth cure, " in the freshness of open-air impressions, without being genuinely attracted by that kind of art. *Boating in Argenteuil* (1874, Metropolitan Museum, New York), *Rowers, View of Argenteuil* (1874, Tournai, Museum), *Monet Painting on his Boat* (1874, Neue Staatsgalerie, Munich), *The Monet Family in their Garden* (1874, Private Coll., Berlin) are the best examples of this so-called Argenteuil period. However, we note that Manet was unable to turn his back altogether on his former predilection for contrasted values. This urge to use blacks or dark tones to show up light and luminous tonalities estranges him to a certain extent from the true Impressionist manner. Nor does he invariably execute his canvases with the rapidity required by such a technique. Thus in *View of Argenteuil*, exhibited at the Salon in 1875, the painter must have required many sittings of the figures (we recognize his brother-in-law Rodolphe Leenhoff in that of the rower), scrupulously painted, whereas he is content to catch the landscape in its fleeting mood.

For Manet the " subject " always, or almost always, has a fundamental importance. Unlike Claude Monet who in some of his " series " ended by creating a kind

ÉDOUARD MANET — THE RUE MOSNIER DECKED OUT WITH FLAGS. 1878 (25 1/2 × 32 ") — FORMERLY JAKOB GOLDSCHMIDT COLLECTION, NEW YORK

ÉDOUARD MANET — MONET PAINTING ON HIS BOAT. 1874 (32 1/4 × 39 1/4 ") — NEUE STAATSGALERIE, MUNICH

of fiction, a fairyland, Edouard Manet, like the Spanish painters who inspired him, needed reality. He does indeed transpose it with his creative genius but it still remains the basis of his inspiration.

From a stay in Venice, he brought back some views that quiver with reflections, but the dark tones—frequently a black gondola—are always contrasted with the lights. *The Grand Canal, Venice* (Private Coll., New York) is typical of this stay " where the air devours the shores, where everything melts and merges in the splendors of light, " to quote his own words.

His experiments led him to the realization, between 1874 and 1875, of his Impressionist masterpiece *Washing* (dated 1875, Barnes Foundation, Merion, U.S.A.). Berthe Morisot wrote this about it in her notebook [59] : "painted in 1874 in a little garden at Batignolles from the model Alice Legouvé and her child... *Washing* is along with *Argenteuil* his most ambitious effort in open-air painting. " Once again Manet had been unable to resist the attraction of a " subject "; but this canvas, painted entirely in light colors, is a dazzle of brilliance and color. Its boldness proved too shocking to allow its admission to the Salon of 1876, but exhibited by the artist in his studio, 4, rue de Saint-Pétersbourg from April 25 to May 1st 1876, it long remained one of the most discussed of the Master's pictures. " Poor Manet, " exclaimed Degas, " after painting *Maximilien*, the *Christ with Angels* and all that he has painted up to 1875 and then to relinquish his magnificent ' prune juice ' to paint *Washing!* "

It was from the rue de Saint-Pétersbourg from which he looked into the rue Mosnier—the present rue de Berne—that Manet shortly afterwards, in 1878, painted two pictures, one inspired by the patriotic fête of June 30, *The Rue Mosnier deked out with Flags* (Private Coll., New York) and the other by the more realist subject of the road-menders : *Road Menders in the rue de Berne* (Private Coll., London). The former has affinities with a painting of Claude Monet's on the same theme and executed the same year *La rue Montorgueil pavoisée* (Rouen Museum). With Monet, everything consists of fugitive impressions, expressed in a sort of Tachism that conveys the continual movement of the innumerable flags at the slightest puff of wind. With Manet, we have a realistic scene with a one-legged man, a cab and some pedestrians, and, although a few flags lend their bright touches to the sunlit street, we are a long way from the effect of the ceaseless vibrations that Monet rendered so successfully. Other artists were to exploit this theme of hanging out flags, the occasion this time being the Fourteenth of July : Van Gogh, in 1887 (Hahnloser Coll., Berne) and, during the Fauve period, Dufy and Marquet in 1906 (Private Coll., Paris).

After these experiments in open-air painting, Manet, who was fundamentally opposed to it and always kept a certain distance from complete Impressionism returned to his studio and discovered " ... a solution to the conflict of tendencies of which his art is the stake; his idea is to combine the two doctrines and paint, if I may so express it, indoor open air ! He gets his models to pose in a greenhouse, in an arbor, in the undefined light of a small Parisian garden in which a lone chestnut tree suffices to veil the sun. This device enables him to rediscover his familiar lighting, possibly both more intense and more refined, and one that is not alien to his studio-painter's habits, in particular that of imposing interminable sittings on his models [60]. "

Two characteristic canvases mark the synthesis between his studio technique and the lessons he had learned out of doors : first *In the Greenhouse*, painted in 1878 and shown in the 1879 Salon (Nationalgalerie, Berlin-Dahlem) in which we see M. and Mme Guillemet in a lighting which is a compromise between open air and indoors, then in *Chez le père Lathuille*, dated 1879 and exhibited in the Salon of 1880 (Tournai Museum) the models for which were the son of the owner M. Gauthier-Lathuille and Mlle Fresnels, the latter replacing Ellen André who had had to discontinue her sittings. In both works, especially in the second, Manet still shows his liking for subjects of a realist tendency that are reminiscent of Zola or Maupassant.

Manet had rented a villa at Bellevue, on the road to Gardes, during the summer of 1880 and painted several pictures there, including *A Corner in the Bellevue Garden* (Private Coll., Paris), *La Promenade* (Private Coll., New York) and *Girl in a Garden* (Rouart Coll., Paris) informed by a subtle naturalist vision whose considerably diluted Impressionism is in point of fact his own personal impressionism.

In the same spirit he painted *The Seat* (Private Coll., Paris), executed during

ÉDOUARD MANET — GIRL IN A GARDEN. 1880 (59 1/2 × 45 1/2 ") — ROUART COLLECTION, PARIS

the summer of 1881 in the garden of the small villa he had rented, 20, avenue de Villeneuve-l'Etang, at Versailles. In a letter dated September 23, 1881, Manet explains to Eva Gonzalès how, seeking a more ambitious subject, he was reduced to the banal reality of a suburban garden : " ... Thus, having set out to do studies in the park designed by Le Nôtre, I have had to be content to paint merely my own garden, the most dreadful of gardens[61]... "

Shortly before his death, Manet returned to one of his favorite themes, the scenes of Parisian life : *Le Bar des Folies-Bergère*, painted at the end of 1881 and exhibited in the Salon of 1882 (Courtauld Institute, London) sets the seal on the genius of this artist who had a thorough understanding of the nature of the object, of space and planes, who was a born painter and whose Impressionism is much more allied to that of the Spanish, his real masters, than that of Claude Monet and his other friends.

EDGAR DEGAS

CAN Degas be considered an Impressionist ? Yes, if we refer to the history of the movement; he exhibited almost continually with the group whose spirit of independence towards official painting he shared. But a careful examination of his work shows fundamental differences side by side with points in common, particularly where technique is concerned. The basic originality of his art prevents us from connecting him with any definite school; neither purely classical, truly realistic nor frankly Impressionist, Degas is all these and something else. Classical, he is above all sensitive to form and, in this, diametrically opposed to the Impressionists. Enthusiastic about line and its convolutions—though he avoids the reef of pure intellectualism—intoxicated with drawing (which is for him, according to Valéry, " a manner of seeing "), he has the liking for graphism and construction that eludes the Impressionists.

Degas had an academic training and was first attracted by portraiture, his analytical and psychological gifts leading him to scrutinize the human face, that reflection of the spirit, and subsequently by vast historical compositions. The *Portrait of the Bellelli Family* (c. 1858-1860) is a masterpiece from that point of view. And in this canvas, the classicism of the balanced composition, the idealized purity of the faces, inevitably recalling the Florentines, is mingled with the everyday realism of the attitudes and expressions. This synthesis, characteristic of all his work, was acknowledged by the artist himself. " I want to be the classical painter of modern life, " he writes. The *Portrait of Marguerite de Gas*, who was to become Mme Henri Fèvre (c. 1858-1860, Jeu de Paume), which is worthy of a Ghirlandaio or a Botticelli, and finally the *Portrait of Thérèse de Gas, Duchesse de Morbili* (1863, Jeu de Paume), amazingly hieratic, also command our attention.

The historical compositions of the same period recall the technique of the fresco : sober in their color, rigorous in their drawing, they are conceived as mural decorations. The *Young Spartans Exercising* (1860, National Gallery, London) clearly shows Degas' double tendency : classicism in the static pose, the rhythm, the harmony of composition, strong drawing emphasizing the forms; realism in the dynamic attitudes (despite the held poses), expressive gestures, naturalism. *Semiramis founding a Town* (1861, Jeu de Paume), which was left unfinished, is organized like an ancient bas-relief, and Semiramis herself is in the direct line of Greek statuary. The Cabinet of Drawings in the Louvre preserves admirable pencil studies for this canvas in which Degas shows his early mastery of spontaneous movement. Next came *Alexander and Bucephalus* (1861-1864, Smith College, Northampton, U.S.A.) of which two versions exist, and *The Misfortunes of the City of Rouen* (Salon of 1865, Jeu de Paume), the artist's last experiment in historical painting, the pencil studies for which anticipate the *Danseuses* and the *Femmes à leur toilette*.

Between the years 1865 and 1866 Degas associated with the Impressionists, frequented the Café Guerbois and moved in literary and artistic circles. He suddenly neglected the classicism of his early years to discover a new original art in contemporary life and humanity that he could render in terms of *personal impression*. It was in this spirit that he painted scenes of Paris life and, indefatigably, his portraits. In the latter he strove to endow his model with the maximum individuality. He wanted to make " a study of modern feeling... portraits of people in everyday and characteristic attitudes, to give their faces the same variety of expressions as one gives their bodies... " *The Woman with the Chrysanthemums* (1865, Metropolitan Museum, New York) is one of the high points of his art: a new style of composition, doubtless inspired by snapshots, with the figure shifted to the extreme right of the picture; a shrewd psychological analysis of this woman in the autumn of her life, next to those autumn flowers, looking anxiously at her first wrinkles in a mirror outside the canvas. Could the artist who evidently understood this agony of the feminine heart really be a misogynist, as some assert? *The Orchestra of the Paris Opera* (c. 1868-1869, Jeu de Paume) demonstrates the master's boldness in the matter of composition. And here again we remark his penetrating observation of each of the individual personalities who make up the orchestra.

Degas' technique also underwent a transformation; its previous smoothness gave way to a richer paint substance, as we note, for example, in *Mlle Fiocre in the Ballet, " La Source "* (1868, Metropolitan Museum, New York) in which his new plastic experiments under the influence of the theatre, photography and *Japonisme* are in equal evidence. This development can be seen no less clearly in the *Portrait of Mme Camus* (1870, National Gallery of Art, Washington); here the boldness of color and design show Degas to be an exceptional innovator.

Four important paintings with realistic subjects borrowed from the " modernity " of which Baudelaire speaks, still belong to his earlier manner and are treated with a fairly traditional technique: *Carriage at the Races* (1873, Museum of Fine Arts, Boston), shown at the first Impressionist Exhibition of 1874, *The Cotton Office at New Orleans* (1873, Pau Museum), shown at the second Impressionist Exhibition of 1876, *La Bouderie* (Metropolitan Museum, New York) and finally *Le Viol* (c. 1874, Private Coll., Philadelphia). The first two pictures are satisfying in their truth, the latter betray a poignant misanthropy in their author. This period is marked by a whole series of portraits; those of *Mlle Hortense Valpinçon* (1869, The Minneapolis Institute of Art), the *Vicomte Lepic and his Daughters* (1870, Private Coll., U.S.A.) and finally the admirable composition entitled *Double Portrait of Mme Fèvre or the Song rehearsal* (1873, The Dumbarton Oaks Coll., Georgetown, Washington).

Scenes of life in Paris, in the café or café-concert, next assume an important part in the artist's work. *Absinthe* (1876, Jeu de Paume) is the most striking of these, both with regard to the composition, to which could be applied the paradoxical label " asymmetrical symmetry, " and the spirit in which the work has been carried out, that is to say, with neither vulgarity nor caricature but simply the objectivity of a man for whom everyday life and people have no longer any secrets. Concerning the pastel on monotype *Femmes dans un Café le soir* (1877, Jeu de Paume) Georges Rivière wrote the same year in the first issue of the *Impressionniste* : " M. Degas is an observer; he never aims at exaggeration, the effect is always obtained by painting life without any trimmings. It is that element which makes him the most valuable recorder of the scenes which he depicts for us... " The *Café Concert : Les Ambassadeurs*, (1876-1877, Lyons Museum), pastel on monotype, and *Café Singer wearing a Glove* (1878, Fogg Art Museum, Cambridge, U.S.A.), pastel with distemper on canvas, speak more eloquently still of Degas' aptitude as the " painter of contemporary history. "

The sea, the great seducer of the Impressionist circle, appealed to him too. But it is rather the foreshore that claims his particular attention, since he could people it with figures. Like Manet, Degas found it difficult to conceive a painting without human presence. For him the landscape is only a framework, and he prefers that of an intimate interior as being more closely associated with people. But on occasion he restricts himself to interpreting the magic of the sea and sky in studies generally executed in pastel, which are reminiscent of his great predecessors, Boudin and Delacroix (*Au bord de la mer*, 1869, Jeu de Paume).

Degas' work of the post 1870 period falls naturally into " series, " though these are conceived in a very different spirit from those of Claude Monet. " Permanence of a theme " is how François Fosca has correctly described it. And the theme provides the painter with an almost inexhaustible record of forms whose secret he endeavors to penetrate. Degas was constantly renewing himself and never fell a victim of formula. Each work has its own individuality and its own justification and is a stage in his search for the mysterious geometry which determines the unity of nature in its universal rhythm. Paul Valéry has given us the perfect definition of this constant progression, realized without either effort or artifice : " A passionate devotion to the simple line which fixes a figure, and this figure, encountered in everyday life, the street, at the Opera, at the milliner's and even in other places; but always a figure caught in the special ambiance to which it belongs, at a given moment, never static and always expressive—this would be my rough summing up of Degas. He was bold enough to attempt to combine immediacy and painstaking detail in the studio, to enshrine the impression in the careful study and the immediate in the permanency of considered purposefulness. " [62]

His work consists of five series : three numerically not so important : *Racecourse Scenes*, the *Ironers* or *Laundresses*, and the *Milliners;* two, destined to assume considerable importance, *Les Danseuses de l'Opéra* and *Les Femmes à leur toilette*. Already by 1862, the artist had concerned himself with racecourse scenes—a pretext in his case, not for the study of open-air effects but for that of the attitudes of riders and their mounts—in a painting influenced by Géricault, *La Course de gentlemen, avant le départ* (Jeu de Paume). And in 1866 he exhibited a *Steeplechase* in a more

personal idiom. *Parade of Race Horses before the Grand stand* (*c.* 1869-1872, Jeu de Paume), typical of this series, creates the illusion of open air, although it was actually executed from memory in the studio. A certain Impressionism is discernible in the treatment of the grass, but the work is conceived in a totally different spirit dominated by the artist's striving after an original composition. Among so many, we must pick out *Race Horses at Longchamp* (1872-1875, Museum of Fine Art, Boston, Mass.), the strange composition of which emphasizes its living character, and the later pastel (1894) from the Mr. and Mrs. J. Watson Webb Collection, *Training*

109

whose distinctive feature is the use of purple and blue-green in the distance.

A charcoal drawing, heightened with chalk and pastel, entitled *La Repasseuse* (*Woman ironing*, 1869, Jeu de Paume), opens the way to the *Blanchisseuses* and *Repasseuses* series, already referred to and so rich in observation. In the same way as Picasso who later treated the same theme, Degas expresses the permanence of an eternal gesture and tirelessly studies its endless variations. We can assess them from *La Repasseuse à contre-jour* (1874, Metropolitan Museum Art, New York), from *Les Repasseuses portant du linge* (1876-1878, Private Coll., New York) or from *Les Repasseuses*, 1884, Jeu de Paume); in these the beauty of effort is exalted with undeniable grandeur.

In the *Modistes* series, fashion once more provides a pretext for a multiplicity of forms (*At the Milliner's*, 1883, pastel, Private Coll., Paris; 1885, Art Institute, Chicago, etc.).

But the most famous series is that of the *Ballet Dancers*. Degas pursues the rhythms indefatigably, analyzing all its modulations without respite, and yet never neglecting color. What wins him a place apart among his contemporaries is this expressive drawing, accompanied by color that is both bold and refined. He renders the reflections of light—which is always that of the footlights and not of the sun—with an Impressionism that never obscures the form. How can one list all these masterpieces? Beginning with oil paintings that were often almost *grisailles*—*Le Foyer de la danse à l'Opéra, rue Le Peletier* (1872, Jeu de Paume)—he ended with the magic of colored vibrations with pastels such as *Fin d'arabesque* (1877, Jeu de Paume), *Dancer with Bouquet taking a Call, Danseuse au bouquet saluant sur la scène* (1878, Jeu de Paume) or *Danseuses à la barre* (Metropolitan Museum Art, New York). Intoxicated with color, he embarked on a series, in blue, green, yellow (or orange) respectively.

Relentlessly pursuing the living form, Degas never ceased to renew himself, and in 1886, at the last Impressionist Exhibition, he showed a series of pastels entitled: "Series of nudes of women bathing, washing, drying, rubbing down, combing their hair or having it combed." A long time before this date, he had tackled the theme (*Women combing their Hair*, 1875-1876, Phillips Gallery, Washington; *Sea Bathing*, 1876-1877, National Gallery, London) which was to give birth to the most outstanding series perhaps of all his work. The female body is now bent to every caprice of the master: he breaks it up the better to reconstruct it, distorts it to define the forms with greater clarity. His experience in this sphere extends so far that he arrives at those "formless forms" to which Paul Valéry refers, and the pastel entitled *Woman combing her Hair* (c. 1887-1890, Jeu de Paume) remains one of the most remarkable examples. Design and color became increasingly daring. *La Toilette* (pastel, 1885, Metropolitan Museum, New York), *The Tub* (pastel, 1886, Jeu de Paume), *After the Bath, Woman drying her Feet* (pastel, 1886, Jeu de Paume), *La Coiffure* (painting 1892-1895, National Gallery, London), *After the Bath, Woman drying her Neck* (pastel, 1898, Jeu de Paume) are works in which boldness of tonality is combined with daring composition and which, in their powerful originality and modernism, opened the way directly to the Nabis and, in particular, to Bonnard.

Although Degas was associated with the Impressionist *milieu* and took part in the majority of its exhibitions, his art is essentially different. If on occasion, chiefly in his pastels, he employs an Impressionist technique—optical mixture of tones, juxtaposition of touches that are dissociated rather than fragmented, setting down

110

EDGAR DEGAS
WOMAN IRONING. 1874
(21 1/4 × 15 1/4 '')
METROPOLITAN
MUSEUM, NEW YORK

luminous vibrations, boldly colored shadows—everything in him is different from
the Impressionist vision, above all his acknowledged hostility to open-air painting.
Vollard records his angry reaction to it : " If I were the government, I would have a
brigade of gendarmerie to police people who paint landscapes from nature. Oh,
I don't want anyone's death, I would be satisfied if they just peppered them with
shot to start with ! " The artist returns to the theme : " Don't mention the word
open air again in my hearing ! " And, defining his position, " Oh well ! A painting
is primarily a product of the artist's imagination. It should never be a copy. If
he proceeds to add two or three touches from nature, that obviously does no harm...
It is much better to draw what you can only see from your memory of it. It is a

112

transmutation during which your imagination collaborates with your recollection; you reproduce only what struck you, that is to say, the essential."

Degas was unequivocally opposed to the Impressionists : " Don't speak to me about the Impressionists, they ought to be... " and picking up a walking stick, he raised it to his shoulder. He inveighed with no less violence against the tones used by Monet and his friends, and when the latter accused him of not being a colorist, retorted : " I am a colorist with line, " and elucidating his remark, " The essential thing is to possess and set the dominating tone around which the harmony of a picture will be established. To emphasize this tone and make it more real, false tones must be employed, in combination with it, if necessary, to bring it out. "

Degas went so far as to react against the term " Impressionist "; he preferred the term " independent " which is, moreover, a more fitting one for this artist, the complexity of whose work cannot be confined within the limits of Impressionism alone.

EDGAR DEGAS — THE TUB. PASTEL. 1886 (23 1/2 × 32 1/2 ") — LOUVRE, PARIS

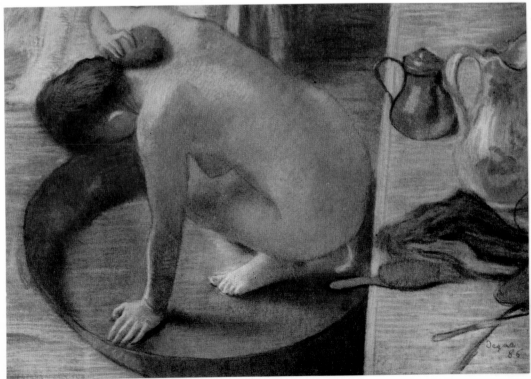

HENRI DE TOULOUSE-LAUTREC — SUZANNE VALADON. 1885 (21 1/2 × 17 3/4 ")
NY CARLSBERG GLYPTOTEK, COPENHAGEN

Born in 1864 and belonging therefore to a generation later than the Impressionists who were mostly born *circa* 1840, Toulouse-Lautrec likewise stands beside them as an " independent. " He did not participate in any of their exhibitions, and his artistic preoccupations are for the most part very different from those of a Monet and his friends. His realism is not that of an Edouard Manet or a Degas; yet we place Lautrec in the direct line of these two masters, for he had the same taste for modernity, for subjects borrowed from everyday life in which people play the main role. Nevertheless, unlike them, he joined Impressionism in his early days, when he embarked on open-air painting—racecourse scenes, landscapes, portraits executed out of doors—only to forsake it shortly afterwards for an art in which nature took little part. He preferred cafés, cabarets, the music hall, the circus, brothels, night life that is at the same time artificial and poignantly real. However, he retained the Impressionist technique : the use of pure, often light tones, touches composed of juxtaposed *hachures*, but free of impasto. He frequently painted on cardboard and diluted his paints with turpentine, a process which gives his works the dull finish of a gouache. But Lautrec, like Degas, is first and foremost a draftsman, and his expressive line, less precise than that of Degas, suggests more than it defines. His predilection for the graphic arts—drawing, lithography and poster— sets him apart from the Impressionists.

His work is informed by the same spirit as that of the writer Octave Mirbeau; his aim is, he says, to be a *witness*. And he adds : " I have endeavored to paint the true, not the ideal. " He sees mankind without indulgence, paints it unmasked, stripping it of all conformism, always seeking to capture the individual tic or tics which characterize each person. By a process of elimination, following the Japanese example, or that of some caricaturists—though he goes beyond the caricature—he succeeds in seizing on the expression in isolation, the peculiar gesture that gives his model, not a fleeting attitude but that which is peculiarly *its own*, the one it bears within itself, permanently from birth to the grave. It was the method of the Japanese reducing a form to an extreme synthesis; it was the method adopted by his contemporary, the caricaturist Sem, who, shedding all picturesque notation or after many preliminary sketches, reduced the portrait of the Prince of Wales, the future Edward VII, to a circle and a cigar—a wonderful likeness without nose, mouth or hair ! We find this same economy and acuteness of observation in Lautrec, who knew how to jettison the element of caricature in favor of the real and profoundly human trait, sometimes underlined with a touch of satire. Without any systematic striving after originality, he achieves it brilliantly in his new and personal vision, his bold designs. His critical sense warns him off well-trodden paths and stimulates him to recreate through the medium of reality a world—that of the " Belle Époque "— which becomes *his* " world. " " Believe me, " wrote Oscar Wilde, whose portrait he painted, " there is no fine art without self-consciousness, and self-consciousness and the critical spirit are one. " (Oscar Wilde, *Intentions*.)

Although Lautrec began by painting some landscapes and coach scenes (*Count Alphonse de Toulouse-Lautrec driving his Mail Coach at Nice*, 1881, Petit-Palais, Paris), he makes the following observation about the Impressionists : " The figure alone exists,

115

HENRI DE TOULOUSE-LAUTREC — MARCELLE LENDER DANCING THE CHILPERIC BOLERO. 1895 (57 1/2 × 59 3/4 ")
THE HONORABLE AND MRS. JOHN HAY WHITNEY COLLECTION, NEW YORK

the landscape is, and should only be an accessory : the pure landscapist is merely a brute beast, the landscape should serve only to make us understand the character of the person better... '', thus sharing Degas' opinion.   And he often adopted a form of expressionism which sometimes anticipates Rouault (*An Ecclesiastic*, 1881, Albi Museum; *Woman pulling on her Stocking*, c. 1894, Jeu de Paume).

Once he was in Paris, 1882, Lautrec was rapidly attracted by the circus, bars, cabarets, the music hall, before seeking his inspiration in brothels.   He then painted *At the Cirque Fernando : Circus Rider* (1888, Art Institute, Chicago).   From 1884 to about 1889 he was fascinated by the subjects of Aristide Bruant and he illustrated his most famous songs : *A Batignolles, A Belleville, A Saint-Lazare* and did a picture of the " chansonnier " in his own cabaret (*Aristide Bruant, at the Ambassadeurs*, 1892, Albi Museum).   He also painted those cynical canvases which reveal his spirit of mockery : *Gueule de bois ou la buveuse*, for which the model was Suzanne Valadon (1888-1889, Fogg Art Museum, Cambridge, U.S.A.), *In Lodgings* (1890, Private Coll.), *A la mie*

(1891, Museum of Fine Arts, Boston), *Alfred la guigne* (1894, National Gallery of Art, Washington); to which we may add his studies for Zola's *Assommoir*. During the same years, the painter executed portraits of profound psychology, whether indoors : *Mlle Dihau at the Piano* (1890, Albi Museum), a symphony in deep blues ; or in the Garden of Père Forest at Montmartre : *Justine Dieuhl*, or again *The Woman in the Gloves, Honorine P.* (c. 1889-1890, Jeu de Paume), and finally *Woman in Père Forest's Garden* (1891, Museum of Art, Toledo, U.S.A.). Nevertheless these assays in the open air bear no resemblance to those of the Impressionists; he treats the landscape as a piece of décor and his only link with these painters is his use of vibrating juxtaposed touches of color, pure tones of blues, greens and violets, binary complementaries.

The somewhat dubious milieu of dance halls became his favorite haunt and led him to frequent the cabarets and the Moulin Rouge, where his verve, raillery, taste for reality and picturesque attitudes had free rein : *Au Bal du Moulin de la Galette* (1890, Henry P. McIlhenny, Philadelphia), *At the Moulin Rouge* (Art Insti-

HENRI DE TOULOUSE-LAUTREC — JANE AVRIL LEAVING THE MOULIN ROUGE. 1892 (32 1/2 × 25 1/4 ") — WADSWORTH ATHENEUM, HARTFORD, CONNECTICUT.

tute, Chicago), *Quadrille at the Moulin Rouge* (1892, National Gallery of Art, Washington). Then came the favorite characters La Goulue (*La Goulue entering the Moulin Rouge*, Private Coll., Paris) and her partner "Boneless Valentin" (*La Goulue and Boneless Valentin*, 1890, Hahnloser Coll., Winterhur) represented later in the two panels, masterpieces of decoration, executed for La Goulue's Booth at the *Foire du Trône* and now preserved in the Jeu de Paume : *La Goulue and Boneless Valentin dancing*, showing two new arrivals in the center (Lautrec situates the ambiance of his models with a single detail; whereas the Prince of Wales had set the fashion in Paris for wearing a cornflower boutonnière, the man in the picture is adorned with a whole bunch), and *La Goulue, or the Almahs* with Paul Sescau, the photographer, playing the piano on the left and among the foreground spectators Maurice Guibert, Dr. Tapié de Celeyran, the painter's cousin, Oscar Wilde, Jane Avril, back-view of Lautrec and Félix Fénéon in profile.

And then Jane Avril again (*Jane Avril dancing*, c. 1892, Jeu de Paume; *Jane Avril leaving the Moulin Rouge*, 1892, Wadsworth Atheneum, Hartford, Conn.); *Loïe Fuller at the Folies-Bergère*, 1893 (Albi Museum); Marcelle Lender (*Marcelle Lender dancing the Chilperic Bolero*, 1895-1896, John Hay Whitney, Coll., New York); the Irish dancer May Belfort. Nevertheless, the painter's favorite model, she whose comedienne's heart he summed up in inimitable fashion, is the entertainer Yvette Guilbert in her black gloves. We find her in innumerable paintings, sketches and drawings : *Yvette Guilbert taking a Call, Yvette Guilbert* (1894, Albi Museum), etc.

A large section of Toulouse-Lautrec's work is devoted to prostitutes. In 1894 he installed himself in the " house " in the rue des Moulins and carried out an important series of sketches, pastels and lithographs, done either from the prostitutes themselves or from life in brothels. Here again he is merciless, without ever falling into exaggeration; he paints this special world with which he had a day-to-day connection intimately, almost clinically. No concessions to the picturesque, just life in the raw; no license but a certain crudity. Despite the obvious vulgarity of his models and sometimes their vices, he passes beyond his subject and paints a study of manners, seeing, as he does, the dramatically human side of this " milieu " : *In the Salon de la rue des Moulins* (1894, Albi Museum). And we cannot omit *In Bed* (1894, Albi Museum, c. 1892-1895, Jeu de Paume), *The Laundryman* (1894, Albi Museum) and numerous studies of prostitutes which show his subtle psychology. To these we may add the suite of lithographs entitled *Elles*.

Towards the end of his career, the artist exploited his favorite themes again in wonderful drawings such as *The Negro Clown Chocolate dancing at Achilles' Bar* (1896, Albi Museum). He returned to scenes of contemporary manners with *At the Bar, the Chlorotic Cashier* (1898, Kunsthaus, Zurich), *A la toilette, Madame Poupoule* (1898, Albi Museum), and portraits, very different in spirit, such as *The English Girl at the Star, Le Havre* (1899, Albi Museum) or *Maurice Joyant* (1900, Albi Museum). His expressionism re-appears in the picture entitled *Examination at the Faculty of Medecine, Paris* (1901, Albi Museum) in which Lautrec once again reveals himself as one of Rouault's immediate precursors.

This art of a " skin-deep " brutality sometimes shocks but it bears within it the poignant secret of a wounded soul, one that is not so much in revolt as striving to understand with love and with charity. Did not Lautrec reply to those who questioned him : " First you do not know and you will never know; all you will know is what someone has been kind enough to reveal to you. "

118

Reaction against
Impressionism

PAUL CÉZANNE

Some of the artists associated with the Impressionist group were interested in its method of painting and at the same time were alive to its drawbacks. Thus a reaction set in, particularly against what was considered a too undisciplined technique. Cézanne wanted a return to drawing and form; Seurat, Signac and their friends tried to reduce the procedures which had hitherto been employed empirically, into a strict code.

"My aim," said Cézanne, "has been to make of Impressionism something solid and enduring like the art in the Museums." And, as opposed to the Impressionists who saw only color at the expense of form, Cézanne did not dissociate color from drawing : "Drawing and color are not separate," he remarked to Émile Bernard. "One draws as one progresses with the painting. The more the color harmonizes, the more the drawing becomes defined... *When color has its greatest richness, form reaches its plenitude.* Contrast and relations of tones, that is where the secret of drawing and modeling lies..." This definition is so fundamental, I think, that it can be said to sum up the whole art of painting.

In point of fact, whereas the Impressionists expressed only the ephemeral, the unstable, and captured the frailty of the impalpable in nature, Cézanne, when he is concerned with this evanescent aspect, is attracted rather to the internal architecture of natural elements and the very structure of the soil itself. Hardly aware of its superficial reflections, he analyzes even water in a classical way, rendering only its density, volume and its mass in depth. Unwilling to neglect form for the envelope, he endeavors to balance the two elements : "Nature is always the same, but nothing remains of her that appears to us... our art should give it the *quiver of its permanence* with the elements, the appearances of all these changes."

The "quiver" is the Impressionist contribution, "permanence" marks the reaction. Starting from this apparent antithesis Cézanne succeeded in creating a perfectly coherent synthesis from contradictory elements. He admits the basic principle of Impressionist light, but with a difference. In his conversations with Émile Bernard and K.-X. Roussel, Cézanne elucidates his idea : "Light is a thing *which cannot be reproduced;* it must be represented by something else, *color.* I was pleased with myself when I made this discovery." Thus, little by little the Cézanne *idea* is elaborated; largely opposed, as will be remarked, to the Impressionists' purely intuitive *vision*, but the artist recognizes the necessity of this pictorial movement : "What is Impressionism? It is the optical mixture of colors, do you understand? The division of tones on the canvas and their reconstitution in the retina. We had to accept that." But later he gives no quarter and concludes : "The Impressionist band who have lacked a master and ideas..." Finally, whereas the typical Impressionist Claude Monet brushed in his canvases, which are not really much more than sketches, rapidly, in a few hours, Cézanne constructed each work with slow deliberation. For years, he "returned" endlessly to the same picture, searching for the right color and tone, redrawing the form to convey the quality of the object, this, not wholly with reference to its external appearance; and after one hundred and fifteen sittings he exclaimed in front of his *Portrait of Vollard*, "I am not displeased with the shirt-front!"

Cézanne's art contains as much reflection as vision; he strove to establish the fusion between the two manners which people nowadays are over-eager to define as "figurative" and "non-figurative"; the objective and subjective are interdependent to the genuine artist, and Cézanne affirms this when he says : "In painting there are two things : the eye and the brain; they should help each other; one should attend to their mutual development, but as a painter : to the eye by one's vision of nature; to the brain by the logic of organized sensations which provide the means of expression."

Far from restricting himself exclusively to what he calls "my little sensation," Cézanne recomposes what his eye registered : "We must become classical again through nature, that is through sensation." But for him this sensation is not reduced to the purely visual image of nature, beloved of Claude Monet and his friends; he was unable to accept the role of "speculum mundi," the mirror of the world of nature. Such an aesthetic conception offered no attraction for the man who aimed at the absolute : "Painting," he remarked to his son, "is not making a slavish copy of the object; it consists in seizing a *harmony* among innumerable relationships, transposing them to a scale of one's own by developing them in accordance with a *new and original logic*." He returns to this theme more succinctly in a letter to Émile Bernard : "Art is *a parallel harmony* to nature." This definition separates him completely from his Impressionist friends and their art; he had now discovered, with the secret of equilibrium, the secret of painting. He innovated within the tradition and he not only continued Delacroix, Poussin and the Venetians, but anticipated Fauvism, Cubism and was a precursor of genius of all contemporary art.

Cézanne's biographers have confined their studies too closely to his work of certain periods and, because of this, have partitioned it up too much. There was, it is true, the "palette-knife" period which René Huyghe calls the Age of Vehemence and which I would define as a time of baroque and romantic exaltation; it extended from his beginnings to about 1870. It was followed by the period that we might call "Impressionist"—the Age of Light for Huyghe (1871 to about 1882). A third period, Huyghe's Age of Style, is what I should consider a phase of synthesis and classical harmony (1882 to c. 1895). Finally the last period (1896 to 1906)—the Age of Lyricism for Huyghe—is the stage of total liberation when the

120

artist, in pursuit of the absolute, is striving to express both the purely visual reality inspired by nature and the strictly cerebral reaction to it, by means of the logic of his organized sensations. I should add that if these four periods serve as a framework to the study of Cézanne's work, the dates which partition them should not be regarded too exactly; otherwise they would tend to limit the range of a work that, composed of continual experiments, and knowing no limits or periphery, was fundamentally fluid, an art for which the painter fought a superhuman battle, frustrated that he was vouchsafed only one life in which to realize all he had to express.

In his early days, Cézanne practiced a technique of vigorous impasto and violently contrasted chiaroscuro in the Caravaggian vein; his style is realistic, informed with a baroque and exuberant romanticism; a certain clumsiness is apparent, particularly in his figures, generally heavy, massive and brachycephalic. Examples are the *Portrait of the Painter Achille Emperaire* (c. 1866, Private Coll., Paris), or *Paul Alexis reading to Zola* (1869, Private Coll., New York); the somber colors, the excess of dark shadows, the thick impasto, the awkwardnesses in the models' anatomy are compensated for by the amazing freedom of the technique. But one is conscious of the artist's struggles with the difficulties of his craft and the solution of the hard problems involved. From this point on, he worked indefatigably, sometimes anxious but never discouraged, facing rebuffs or lack of understanding with patient obstinacy, moving slowly forward, getting rid of the imperfections of his art, ceaselessly developing towards freedom from all stereotyped formula or method whether academic, classical or baroque, imbued with his mission which was to be one of the most glorious in the whole history of painting. In the same spirit as the two previously mentioned works but executed with a broader and more assured technique the *Portrait of the artist's Father, Louis-Auguste Cézanne, reading " L'Evénement "* (1866, Private Coll., Paris) should be mentioned. Zola had just published in that journal an account of the Salon, in which he conducted a violent attack on official painters and a vigorous defence of his " independent " friends. It was doubtless therefore no coincidence that Cézanne painted his father reading this (as far as he and his friends were concerned) eulogistic article. Still about this same period, he executed several *Portraits of " Oncle Dominique "* (Private Coll., Paris).

The Negro Scipio (1865, Michel Monet Coll., Giverny) and *Mary Magdalene or Sorrow* (c. 1866-1868, Jeu de Paume) bear witness to somewhat different experiments : the combination of various influences, particularly that of El Greco in the elongation of the human form, Caravaggio's in the chiaroscuro and Géricault's in the technique. *Mary Magdalene*, characteristic of this exacerbated baroque spirit (his " supernatural reality " is worthy of the Spanish School), along with *Christ in Limbo*, formed part of decorations executed by the artist at his house at Jas de Bouffan and later transferred to canvas.

Following the Spanish example, Cézanne embarked on still-life painting. And he demonstrated his gift for revealing that " silent life " of things and expressing its poetry. He and Chardin are perhaps the only two who have conveyed the inexpressible of the inanimate. He began with two masterpieces, *The Black Clock* (1869-1870, Niarchos Coll.) and *Still Life with pewter Kettle* (1869-1870, Private Coll., Paris). The former, in particular, painted in broad contrasted planes, is astonishingly poetic with its handless clockface (a symbol of arrested time ?);

121

the pink of the shell and the yellow of the lemon set off the deep black of the clock and the brilliant white of the duster with its intensely black folds. Also belonging to this so-called romantic period is a vigorous portrait, still treated in the Spanish manner, *The Man in the Straw hat, or Portrait of Boyer* (1869-1870, Metropolitan Museum, New York) and a landscape *Melting Snow at l'Estaque* (1870-1871, G. Wildenstein Coll., Paris) in which everything is violent and dramatic; the dark sky with sweeping opaque clouds, the modelled technique anticipate some of Vlaminck's landscapes.

About the year 1870, while under Impressionist influence, Cézanne lightened his palette and banished black. On Pissarro's advice, he worked to some small extent in the open air but it did not suit him very well; he preferred creating in the studio, since nature for him was a means and not an end. His excessively thick paint was exchanged for a rather gritty finish like that of his friends. Two works, both inspired by Manet, marking this transition, *A Modern Olympia* (1870, Private Coll., Paris and 1873, Jeu de Paume) are still very much Baudelairean in spirit, but in my opinion, the tone relationships are inharmonious and the two paintings have only an experimental value. *La Maison du Pendu at Auvers-sur-Oise* (1873, Jeu de Paume) is the decisive work of this period of Cézanne's development towards Impressionism. Pissarro's influence is evident; it appears particularly in the " earthy " tone; not much sky, a very high horizon—unlike Claude Monet, Sisley or Renoir—and in the preoccupation with construction : the structure of the houses, trees and soil show clearly the attraction that everything solid and defined had for Cézanne. The tonalities here are extremely clear, the air and light certainly those of the open air. In the majority of the landscapes of this so-called Impressionist period the artist is haunted by the vastness of space—in depth—the brush strokes are oblique and applied in planes that are already to some extent geometrical, form has pride of place and structure is respected even in the foliage (*Auvers, panoramic view*, 1873-1875, Art Institute, Chicago; *Pontoise, the Hermitage*, 1875-1877, Municipal Museum, Wuppertal; *Pond at Jas de Bouffan*, c. 1878, Private Coll., Paris; *La Côte du Jalais at Pontoise*, 1879-1882, Private Coll., Philadelphia; *The Poplars*, 1879-1882, Jeu de Paume ; *The Pont de Mennecy*, called *The Little Bridge*, c. 1882, Jeu de Paume, etc.).

His still lifes show a similar development from the *Bouquet au petit Delft* (c. 1873-1875, Jeu de Paume) to the *Still life with Soup Tureen* (c. 1883-1885, Jeu de Paume) and in all these, including the latter, the Impressionist manner still predominates. And if the forms are not always balanced or symmetrical, we should not follow the example of some critics and see an optical distortion as the cause, but rather a certain indifference on Cézanne's part with regard to the exact and photographic rendering of the object whose intrinsic quality was what he wanted above all to express. Several portraits date from this period : some *Self Portraits* (1873-1876, Private Coll., Paris; 1879-1882, Kunstmuseum, Berne), some *Portraits of Madame Cézanne* of which the one known as *The red Armchair* (1877, Museum of Fine Arts, Boston, Mass.) is the masterpiece; finally the *Portrait of Victor Chocquet* (1876-1877, Private Coll., London). He further painted various studies of *Baigneuses*, (1873-1877, Private Coll., Paris; Barnes Foundation, Merion, U.S.A.).

122

The third so-called period of synthesis when Cézanne's constructive genius, profoundly pictorial sense and originality asserted themselves, is dominated at first by the *Views of l'Estaque, near Marseilles* (1883-1885, Jeu de Paume; Metropolitan Museum, New York; Art Institute, Chicago, etc.) in which Cézanne conveys the Impressionist " quiver ", particularly in the foreground trees, but also the immutable character, the permanence of the natural elements; the water has no reflection mirrored on its surface; it is dense, profound, offering a mass, a volume, obtained solely by the balancing of tints and tones : " When color is at its greatest richness, form reaches its plenitude ! " Finally, the distant hills are treated in simple geometric planes, the geology of the soil appears in its reconstituted structure. We see the first precursory elements of Cubism in the foreground, in the chimney stack—a cylinder and in the houses—cubes, " Treating nature in terms of the cylinder, sphere,

PAUL CÉZANNE — MONTAGNE SAINTE-VICTOIRE. 1904 (11 × 14 1/4 ") — MUSEUM OF ART, PHILADELPHIA

123

cone, all set down in perspective... Nature for us men is more in depth than on the surface !... " was now the great Cézanne lesson.

The admirable series of *Views of Montagne Sainte-Victoire* occurs between 1885 and 1887 (Metropolitan Museum, New York; National Gallery, London; National Gallery, Washington, D.C.; Private Coll., Paris, etc), a theme to which the artist never tired of returning right up to his death (*c*. 1900, water color, Private Coll., Paris; Museum of Art, Philadelphia, etc.). Cézanne found in this subject, which he treated with a masterly synthesis of baroque temperament and classical aspiration, the great universal rhythm of life, "the parallel harmony to nature" which puts him in the direct line of Nicolas Poussin. The same fugal composition, interpenetration of planes, the same sense of space, the same concordance of voids and solids. He attains that perfect equilibrium in which light and form are closely associated to

PAUL CÉZANNE — AMBROISE VOL-LARD. 1899 (39 1/2 × 32 ") — PETIT-PALAIS, PARIS

PAUL CÉZANNE
THE CHEST OF DRAWERS. 1883-1887 (28 3/4 × 36 1/2 ") — NEUE STAATSGALERIE, MUNICH

express nature's opulence. " The planes are in the color, the planes ! " he said.
" The colored place where the soul of the planes vibrates, prismatic warmth achieved,
the encounter of the planes in the sun. I make my planes with tones on my palette,
do you understand ?... You must see the planes. Clearly... but fit them together, merge them. It must all turn and interlock at one and the same time. The
volumes alone matter. " He returned to this theme : " I try to express perspective by means of color alone. " This depth, he asserts, can only be translated
by... " introducing in our vibrations of light—represented by reds and yellows
—a sufficient amount of blue tones to make us feel the air. "

His still lifes emanate from a similar spirit : reconstruction in space, sensibility in color values, quality and poetry of the object (*The Blue Vase*, 1883-1887,
Jeu de Paume; *The Chest of Drawers*, 1883-1887, Neuestaatsgalerie, Munich; *Milk-
jug and Fruit on a Table*, 1888-1890, National Gallery, Oslo; *Still Life with Apples and
Primroses* 1890-1894, Metropolitan Museum, New York).

The portraits appear sculptured, to such an extent does Cézanne model faces,
hands and costumes in geometric planes; he makes the form convex or concave by
his astonishing use of relief and yet evokes all the subtlety of his sitters' inner life
(*Madame Cézanne in the yellow Armchair*, 1890-1894, Private Coll., Saint-Germain-

125

PAUL CÉZANNE — THE LAKE AT ANNECY. 1896 (25 1/4 × 31 ″) — COURTAULD INSTITUTE, LONDON

en-Laye; *The Boy in the Red Waistcoat*, 1890-1895, several variants; *Gustave Geffroy*, 1895, Private Coll., Paris).   The most remarkable, doubtless, is the *Woman with the Coffee pot* (1890-1894, Jeu de Paume) whose face with its solemn expression recalls the finest Greek carvings, and the folds of whose dress evoke the flutings on Doric pillars.   Then, again we have compositions containing several figures, such as *Shrove Tuesday* (1888, Museum of Modern Western Art, Moscow) which antici-pates Picasso, Derain and many other contemporary artists; numerous studies of *Men and Women Bathers* of which I shall have something to say later; and above all the *Card player* theme (*c.* 1890-1892) with five figures (Barnes Foundation, Merion, U.S.A.), four (Private Coll., New York) or two (Courtauld Institute, London; Pri-vate Coll., Paris and Jeu de Paume).   Personally, I think that Cézanne first envis-aged his canvases with several players before reducing the scene to two men, two intelligences face to face; one calculating, methodical, the other impulsive and excitable.

The master's final period, while preserving the sense of rhythm, harmony and the spirit of synthesis, appears more lyrical, sometimes more impassioned, and still more original in the domain of Pre-Fauvism and Pre-Cubism. The landscapes are constructed more and more in defined planes with vibrant and rhythmic facets (*Le Lac d'Annecy*, 1896, Courtauld Institute, London; *The Mill stone*, 1898-1900, Private Coll., Paris; *Rocks in a Wood*, 1896-1898, Kunsthaus, Zurich; *Rocks and Branches at Bibémus*, c. 1904, Petit-Palais, Paris; *The Château noir*, 1904-1906, Private Coll., Paris). The Petit-Palais canvas in particular is already a Cubist painting before its time, and the *Views of l'Estaque* by Georges Braque in 1907 or the *Landscapes of la Huerta de Ebro* by Picasso about 1908 reveal similar preoccupations on the artist's part.

Two of the still lifes are especially typical : the *Still Life : Onions and Bottle* (1895-

PAUL CÉZANNE — LES GRANDES BAIGNEUSES. SKETCH. 1883-1885 (13 3/4 × 17 1/2 ") — JOSEPH MULLER COLLECTION, SOLOTHURN

1900, Jeu de Paume) and *Still Life with Apples* (1895-1900, Museum of Modern Art, New York); the paint is now supple and rich, the composition perfectly organized, and finally, a glass of wine in the first canvas, viewed simultaneously in perspective and from above in accordance with the Cubist formula, is one of Cézanne's boldest realizations. Again, portraits, including that of *Ambroise Vollard* (1899, Petit-Palais, Paris) and of *Vallier* (1906, Private Coll., Paris), both treated in geometric planes and multi-faceted, anticipate similar studies of a only a few years later by Braque and Picasso.

Finally, the lyric element in Cézanne is noticeable in all the late studies of *Men and Women Bathers;* they are many and dispersed in galleries and private collections throughout the whole world. Memories of El Greco are discernible in some: elongation of the human body, mannerist and baroque postures. We are aware too of a certain pantheism and even classicism. A study (Muller Coll., Switzerland) reflects the artist's preoccupation with that unfinished masterpiece, *Les Grandes Baigneuses* (1898-1905, Museum of Art, Philadelphia), a symbol of power and rhythm, grandeur and harmony. The balancing of the forms in space and the rightness of the colors are inimitable. We think of Titian's and Poussin's *Bacchanalia* and Picasso's *Les Demoiselles d'Avignon*. " Imagine Poussin done over again from nature, that is classicism as I understand it, " said Cézanne.

Conscious, like Delacroix, of his own worth, without either under- or over-estimating himself, Cézanne in a conversation with Vollard one day, ventured to situate himself in the art of his time : " You know very well that there is only one painter in the world and it is myself... "

NEO-IMPRESSIONISM

SEURAT AND SIGNAC

Reaction against Impressionism, parallel to that brought about by Cézanne but based on purely scientific premises and a methodically established theory, was to see the light of day in 1886. It took shape at the Société des Artistes Indé-pendants, founded June 30, 1884, and at their first Salon, organized that year in a temporary building in the courtyard of the Tuileries. However, it was at the eighth (and last) Exhibition of the Impressionist Group which took place May 15 to June 15, 1886, No. 1, rue Laffitte, that works executed in pure colors, divided off, balanced and optically mixed according to a logical method, made their first appearance. Georges Seurat, inaugurator of this new manner, showed there his *Sunday Afternoon on the Island of La Grande Jatte* and rallied round him Paul Signac, Camille Pissarro and the latter's son Lucien. Shortly afterwards, from August 21 to September 21, Seurat, accompanied by several of his friends, Signac, Dubois-Pillet, Henri-Edmond Cross, Lucien Pissarro, Angrand, exhibited the same picture again in the rue des Tuileries at the second Exhibition of the Société des Artistes Indé-pendants. The term Neo-Impressionism was used for the first time by the critic Arsène Alexandre in an article which appeared on December 10 in *Événement* concerning a pamphlet entitled *Les Impressionnistes en 1886* in which Félix Fénéon presented the various " independent " exhibitions of the year.

If the Neo-Impressionists come close to the Impressionists from certain angles —light, color, taste for nature—they part company when they claim to be employing a rational and scientific method. Dismissing Monet's purely intuitive empiricism, Seurat promulgated a strict theory based on reason and discipline. Since art is harmony (a view he shares with Cézanne) and harmony is the free construction of the mind, man the architect, he explains, should re-assert his rights over man the spectator.

Inspired by the scientific aesthetic elaborated by Charles Henry, Seurat began by using *contrasts of tone* (1883-1885), drawing with Conté crayon, sometimes with charcoal, and obtaining striking and vibrating chiaroscuro effects solely with black and white; he then proceeded by *contrasts of color* (1884-1886), systematically employing complementaries and binary complementaries as he does in his painting *La Grande Jatte* (Art Institute, Chicago), and ended with *contrasts of lines* (1881-1891) which, according to their positions with reference to the horizon, determine the composition, be it static and balanced like *La Parade* (Clark Coll., New York) or dynamic like *Le Chahut* (Kröller-Müller Museum, Otterlo) or *The Circus* (Jeu de Paume).

This method led the artist to a systemization taken to its logical extreme, and he built up a theory from these governing principles which seemed to him to have all the evidence of a mathematical problem. " Art is harmony; harmony is the analogy of contraries, the analogy of likes in tone, hue, line : tone, that is to say light and dark; hue, that is to say red and its complementary green, orange and its complementary blue (we should correct this to blue and its complementary orange), yellow and its complementary violet; line, that is to say the directions in relation to the horizontal.

" These various harmonies are combined into calm, gay or melancholy ones: gaiety of tone has a dominant of light; of color, a dominant of warmth; of line, rising lines (above the horizontal); calm is the equality of dark and light, of warm and of cold where color is concerned; and is the horizontal in the matter of line; melancholy in tone means a dominant of darkness; in color, a cold dominant, and in line, lowered directions.

" The means of expression in this technique is the optical mixture of tones, colors and their interplay (shadows) in accordance with very rigid laws. "

The propagator and defender of this doctrine—which was to give rise to a School of painting—was Paul Signac. In his profound study published by the *Revue Blanche* in 1899 and entitled *D'Eugène Delacroix au Néo-Impressionisme*, he replaces the term chromo-luminarism by *divisionism* and *pointillism*. Further, he defined this new aesthetic and this new technique, separating them clearly one from the other [63] :

" Neo-Impressionism does not use *dots*, it *divides*. Now *dividing* is:

" Obtaining all the benefits of *luminosity, coloration and harmony* by:

" 1. The optical mixture of pigments in their pure state (all the prismatic colors and all their tones);

" 2. The separation of the various elements (local color, color of lighting, their interplay, etc.).

" 3. The balancing out of these elements and their proportion (according to the laws of *contrast, gradation* and *irradiation*);

" 4. The choice of a touch proportionate to the picture's dimensions. "

And Signac explains [64] :

" *Division* is a complex system of harmony, an aesthetic rather than a technique, the *point* is only a means.

" *Dividing* is striving after the power and harmony of color, by representing colored light with its pure elements and by using the optical mixture of these pure elements, separated and loaded in accordance with the essential laws of contrast and gradation.

" Separation of these elements and optical mixture are a guarantee of purity, that is to say, luminosity and intensity of colors; gradation enhances their brightness; contrast, by regulating the harmony of likes and the analogy of contraries, subordinates these elements, powerful yet balanced, to the laws of harmony. The basis of *division* is contrast; is that not what art is—contrast ? *Pointillism* is the mode of expression chosen by the painter who applies color on the canvas in small touches rather than spreading it in flat areas. It is covering a surface with small, juxtaposed multicolored touches of pure or dull color, at the same time striving by means of the optical mixture of these many elements to imitate the varied colors in nature, without any conscious effort to achieve equilibrium or contrast. The *point* is merely a brush-stroke, a method and, like all methods, is not important. "

GEORGES SEURAT — LA PARADE. 1887-1888 (39 1/2 × 59 ") — STEPHEN C. CLARK COLLECTION, NEW YORK

We should add that *pointillism* recalls the little colored cubes of Byzantine mosaics, or the " points " in tapestry or Oriental carpets.

The Neo-Impressionist palette remains identical with that of the Impressionists; it is composed solely of pure colors approximating to the solar spectrum. The fact that optical mixture was practiced by both Schools should not blind us to the fact that the Impressionists did not completely abandon palette mixing, as did the Neo-Impressionists; the touches in commas or broad sweeps of the former were replaced by *divided* touches. This methodical division, the fundamental problem of Neo-Impressionism, is founded on observation of the scientific theory of colors. The painter, taking as his basic principle the contrast of two colors, opposes, gradates and loads his various elements and builds up his composition on a system of contrasts.

The experts on this theory assert that it guarantees a maximum luminosity (an opinion I do not always share), coloration (note that systematization sometimes produces excess of colors and a certain vulgarity in their relationships which lack subtlety, to put it mildly), and, last but not least, harmony.

Georges Seurat

U NLIKE the majority of the Impressionists, Georges Seurat returned to the lessons of the museums, the study of the old masters and of the works of theorists such as Charles Blanc, Chevreul, Sutter, Rood or Charles Henry. A text by D. Sutter had so impressed him that he applied himself obstinately to the problem : " ... We must therefore find the clear and precise formula of the rules governing the harmony of lines, light and color and produce the *scientific* justification of these rules... "

Doubtless, Seurat next sought out the secret of the old masters' compositions, balanced according to certain governing principles, and his study of the Golden Number revealed it to him. According to the works of Matila C. Ghyka and Elisa Maillard [66] : " This *Divine Number* or *Symbolic Number of the Universe* is the Decade, the principle of everything counted in tens and the most perfect of all Numbers. The Decade possesses the transcendent qualities of dynamism and triangular growth to be found in Pythagoras' Tetractys, which is the sum total of the four first numbers whose relation to each other represents the basic musical harmonies. Both emanate from the quaternary formation : $1 + 2 + 3 + 4 = 10$.

" The *mystique* of the Number attributes to the Pentade—the principle of all the five's—all the basic qualities and importance of the Decade as being half of the latter and its condensed graphic image. This image is the Pentalpha or *starred Pentagon, mathematical symbol of the Golden Number and emblem of living harmony* realized in the human body by health and beauty. The relation between the Decade and the Pentade corresponds to the concept of analogy between the great rhythm of the Soul of the World or of Universal Life and the rhythms of the soul and the body of Man, the body of Man being considered as the projection of the Soul in the material plane.

" The Golden Number is an irrational relationship, the most logical of those that can result from the division of a length into two unequal parts. When this relationship exists between the two parts of a whole (for example between the segments *a* and *b*, the sum of which corresponds to the segment *c*), it determines a remarkable proportion between the said whole and its parts : The relation between the greater of the two parts and the lesser is equal to the relation between the whole and the greater of the parts. " This relation is expressed in algebra by $\frac{a+b}{b}=\frac{b}{a}$. The proportion of the Golden Number, an ideal sequential proportion, is called in modern geometry the " division into a mean and extreme ratio. "

The constructive urge is, then, manifest in Seurat. Every form is defined in accordance with a geometric diagram; he assimilates painting to an architecture that is submitted to unchanging rules. In point of fact he becomes a classic again, not by sensation as Cézanne did, but by a return to theories of which the essential elements are composition, drawing, rhythm and repose. And if Seurat and Cézanne practice landscape painting it is in a very different way from the Impressionists; however, in the end, and this is important, both went back to a pictorial conception in which man is frequently present—another indication of classicism. Between 1882 and 1883 Seurat drew almost exclusively in Conté crayon and as a result of his experiments in contrast of cunningly balanced tones built up an extremely original idiom of forms (*Portrait of the painter Aman-Jean*, Stephen C. Clark Coll., New York; *The Black Bow*, Private Coll., etc.). He was furthermore to continue to execute wonderful drawings —the most distinguished aspect of his talent in my opinion—to the end of his career, the finest examples being *The Girl with the Sunshade* (c. 1884-1885, Museum of Modern Art, New York), *Au Café Singer* (1887, Van Gogh Coll., Laren, Holland) and the *Portrait of Paul Signac* (1889-1890, Private Coll., Paris).
In his painting *Bathing at Asnières* (1883-1884, Tate Gallery, London), exhibited at the first Salon des Indépendants in May 1884, Seurat was already applying the laws of contrast in a strict manner; the composition is balanced, stable but the colors are dull. The following year, the artist painted a series of seascapes at Grandcamp (*Le Bec du Hoc*, Sir Kenneth Clark Coll., London; *The Bay of Grandcamp*, Lefevre Gallery, London; *Sunset, Grandcamp*, Dr and Mrs David M. Levy, Coll., New York).

Through Signac, Seurat made the acquaintance of Camille Pissarro and the work of the Impressionists. Realizing the advantages offered by pure color, he now proceeded to use color contrasts and it was with that technique that he executed his vast composition, which I consider his masterpiece, *Sunday Afternoon on the Island of La Grande Jatte*, completed in 1886 and submitted that same year to the eighth (and last) Impressionist Exhibition, shortly afterwards to the second Salon des Indépendants, and finally to the Exhibition of the XX in Brussels at the beginning of the year 1887. The artist carried out many drawings and sketches before producing—in accordance with his new methodical and scientific principles—this huge static canvas, perfect in rhythm and balance and, this time, thanks to the use of carefully contrasted complementaries and binary complementaries, both light and luminous. Félix Fénéon may well have been struck by this new pictorial conception, but such was not the case with the public and critics, who regarded it with dismay and some hostility.

132

GEORGES SEURAT — THE SEINE AT LA GRANDE JATTE. 1887 (25 1/2 × 32 1/4 ") — MUSÉE DES BEAUX-ARTS, BRUSSELS

During the summer of 1886 Seurat painted a series of seascapes that were delicate and subtle in their tonalities and invariably logically constructed (*The Harbor Entrance, Honfleur*, Barnes Foundation, Merion, U.S.A.; *L'Hospice et le Phare de Honfleur*, Mrs Chester Beatty Coll., London; *The " Maria ", Honfleur*, Museum of Modern Art, Prague), and two very fine landscapes treated in the same spirit, *The Bridge at Courbevoie* (1886-1887, Courtauld Institute, London) and the *Seine at Courbevoie, La Grande Jatte* (c. 1887, Musée des Beaux-Arts, Brussels).

Seurat then tackled some more important works again, *Les Poseuses* (1887-1888, Barnes Foundation, Merion, U.S.A.), then *La Parade* (1887-1888, Stephen C. Clark Coll., New York), both shown at the Salon des Indépendants in 1888. This

133

time, line contrasts are added to contrasts of tone and color. A perfect balance is achieved in these two pictures; the artist aimed at an effect of serenity, realized by the equality of the tones (light and dark), the colors (warm or cool, major or minor) and lines (vertical and horizontal); the repose of the attitudes also contributes to the general feeling of calm. It should be remarked that in *Les Poseuses* the artist has represented his model respectively front face, back view and in profile. He " turns " round the same person as the Cubists did but without evoking these three aspects simultaneously in one single figure.

During the summer Seurat devoted himself to increasingly systematized landscape painting (*Port-en-Bessin, Outer-Harbor at Low-tide*, 1888, Jeu de Paume; *Le Crotoy, up stream*, 1889, Private Coll., New York).

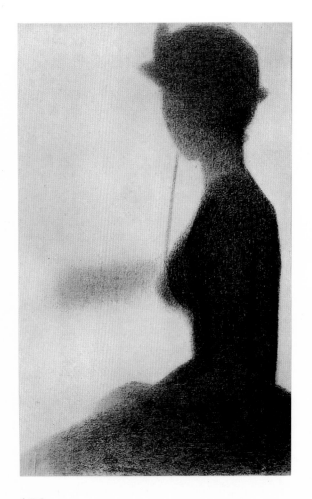

GEORGES SEURAT — GIRL WITH A SUNSHADE. DRAWING. 1884-1885 (19 × 12 1/4 ") — MUSEUM OF MODERN ART, NEW YORK

GEORGES SEURAT
LADY WITH A SUN-
SHADE. SKETCH. 1884
(9 3/4 × 6 ") - BÜHRLE
COLLECTION, ZURICH

135

HENRI-EDMOND CROSS — COAST NEAR ANTIBES. 1892 (25 1/2 × 35 1/2 ") — THE HONORABLE AND MRS. JOHN HAY WHITNEY COLLECTION, NEW YORK

New compositions follow: *Le Chahut* (1889-1890, Kröller-Müller Museum, Otterlo) and the *Woman powdering herself* (1890, Courtauld Institute, London), both shown at the Salon des Indépendants of 1890. *Le Chahut* is the archetype of Seurat's lively and gay but *contrived* composition, realized therefore technically by light tones, warm or strong colors and ascending lines; but despite these formulas the figures seem crystalized in apparently dynamic attitudes which are in reality fundamentally static.

Seurat sums up his theories in his last important painting, *The Circus* (1890-1891, Jeu de Paume), unfinished but nevertheless exhibited at the Salon des Indépendants in 1891. In my opinion this picture—with its essentially dynamic subject—is frozen and lacks life, color and light. It demonstrates the bankruptcy of theories which, as Renoir said, " do not make a good picture and more often than not merely serve to cover up the inadequacy of the means of expression. "

PAUL SIGNAC — THE BOSPHORUS. WATER COLOR. (6 1/2 × 9 3/4 "). — CACHIN-SIGNAC COLLECTION, PARIS

Paul Signac

THE artist who codified Neo-Impressionism in his remarkable work entitled *D'Eugène Delacroix au Néo-Impressionnisme* expressed himself in paint in colors of a high key, raising the tones to almost hysterical heights, and sometimes, it must be confessed, to the point of disharmony. He enlarged the " point " into square or rectangular patches that recall cubes of mosaic. Signac's aim was realism, but a tendency towards stylization and decoration is prominent in most of his paintings, particularly in his views of harbors, endowing them whith a somewhat artificial character (*The Palace of the Popes at Avignon*, 1900, Musée d'Art Moderne, Paris). His water colors on the other hand with their lively freedom are remarkably sensitive in both technique and color, and are sometimes reminiscent of Jongkind (*The Bosphorus*, Cachin-Signac Coll., Paris).

137

Henri-Edmond Cross joined the Neo-Impressionists about 1891; from that time on his colors became increasingly intense and on occasion he uses strident colors in some of his Midi or Italian landscapes, which are stylized in a somewhat theatrical manner. However, in a canvas like the *Golden Isles* (Musée d'Art Moderne, Paris), he shares the subtle delicacy of Seurat.

Among the best artists connected with Neo-Impressionism we should mention Maximilien Luce, Hippolyte Petitjean, Lucie Cousturier, Théo Van Rysselberghe and even the Academic painters such as Henri Martin who borrowed their technique.

Far from liberating and renewing Impressionism, Neo-Impressionism merely paralyzed and impoverished the original vision in which its value lay and dessicated it with its purely intellectual and scientific methods, whereas Cézanne, with the human warmth of his organized sensations, had breathed new life into it.

Periphery of
Impressionism

FANTIN-LATOUR

Associating with the Impressionists without being of them, certain painters stand out as independents. Among them, occupying a place somewhat apart, Fantin-Latour found himself involved in the Café Guerbois reunions, took part in the discussions and was a great admirer and passionate defender of Edouard Manet. Yet he showed little taste for landscape, preferring portraiture, large compositions of group figures and still lifes with flowers. We have evidence of these tendencies in his *Homage to Delacroix* (1864, Jeu de Paume); in it, along with the artist's self-portrait we find Whistler, Edouard Manet, Bracquemond, Balleroy, Legros, Cordier and the critics Duranty, Champfleury and Baudelaire.

But he became more strongly attached to the new school and produced a kind of manifesto in support of his friend Manet, in which he portrayed the latter surrounded by some of the Impressionists—Bazille, Monet and Renoir—and some of their champions, the critics Zacharie Astruc, Émile Zola, the musicologist Edmond Maître and the German painter Schölderer. This painting, entitled *The Studio in Batignolles* and dated 1870 (Jeu de Paume) is treated in a brown key, very far removed from the light and vivacious tonality of the Impressionists. Two further compositions follow, one devoted to the poets, *The Table* (1872, Jeu de Paume) in which we see, in particular, Paul Verlaine and Arthur Rimbaud; the other, *By the Piano* (1885, Jeu de Paume) is in homage to some contemporary musicians grouped round the composer Chabrier who is seated at the piano.

In the genre at which he excels, flower paintings, Fantin uses brighter colors and is more preoccupied with reflections and transparent effects; his vision becomes more impressionist and yet his technique undergoes no transformation (*Flowers*, 1865, Jeu de Paume; *White Roses*, Private Coll., Paris).

Nor should we forget Forain, influenced by Edouard Manet and Degas. He appeared with the latter in various exhibitions of the Impressionist group, particularly in 1879, 1880, 1881 and 1886. However his painting, which is not without a touch of satire, remains definitely traditionalist and his studies of ballet dancers are very different from those of Degas (*Pink Dancer, dancing with Arms outstretched*, pastel, Jeu de Paume).

We cannot mention the innumerable " minor masters " who gravitated round the Impressionists and Independents; their role, less significant in the history of the movement, is dealt with in the notes.

VINCENT VAN GOGH

T HE influence of Vincent Van Gogh extended far beyond Impressionism and led to Fauvism. His intense and violently expressionistic art is an extreme manifestation of the baroque. Writing from Wasmes to his brother Theo, June 1879, he confides : " I know no better definition of art than this, ' Art is man added to nature, ' nature, reality, truth, but with a significance, a conception, a character, which the artist brings out and to which he gives expression, ' which he sets free, ' disentangles, liberates, illumines... " No artist illustrates this definition more convincingly than Van Gogh; no artist pledged his life—to the point of madness and death—with so much zeal, tragic passion, unbridled violence, agonizing doubts and impassioned victims.

His art connects the twin poles of human nature : matter and spirit. It is matter in its direct, intuitive, somewhat barbarous force, in the aggressiveness of the brilliant tones raised to the height of pure tones, in the harshly underlined asymetrical forms, in the early realism and spontaneous naturalism which partakes of the great universal rhythm and vast cosmic cataclysms. But the continual transition from the reflex to the instinctive leads Van Gogh from the instinctive to the deliberate, at which point his art becomes spiritualized. It is spirit in its " groping for the infinite, " to use his own words. The realist is transformed into a visionary; from his hallucinations he recreates the universe and colors it from the image he makes of it : " Instead of striving to render exactly what I have in front of me, " he says, " I use color more arbitrarily to express myself with greater force. " This " colored shock " perceived in nature is experienced so intensely by Van Gogh that its deep resonances are amplified to the maximum and drive the painter to take color to the point almost of paroxysm. Actual forms are abolished and replaced by spatial forms which turn and writhe like flames, surge and leap like balls of fire. This frenzy is expressed in thick brush strokes continually broken up into commas, spots, dots, dashes which vibrate endlessly and convey a miraculous sensation of life.

The world created by Van Gogh in his inner vision is not our terrestrial world as we know it. This cosmos in perpetual evolution, continual renewal, is outside time and space; it belongs to the realm of the miraculous and transcends the limits of the communicable.

It is common knowledge that Van Gogh began his career late—he did not begin to paint until he was close to thirty. It was both extremely short and extremely productive. During his first Dutch and Belgian period (1880-1886) he executed some still lifes, landscapes, portraits and scenes of peasant or working-class life. Manifest in these is a powerful realism closely associated with the contemporary Belgian literary movement, or with the work of a Zola whose books, he said, are " the best that treat of the present period. " The most direct, sometimes the most crude or commonplace elements of materialism are as evident in the object as in the human figure, but the painter was able to add poetry of great evocative power. On the technical side, he used thick paint, applied it in broad touches, violently

140

emphasized shadows and lights, and made use of a deliberately restricted scale, limited in fact almost to ochres, earth-colors, Prussian blue, blacks and some whites.

The chief still lifes of this period, *Potatoes, Sabots, The Pitchers* (all in the Kröller-Müller Museum, Otterlo), *The Nests, The Mortar, The Open Bible* (V.W. Van Gogh Coll., Laren), *The Shoes* (Private Coll., Antwerp), often represent everyday and familiar objects, indispensable to the material and spiritual lives of poor people.

The landscapes, mostly executed *circa* 1885 at Nuenen or Antwerp, have a tragic melancholy; man seems confined within hostile nature : " Yesterday I sketched some rotten oak tree stumps, known as bog oak... These stumps were in the black slime of a pond... Above, a stormy sky. This pool in the mud with these rotten tree stumps was melancholy and dramatic... [67] " This is the spirit of such landscapes as *Sunset* (Private Coll., Paris), *The Vicarage Garden* (L.J. Smit Coll., Kinderijk), *Nuenen Vicarage, Cottage at dusk* or *The Quay at Antwerp* (V.W. Van Gogh Coll., Laren).

In these first portraits or compositions with figures his sole interest is in the human element—workers or peasants—those who suffer without complaint, toil without respite. Weariness, exposure to the elements, is deeply engraved on these coarsely modelled faces, fashioned in the image of the earth. His realist canvases with dark tonalities also go back to the Nuenen period : *Interior with a Weaver*; *Peasant at Table, Peasant with a Pipe* (1884, Kröller-Müller Museum, Otterlo), *Peasants digging up Potatoes*, inspired, these, by Millet's work (1885, Kröller-Müller Museum, Otterlo) or that dramatic *Head of a Peasant Woman* (1885, V.W. Van Gogh Coll., Laren), a study for the celebrated composition *The Potato Eaters* (May 1885, V.W. Van Gogh Coll., Laren) whose fervent expressionism anticipates Vlaminck, Soutine or Kokoschka. It is not the grievances of the people but the wretched life of these peasants or artisans, crowded in the dingy room of a dilapidated cottage, that Van Gogh set out to express. The stigma of human bestiality can be read in the lines of these faces, so prematurely aged, degraded, wearied and resigned. He confides his thoughts to his brother Theo : " ... I have striven conscientiously to convey the idea that these people who, beneath the lamp, eat their potatoes in their hands which they dip in their plates, have also tilled the soil, and to make my picture acclaim manual labour and the food which they have themselves so honestly gained. I wanted them to cause people to think of an entirely different way of living than ours, that of civilized beings. Consequently I do not want everybody to think the picture beautiful or good... "

Van Gogh goes much further on this road than either Louis Le Nain or Millet; and if he does not achieve the former's nobility and gravity, he far surpasses the sentimental socialism of the latter. He is moreover much more inspired by Millet's admirable drawings with their direct and forceful realism than by his paintings, despite the fact that he asserts : " His peasant seems painted with the earth in which he sows his seed [69] ! "

His brief Paris period (March 1886-February 1888) is stamped with a twofold influence : that of Impressionism and that of *Japonisme*. He writes : " It is now as necessary to pass regularly through Impressionism as it was formerly to pass through a Paris studio... " However he makes certain reservations in a letter to Theo : " ... Now it is true, I see the resurrection of Eugène Delacroix in Impressionism, but as the

141

interpretations are divergent and somewhat irreconcilable, it is not going to be Impressionism which will formulate the doctrine. "

He was also greatly interested in the art of Seurat and Signac. As for *Japonisme*, he often speaks about it : " ...Look, is it not almost a true religion that we are being taught by these simple Japanese who live in nature as if they themselves were flowers... One cannot study Japanese art, it seems to me, without becoming much gayer and happier... I envy the Japanese the extreme cleanliness that everything has in their lives. It never seems tedious, never done over-hastily. Their work is as simple as breathing and they draw a figure in a few sure strokes with the same ease... Ah ! I must learn to draw a figure in a few strokes... "

Two works at the beginning of his Paris period mark the development of his dark manner towards the light tones borrowed from the Impressionists : *Le Moulin de la Galette* (Kröller-Müller Museum, Otterlo), and *La Guinguette* (Jeu de Paume). From now on, light and luminous colors bear witness to the influence of his new friends and his technique, too, gets closer to theirs; schematization and " stick-like strokes " learned from the Japanese are combined with impressionist vision and commas or sweeping brush strokes with the occasional introduction of Seurat or Signac like " points. "

Among the still lifes we should pick out : *The Yellow Books* (G. Boner Coll., Zurich), *Flowers in a Bronze Vase* (Jeu de Paume), *Sunflowers* (Kröller-Müller Museum, Otterlo).

The landscapes are still more vibrant and quivering with life : *Montmartre* (1886, The Art Institute, Chicago), *Garden Plots on the Butte Montmartre*, (Rijksmuseum, Amsterdam), *In front of a Restaurant at Asnières, Boulevard de Clichy* (1887, V.W. Van Gogh Coll., Laren), *Fishing in Springtime* (1887, Chauncey McCormick Coll., Chicago), *Interior of a Restaurant* (1887, Kröller-Müller Museum, Otterlo), *Restaurant " La Sirène " at Joinville* (1887, Jeu de Paume).

Impressionism and *Japonisme* are combined in the astonishing *Portrait of Père Tanguy* (1887, Musée Rodin, Paris), sitting before a background covered with Japanese prints. A similar method occurs in *The Woman with the Tambourines* (1887, V.W. Van Gogh Coll., Laren). The artist was moreover interpreting prints of Hiroshige's *(Rain)* and Keisai Yensen (*Japonaiserie*, V.W. Van Gogh Coll., Laren). *Woman near a Cradle* (1887, V.W. Van Gogh Coll., Laren) is more in the traditionalist spirit, whereas the *Self-Portrait* (1887, V.W. Van Gogh Coll., Laren) reveals the anxiety visible in the troubled expression of the artist in front of his own image.

From this point onwards Van Gogh rapidly passed beyond Impressionism—too limited in his eyes—but became more and more intoxicated with *Japonisme*. He dreamed of going to Japan and went... to Arles, from where he writes to Theo : " ... As far as remaining in the Midi is concerned, even if it is more expensive, let's see : we like Japanese painting, we have fallen under its influence, all the Impressionists have that in common, and are we not to go to Japan, that is to say its equivalent, the Midi ? I think that when all is said and done the future of the new art is in the Midi... "

The Arles period (February 1888 to May 1889) saw Van Gogh's genius reach a vertiginous climax. Over this soil burnt by the sunlight, the painter now saw everything in terms of an immediate and violent impact of color (very different from

VINCENT VAN GOGH — BRIDGE AT ASNIÈRES. 1887 (20 1/2 × 25 1/2 ") — BÜHRLE COLLECTION, ZURICH

what Gauguin's was to be) and the brilliance of his colors renders both his vision and his emotion and becomes his chief medium of expression. The artist found his release in color, and, full of burning enthusiasm, applied it to his canvases in its pure state, squeezing it out of the tube in a kind of frenzy. Despite this brutal frankness, there is no clash in his harmonies.

Provence with its vast horizons revealed furthermore to Van Gogh a great sense of space, but, unlike Cézanne, who resolved it in volume, he experienced it in depth, unbounded, infinite. His brush strokes increasingly broken up into a series of dashes, replaced perspective and in themselves gave the illusion of vastness.

His interest began to shift towards the outer universe : the sun, the stars; he was eager to render their immense glow and dazzling brilliance. He was a prey to anxiety; contact with the night excited him, and when daylight came, he evoked the intensity of all things beneath the luminous brilliance of the burning sun in a riot of color. The fascination which outer space exercised over him was overwhelming. He hoped to achieve an equilibrium between his excitable baroque temperament and this land of Provence whose classicism he was so eager to comprehend; but, instead of realizing a harmonious synthesis, as Cézanne did, he saw only the burning and all-consuming light : henceforward Provence was to be for him no longer a symbol of life but of death. For his pursuit of this equilibrium already referred to resulted in the loss of his own. The crisis occurred at Arles on Christmas eve, 1888, when after a violent dispute with Gauguin, he cut off his own ear. A few months later, at his own request, he was shut away in the Asylum of Saint-Rémy.

In the early stages of his stay at Arles, his landscapes were still gay and serene, although pitched in a high key. He chose themes which he repeated : *The Draw-*

VINCENT VAN GOGH — VIEW OF LA CRAU. 1888 (28 1/2 × 36 1/4 ") — V. W. VAN GOGH COLLECTION, LAREN

Bridge or *Pont de l'Anglois* (V.W. Van Gogh Coll., Laren and Kröller-Müller Museum, Otterlo), *Fruit Trees in Bloom* inspired by the painter Mauve but even more by the Japanese (V.W. Van Gogh Coll., Laren and Kröller-Müller Museum), *Cornstacks* (Kröller-Müller Museum), *The Sower*, after Millet (V.W. Van Gogh Coll., Laren and Kröller-Müller Museum), *Sailing Boats at Les Saintes-Maries* (V.W. Van Gogh Coll., Laren).

Then we see him trying to express space in pen drawings such as the *View of La Crau, seen from Montmajour*, or in paintings: *View of Arles, La Crau: Market Gardens* (all in the V.W. Van Gogh Coll., Laren). The contrast with the *Sainte-Victoire* series of Cézanne's is striking. And when Van Gogh painted *The Alyscamps, Arles* (Kröller-Müller Museum, Otterlo) the famous avenue for him is merely a " *Japonaiserie.* "

VINCENT VAN GOGH — STARRY NIGHT. 1888 (28 1/2 × 36 1/4 ") — PRIVATE COLLECTION, PARIS

We see him fascinated by the brilliance of artificial light (*The Night Café*, Stephen C. Clark Coll., New York), by the mirage of nights in Provence (*Night Café*, Kröller-Müller Coll., Otterlo) and the glittering reflections of the stars in the water.

"But when, " he writes to Emile Bernard (letter No. 7) "shall I paint the starry sky, the picture which haunts me ? " And, shortly afterwards in a letter to Theo (No. 543 with a sketch) he describes the picture he has just painted (*Starry Night*, Private Coll., Paris) : " Enclosed small sketch of a canvas 30 square cm. at last the starry sky painted actually at night under a gas jet. The sky is blue-green, the water royal blue, the ground lilac. The town is blue and violet, the gas yellow and the reflections are reddish gold and descend to green-bronze. Over the blue-green of the sky the Great Bear gives a green and pink glow the discreet pallor of which

VINCENT VAN GOGH — YOUNG PEASANT. 1889 (24 × 19 3/4 ") — PRIVATE COLLECTION, FLORENCE

contrasts with the brutal gold of the gas. Two small colored figures of lovers in the foreground. "

During his stay in the hospital he drew and painted in a tormented, baroque vein which knew no limits : *The Asylum Garden at Arles* (sepia, V.W. Van Gogh Coll., Laren, and painting, Oscar Reinhart Coll., Winterthur).

Three works are particularly famous among the still lifes : *Sunflowers*, a brilliant symphony of yellows, *Gauguin's Armchair* with a lighted candle (V.W. Van Gogh Coll., Laren) and *The Yellow Chair* (Tate Gallery, London), a simple object that symbolizes a presence.

The asymmetry of the faces sometimes of a very oriental character, the strained anxiety of the eyes, the odd color of the pupils—yellow or orange—the odd choices of color (green or yellow hair) contribute to create a strange aura round his personalities : *The Arlésienne* (Sam A. Lewisohn Coll., New York), *An Actor* and *Lieutenant Milliet* (Kröller-Müller Museum, Otterlo), *The Belgian Painter Boch* (Jeu de Paume), *The Zouave* (A.D. Lasker Co Coll., New York and V.W. Van Gogh, Laren), *The Postman Roulin* (Museum of Fine Arts, Boston, and Kröller-Müller Museum, Otterlo), *Girl against a pink Background* and *La Berceuse* (Kröller-Müller Museum) or, finally, the dramatic *Portrait of the Painter with his severed Ear* (Mr. and Mrs Leigh B. Block, Chicago).

The Saint-Rémy period (May 1889 to May 1890) reveals the artist's mental instability; the baroque element is wilder than ever; it is a " flamboyant " period in which cypresses and olive trees writhe in huge flames towards the sky; the undulating earth reels; the very sky seems to dissolve and rolls with incandescent balls and clouds in spirals like huge waves. It is an oddly mobile world which seems to be perpetually evolving, forming, breaking up and re-forming ideally : *Cornfield and Cypress Trees* (Tate Gallery, London) *The Cypresses* (Metropolitan Museum, New York), *Starry Night* (Museum of Modern Art, New York) and the amazing *Road with Cypress Trees* (May 1890, Kröller-Müller Museum, Otterlo), in which the road looks like a river of mud or lava. Then, tortured, it would seem, by infernal forces, *The Olive Trees* (J.H. Whitney Coll., New York) or *The Olive Grove* (Kröller-Müller Museum), followed by *At the Alp Foothills* (Kröller-Müller Museum), *The Road-menders* (Museum of Art, Cleveland) and *The Hospital of St. Paul at St. Rémy* (Private Coll., Switzerland); then The *Irises* (Mrs Charles Payson, New York), a bed of stylized flowers, or interiors like *Van Gogh's Bedroom at Arles* (V.W. Van Gogh Coll., Laren), *The Hospital Ward at Arles* (Oscar Reinhart Coll., Winterthur) and the tragic *Prison Yard*, after Gustave Doré (Pushkin Museum, Moscow), in which the infernal round of the prisoners seems to symbolize Van Gogh himself, imprisoned in his own madness. He also drew inspiration from works by Rembrandt and Delacroix and above all Millet, which he interprets with his own strong personality.

More and more the portraits become renderings of the haunting violence of their author : *L'Arlésienne* after Gauguin (Kröller-Müller Museum), *The Chief Superintendent of the Asylum at St. Rémy* (Mrs G. Dübi-Müller Coll., Solothurn) and those two masterpieces, *The Young Peasant* (Private Coll., Florence) and *On the Threshold of Eternity* (Kröller-Müller Museum), the dramatic despair of a man chasing his own shadow.

Finally during the last period, that of Auvers-sur-Oise (May 31 to July 29,

VINCENT VAN GOGH — THE PRISON YARD. 1890 (31 1/2 × 25 1/4 ″) -- PUSHKIN MUSEUM, MOSCOW

1890), Van Gogh stayed at the house of Dr. Gachet whose affectionate devotion appeared to soothe him. But suddenly this solitary soul fell once more a prey to his inner anguish, and all his final paintings testify to the tragedy of his fate. Van Gogh seems to want to express this temporary lull in that most soothing of colors, green; for, in a letter to Theo, dated June 10, he writes : " ... two studies of houses set among green trees... " He was doubtless refering to the *Cottages at Cordeville*, formerly known as *Cottages, Montcel* (Jeu de Paume) and perhaps the *View of Auvers* (V.W. Van Gogh Coll., Laren). His obsession with space re-occurred in *Landscape at Auvers* (Museum of Modern Western Art, Moscow) and more particularly in *Fields in a gathering Storm* (V.W. Van Gogh Coll., Laren) in which our eyes and mind do indeed wander across the infinite space.

Van Gogh re-discovered the spirit of his childhood to paint *The Mairie at Auvers, 14th July* (Mr. and Mrs Leigh B. Block, Chicago) whilst the *Church at Auvers* (Jeu de Paume) achieved an expressionistic virulence, for " ... the color is more expressive, more sumptuous " he writes. The intensity of the blue sky is such that we are dazzled as we look at it. As for the church itself, it seems to collapse on its foundations and the surrounding footpaths look as if they were carrying away streams of lava. This apocalyptic world betrays the tumultuous chaos in which the painter's reason was foundering.

In the portraits there is a return of contradictory elements. *Mlle Gachet in the Garden* (Jeu de Paume) is a fairylike apparition, white and evanescent in the soothing foliage. Then *Mlle Gachet at the Piano* (Basle Museum) and the *Portrait of Dr. Gachet* (Jeu de Paume) done, says the artist " ... with an expression of melancholy which often to those who looked at the canvas might seem a grimace. And yet it is like that it should be painted, because we can then take account of how much expression and passion there is in our heads at this present time in comparison with the calm portraits of the old masters... "

Finally, the *Self-Portrait* (Jeu de Paume), executed in a general harmony of blues against a spiral background, is strange, haunting and tragic. The man and the artist surrender themselves entirely in this battle with the angel. This masterpiece seems to sum up the last devastating phrase of the final letter addressed to Theo and found on Vincent at the hour of his death : " ... As for my work, I am staking my life on it and my reason has half foundered on it—all right—but you are not, as far as I can judge, among the dealers in men and you, I think, can take your stand, acting truly for humanity, but what would you... ? "

Certainty and doubts, matter and spirit, these are the contradictions in Van Gogh's genius whose tragic art is appreciated both by the masses and the élite; a rare thing for an artist, but doubtless arising from the fact that he was able to give the worst and the best of himself.

PAUL GAUGUIN — NAFEA FOA IPOIPO. 1892 (40 × 30 1/4 ") — KUNSTMUSEUM, BASLE

Symbolism
OR
the Revolt

SIDE by side with the reaction of Cézanne and the Neo-Impressionists against the visual realism of the Impressionists, a vast movement, which first appeared in 1879, was to drive the opposition into rebellion. This revolt against submission to nature now led the painters to evoke the *idea* rather than the *sensation*. And, repeating Baudelaire's affirmation :

> " Nature is a temple where living pillars
> Sometimes allow mysterious words to escape;
> Man passes there through forests of symbols... "

they anticipate the writers of their generation in creating various related schools —Symbolism, Synthetism, Neo-Traditionalism—all of which reflect the same preoccupations. We are able to identify them, thanks to the definition of the work of art, given in 1891 by Georges-Albert Aurier in an important article entitled " Symbolism in Painting " and published in the *Mercure de France*.

" The work of art, " he proclaims, should be :

" 1. *Ideist*, since its sole ideal will be the expression of the Idea.
" 2. *Symbolist*, since it will express this idea in forms;
" 3. *Synthetist*, since it will write these forms, these signs, according to a method of general comprehension;
" 4. *Subjective*, since the object will never be considered as an object *per se*, but as symbolizing an idea perceived by the subject.
" 5. (A result of this) *Decorative*, for decorative painting in the true sense of the word, as conceived of by the Egyptians and, in all probability, the Greeks and the Primitives, is nothing other than a manifestation of art that is subjective, synthetic, symbolist and ideist at one and the same time.

"But the artist endowed with all these talents would be merely a scholar, were he not possessed of the gifts of *emotivity*... That great, precious, transcendant emotivity which quickens the soul before the shifting drama of abstractions."

This definition in which we see intellectual speculation dethroning Impressionist vision and resolutely destroying it, justifies our use of the term "revolt."

This hotchpotch of ideas makes one think of a letter written by Cézanne to Émile Bernard, July 25, 1904, warning him, no doubt, against this conception : "... *Avoid the literary outlook* which so often causes the painter to deviate from his *true path :* the concrete study of nature." "... I do not want to be right *theoretically* but from nature." And, confirming this stand, he wrote to Gasquet : "Everything except contrast and tone relations is *poetry*, which one should perhaps have in one's brain but never, *under pain of literature*, attempt to put on one's canvas. It comes there of its own accord."

But Cézanne's wise counsels were of no avail to stem the tide of Symbolist phraseology. Painting now lost its claims to painting : it became literature... or, on occasion, music; did not Redon call himself the musician-painter ? Technique almost ceased to count; a picture was considered painted well enough once it was "thought."

Gustave Moreau was the promoter of this new outlook, and if Huysmans set him up as a god, Degas, on the other hand, irritated by the clinking jewelry which the artist was so fond of, exclaimed one day : "He would have us believe that the gods wore watch chains !" And M. Germain Bazin, very justifiably, compares Gustave Moreau's methods to those of the Parnassiens. A fake orientalism in which the picturesque element of the details seems borrowed from literature, dominates his work. Some of his canvases however had a certain influence on the elaboration of Symbolism. And we cannot pay too much respect to the professor who developed the talent of the most illustrious painters of our generation in his studio.

Puvis de Chavannes is too neglected today, although his ascendancy over the Symbolist circle is undeniable. Gauguin and the Nabis admired him and considered him a precursor. The former moreover dreamed of doing "Puvis in color" and wrote to Fontainas in March 1899 : "Puvis overhelms me with his talent."

In his work *The Idealist Movement in Painting* (published in 1896), Mellerio shows the innovating role of Puvis and sums him up in three essential characteristics : "Improved direct sensation, simplified drawing, decorative tendency." These are very close to the principles formulated by Gauguin. Both masters renounced volume : they like large flat surfaces and color applied, like an illumination, within the simplified and synthetic forms. But Puvis de Chavannes has an extremely limited palette, restricted to faded and diluted colors which create the illusion of the mat surface of the fresco; Gauguin, on the contrary, in a riot of brightness, uses discordant, or at least inharmonious colors, indiscriminately, since he dispenses with nuances and values. Puvis and Gauguin, in point of fact, both reduce painting to a purely decorative art; but the former is mostly bound up with academic classicism whereas the latter belongs to the most ancient primitive tradition. But if Puvis de Chavannes was able to create vast murals which are, according to Focillon, "the moral landscape which suited the thoughts, ideals, sadnesses and tender optimism of the last two generations, " Gauguin, too, judging by his masterpiece : *D'où venons-nous? Que sommes-nous? Où allons-nous?* could have been a great decorator. When confined within the proportions of easel-paintings, the majority of his canvases are completely lacking in profundity.

THE SCHOOL OF PONT-AVEN
CLOISONNISM AND SYNTHETISM

A brief historical survey is required at this point to situate the evolution of Symbolism. In 1879 Puvis de Chavannes had just completed his decorations based on the *History of Saint Geneviève* in the Panthéon. Odilon Redon was publishing his first album of lithographs entitled *Dans le Rêve.* Two years later, Puvis de Chavannes painted his most famous symbolist picture *The Poor Fisherman* (Louvre), Redon was exhibiting for the first time in *La Vie Moderne* while Paul Verlaine published *Sagesse.* In 1884 Seurat and Signac founded the *Société des Indépendants* under the presidency of Redon; Félix Fénéon started the *Revue Indépendante*, and Huysmans published *A rebours;* the following year Jules Laforgue's and Henri de Régnier's first collections of poetry saw the light of day, and Émile Dujardin founded *La Revue Wagnérienne.*

The date 1886 assumed great importance, since in that year the positions of the Symbolist painters and poets were clarified. In *Le Figaro* of September 18, Jean Moréas published the famous *Symbolist Manifesto* and, creating the term, defined this new conception of art "...as the only one capable of properly conveying the present-day tendency of the creative spirit in art. " Mallarmé's determination to eliminate Reality in favor of the Idea remained at its basis : " Symbolist poetry aims at investing the Idea with a tangible form... All concrete forms are incapable of manifesting themselves in themselves; they are merely tangible appearances destined to represent their esoteric affinities with primordial Ideas. "

A series of reviews then appeared : *La Pléiade, Le Décadent, La Vogue*, and —founded by Moréas and Gustave Kahn—*Le Symboliste.* During this same year, 1886, Gustave Moreau exhibited his illustrations to La Fontaine's *Fables* at Goupil's. Finally Gauguin, who had submitted works to the Eighth Impressionist Exhibition, broke away from Pissarro's influence and went to Brittany for the first time, where at Pont-Aven he found his old friend Schuffenecker who introduced him to Émile Bernard. The latter was working there with Anquetin and in 1887 joined forces with Van Gogh, whilst Gauguin went on a voyage to Martinique and on his return in 1888 organized the first one-man exhibition of his works.

Gauguin's second stay in Brittany that year was decisive for the history of the movement at that time : the artist found Émile Bernard once again at Pont-Aven. From this encounter, their conversations and their studies were born Cloisonnism and Synthetism. Later a lively controversy broke out between them, for they both claimed to have invented this new technique. The researches of Charles Chassé and

153

M. Germain Bazin lead us to suppose that it was Émile Bernard's experiments that resulted in the discovery of this technique which Gauguin exploited and made his own.

What is Cloisonnism? It consists of separating off the various objects or portions of objects represented with a line drawn by the brush. Émile Bernard explains : " Dujardin had baptized this first stage of the experiment ' Cloisonnism ' because of the systematic separating off of each tone which gave the picture a partitioned appearance. Actually, it was a large stained glass window rather than a painting, with decorative elements of color and line. " The line, generally dark, black, brown, green or blue, recalls the lead of stained glass and divides off pure colors applied in flat areas : forms and colors are thus partitioned. From Cloisonnism came Synthetism which was the resultant synthesis of form and of color. This schematization taken to an extreme was directly inspired by the masters of the Japanese print who also reduced forms and colors to their minimum and thereby obtained much more striking effects. " Synthetizing, " wrote Maurice Denis, " is not necessarily simplifying in the sense of suppressing certain parts of the object : it is simplifying in the sense of making it intelligible. It is in short hierarchizing, submitting each picture to a single rhythm, to a dominant, sacrificing, subordinating, generalizing. "

Émile Bernard used this technique for his canvas *Breton Women in the Meadow*, painted at Saint-Briac before rejoining Gauguin. The latter, surprised and very intrigued by this method, used it again in his *Vision after the Sermon*. So, in this summer of 1888, several friends grouped themselves round these two masters : Chamaillard, a lawyer at Quimper, Charles Laval, Henry Moret, Schuffenecker, the Dutchman Jean Verkade and finally Paul Sérusier. Thus the School of Pont-Aven was formed. Émile Bernard states that : " The Pont-Aven School is the result of various groupings, it takes the form not of an academy with a leader and disciples following his teaching, but it is like a band of individual intelligences, all directed towards the search for an apparently common ideal... Le Pouldu has been wrongly cited as the historic spot of the so-called School of Pont-Aven... Pension Gloanec at Pont-Aven where we all lived and Gauguin had his studio could possibly be called the focal point of our activities. There in fact were planned the works which caused all the fuss later on. Le Pouldu was a temporary dwelling and the decoration of the room was the work only of Gauguin, Sérusier, de Haan and Filiger. But the real place where the school blossomed forth was Père Tanguy's shop. "

In that same year 1888, Paul Sérusier executed from life, at the spot called the Bois d'Amour and according to Gauguin's directions, a synthetized landscape which he later named *Le Talisman*. " How do you see these trees ? " asked Gauguin. " They are yellow. All right, put down yellow; this shadow is bluish, paint it with pure ultramarine; these red leaves, put down vermilion. " Back in Paris in the autumn, Sérusier showed his canvas to his friends of the *Académie Julian* — Maurice Denis, Ibels, Ranson, K.X. Roussel, Vuillard and Bonnard with whom this new adept of Symbolism, who was to become its theorist, a little later formed the group called the Nabis.

The theories of the new school were so to speak consecrated by a huge manifestation in the year 1889. An *Exhibition of the Painting of the Impressionist and Synthetist Group* took place at the Café Volpini, in the Champ-de-Mars, Paris. Gauguin showed seventeen canvases, Émile Bernard twenty-three, among works by Louis

154

ÉMILE BERNARD — LANDSCAPE AT PONT-AVEN. 1888 (21 1/4 × 25 1/2 ") — GALERIE SALUDEN, QUIMPER

Anquetin, G. Daniel, Léon Fauché, Charles Laval, Louis Roy and Émile Schuffenecker.

During this same year Gauguin left Pont-Aven for Le Pouldu, Verlaine published *Parallèlement*; Bergson *Les Données immédiates de la Conscience;* Schuré *Les Grands Initiés* and Léon Deschamps founded the symbolist review *La Plume* in May. January 1890 saw the birth of the *Mercure de France*, an offshoot of *La Pléiade* and directed by Alfred Vallette; Georges-Albert Aurier was to write in it an enthusiastic article on Gauguin, from now on the crowned chief of pictorial Symbolism. Paul Fort created the *Théâtre d'Art*, Gauguin made a long stay at Le Pouldu in the company of Meyer de Haan, Filiger and Seguin, and Maurice Denis published in the review *Art et Critique* (April 23 and 30, 1890) his celebrated manifesto on the *Definition of Neo-Traditionalism* which should be " ... The universal triumph of the imagination of aesthetes over the efforts of stupid imitation... " and " ... The triumph of the emotion of the Beautiful over the naturalist lie. " Finally he adds : " Remember that a picture—before it is a war horse, a nude woman or an anecdote— is essentially a plane surface covered with colors assembled in a certain order. "

In 1891 the Natanson brothers founded *La Revue Blanche;* many Symbolist meetings took place at the Café Voltaire. Gauguin set off for Tahiti on April

155

4. In December a series of fifteen manifestations which continued until 1897 at Galerie Le Barc de Boutteville, rue Le Peletier, began with the *First Exhibition of Impressionist and Symbolist Painters*, prefaced by Charles Césaulx. There the works of the following were on view: Anquetin, Bernard, Bonnard, Henry Cross, Maurice Denis, Dulac, Filiger, Gauguin, Giran-Marx, Louis Hugues, Ibels, Louis Legrand, Lepère, Maximilien Luce, Manet, Petitjean, Peduzzi, Ranson, Lucien Roy, K.X. Roussel, Schuffenecker, Sérusier, Signac, Toulouse-Lautrec, Vuillard, Willette, the Dane Willumsen, and the Spaniard Zuloaga. The Symbolists and Nabis hung side by side with Impressionists, Neo-Impressionists and even some of the academic school.

In 1892 Sérusier, Bernard, Verkade and Seguin were back at Pont-Aven. The following year Lugné-Poë founded the *Théâtre de l'Œuvre;* programs, costumes and décor were provided by Bonnard, Maurice Denis, Munch, Ranson, Sérusier, Toulouse-Lautrec, Vuillard, etc.

Gauguin returned to Paris while Émile Bernard went away to the Far East. André Gide published *Le Voyage d'Urien*, with illustrations by Maurice Denis, a new and original conception of the book illustrated according to contemporary tendencies.

During the year 1895 Seguin had an exhibition introduced by Gauguin; the latter then set off for Tahiti again; the Swiss painter Vallotton and the sculptor Maillol joined the Nabi group. The following year was that of Paul Verlaine's death, and Bonnard's first exhibition.

André Mellerio published *The Idealist Movement in Painting;* setting aside Gauguin, a recluse at Tahiti and now the "Doyen of the Nabis," he "classed" the movement into four curiously constituted groups:

1. *The Chromo-Luminarists:* Angrand, Maximilien Luce, Lucien Pissarro, Théo Van Rysselberghe, Seurat and Signac.

2. *The Neo-Impressionists:* Anquetin, Guillaume, Guilloux, Ibels, Maufra, Schuffenecker, Toulouse-Lautrec.

3. The *Synthetists* or *Neo-Traditionalists:* Bonnard, Ranson, K.X. Roussel, Sérusier, Vallotton and Vuillard.

4. *The Mystics :* Meyer, Ballin, Émile Bernard, Maurice Denis, Filiger, Jean Verkade.

In the course of a journey in Central Europe in 1897, Paul Sérusier met Verkade at the Benedictine Monastery of Beuron in the Black Forest and was initiated into the theories of the "Sacred Dimensions" and the "Golden Number" — the subject of studies by Père Didier.

The year 1898 saw the disappearance from the scene of the two painter precursors of Symbolism, Gustave Moreau and Puvis de Chavannes and also the greatest of the Symbolist poets, Mallarmé.

Finally in 1899, at the Galerie Durand-Ruel, a general exhibition entitled *Hommage à Odilon Redon* was held, in which the following participated: André, Émile Bernard, Cross, Maurice Denis, d'Espagnat, Ibels, Luce, Van Rysselberghe, Sérusier, Signac, Vallotton and Vuillard.

Nabism, that offshoot of Symbolism, was now to take its place in the history of contemporary painting.

156

IT was not until fairly late in life that Paul Gauguin discovered his painter's vocation. About 1874 he began to build up a collection of Impressionist pictures. He then met Pissarro who was to exercise a certain influence on the development of his personality and introduced him to the circle of his friends. Thus, although Gauguin contributed only one item, a piece of sculpture, to the Fourth Impressionist Exhibition, from the year 1880 on he participated in their last four exhibitions, that is, up to the year 1886. During that period his art was closely bound up with the technique and vision of the Impressionists and followed Pissarro's example to such an extent that Huysmans considered his landscapes shown at the Sixth Impressionist Exhibition, in 1881, as a "Dilution of Pissarro." *The Seine at the Pont d'Iéna* (1875, Jeu de Paume) is very reminiscent of the snow landscapes of the Pre-Impressionists —Lépine—and the Impressionists at their early stages—Sisley or Monet. A *Landscape near Rouen* (1884, Private Coll., Basle) is clearly inspired by Pissarro's orchards and views of Pontoise. The canvas entitled *Entrée de village* (1884, Museum of Fine Arts, Boston) has a close kinship both with Pissarro and Guillaumin.

The artist's first stay at Pont-Aven, from June to November 1886, shows no marked change in idiom. Gauguin was still in fact a respectable Impressionist, possessed of a limited talent.

But a short voyage to Martinique, from April to December 1887, brought about, if not a complete break, at any rate a fairly well defined separation from Impressionism. Shortly before his return Gauguin wrote to his friend Schuffenecker : " I shall be bringing back a dozen canvases, four of which are far superior to my period at Pont-Aven. " Among these we should mention *Seashore* (Private Coll., Paris) in which the tones are less compromising, the whole design more composed.

After regaining Paris, the artist paid a second visit to Pont-Aven where he rejoined Émile Bernard and stayed until October 1888. We have already seen the importance of this meeting and the experiments of the two artists which resulted in Cloisonnism and Synthetism. *The Vision after the Sermon* or *Jacob wrestling with the Angel* (National Gallery of Scotland, Edinburgh) is typical, the first inspired by this new technique which liberated Gauguin from Impressionism. " Far away, very far away, " notes A. Aurier [71], " on a fabulous hill, the soil of which seems glowing vermilion, takes place the Biblical subject of Jacob wrestling with the Angel. While these two legendary giants, seen in the distance looking like pygmies are engaged in their formidable fight, women look on, interested and naive, not too clear doubtless, as to what is taking place over there on this fabulous crimson hill. They are peasants... " The stylization, the schematization of the Breton headdresses, " spread like seagulls wings, " the outline which imprisons the forms and colors applied in broad flat areas, this " Cloisonnism " and this " Synthetism " give a strange, novel character to this work, inspired by the stained glass artists of the Middle Ages. Gauguin was to extract original, essentially ornamental and decorative pictures from this new idiom, and their influence on certain forms of contemporary painting is undeniable. Technically, they are not always well painted : the drawing is some-

PAUL GAUGUIN — THE AWAKENING OF SPRING. 1890-1891 (25 × 52 ") — COLLECTION WALTER. P. CHRYSLER JR., NEW YORK

times incorrect, the colors flat and harsh, inharmonious. And one can often almost share Cézanne's opinion : " Planes ! That is what Gauguin has never understood !... Never have I wanted and never will I accept this lack of modeling or gradations. It makes nonsense. Gauguin was not a painter; he has merely produced Chinese prints. "

Among his first Cloisonnist experiments we should mention such interesting examples as *Still Life at the Gloanec Fête* (Private Coll., France), a *Decorative Landscape* (Stockholm Museum) or that *Portrait of Gauguin dedicated to Vincent* (Coll. V.W. Van Gogh, Laren) of which he himself wrote : " I have painted a portrait of myself for Vincent (Van Gogh) which he had requested. It is, I think, one of my best things : absolutely incomprehensible (for example) so abstract is it... "

And when he found himself in Van Gogh's company (October to December 1888), Gauguin executed landscapes in violent colors that already anticipate the Fauves " *Les Alyscamps,* " *Arles,* Jeu de Paume, or *Arles Landscape,* National Museum, Stockholm).

158

After a brief stay in Paris, the artist set off for Brittany again where he spent some time (April 1889 to November 1890) first at Pont-Aven, then at Le Pouldu in the little inn called "Marie Poupée." Some fine compositions which show Gauguin's development towards a more and more absolute primitivism date from this time. He drew inspiration from Breton wayside calvaries as in *The Yellow Christ* (Albright Art Gallery, Buffalo) and *The Calvary* (Musée des Beaux-Arts, Brussels) or he executed canvases of a more symbolist, more literary nature such as *La Belle Angèle* (Jeu de Paume) which Degas considered a masterpiece. Then there are the Breton landscapes of which *Bonjour, Monsieur Gauguin* (Museum of Modern Art, Prague) remains the outstanding example.

PAUL GAUGUIN — THE YELLOW CHRIST.
1889 (36 1/2 × 28 3/4 ") — ALBRIGHT
ART GALLERY, BUFFALO

From Paris, where he associated with the Symbolists at the Café Voltaire, stem those two amazing works : *The Awakening of Spring* (Private Coll., New York), christened *The Loss of Virginity* by the artist and *Nirvâna*, a portrait of Meyer de Haan (gouache, Wadsworth Atheneum, Hartford, U.S.A.) which has a disquieting strangeness. But like Mallarmé and the Symbolists, Gauguin dreamed of distant lands : *Partir, partir là-bas...*

He embarked for Tahiti (first stay from June 1891 to July 1893). This return to the " source " which he had already looked for on Breton soil he carried out on that famous and still more archaic, more mysterious, more mystical island.

Many paintings echo this feeling : *Ia Orana Maria : I salute thee, Maria* (Mr. and Mrs. Samuel A. Lewisohn Coll., New York), *The Meal : Three little Tahitians behind a Table* (Private Coll., Paris), *Tahiti Women on the Beach* (Jeu de Paume), *I Raro te oviri : Under the Pandanus* (Institute of Art, Minneapolis), *Naked Tahiti Women on the Beach* (Robert Lehman Coll., New York), *Vahine no te vi : Woman of Tahiti* (Museum of Art, Baltimore), *Nafea foa ipoipo : When will you marry ?* (Kunstmuseum, Basle), that amazing masterpiece *Ta Matete : The Market* (Kunstmuseum, Basle) with its mysterious, almost Egyptian beauty, *Hina te Fatou : The Moon and the Earth* (Museum of Modern Art, New York), *The House of the Maori* (Private Coll., Rheinfelden), *Manao Tupapau : The Spirit of the Dead keeps Vigil* (A. Conger Goodyear Coll., New York).

Back in France (August 1893 to February 1895), Gauguin spent most of his time in Paris and Brittany and leaves us, *inter alia*, a painting evoking *Annah the Javanese* (Private Coll., Winterthur) with whom he lived at this period. But he went off to Tahiti (July 1895 to September 1901). In his celebrated correspondence with Daniel de Monfreid he complains of his solitude. " ... I am so demoralized that I do not believe that any greater misfortunes could happen to me... " But later, he regained his confidence when he writes to André Fontainas : " Here, near my hut, in total silence, I dream of violent harmonies among the natural scents which intoxicate me. Bliss heightened by a strange sacred horror that I sense from time beyond memory. "

From this period date the following : *Nave, Nave, Mahana : Delightful Days* (Lyon Museum), *The Day of the God* (Art Institute, Chicago), *Nevermore* (Courtauld Institute, London), *The White Horse* (Jeu de Paume), *Breasts with the Red Flowers* (Metropolitan Museum, New York). However, his masterpiece is still the great composition of 1897 : *D'où venons-nous ? Que sommes-nous ? Où allons-nous ?* (Museum of Fine Arts, Boston, Mass.). He explains it in a long letter to Daniel de Monfreid : " ... Then, before I died I wanted to paint a large canvas that I had in my head; and especially all this month I have been working in an unparalleled frenzy. Heavens, it's not a canvas painted like a Puvis de Chavannes, a study from life, then a preliminary sketch, etc. It is all done without a model, with the tip of my brush straight on to a coarse canvas full of flaws and roughnesses; so it looks terribly crude. You would say that it had been abandoned... unfinished. It is true that oneself is not the best judge, but all the same I think that not only does this picture surpass all my previous ones, but that I shall never do a better, or even one like it. I have put into it, before I die, all my energy, such a painful emotion in dreadful circumstances and so clear and uncorrected a vision that the element of haste vanishes, and life surges

160

PAUL GAUGUIN — HORSEMEN ON THE BEACH. 1902 (29 × 36 1/4 ")

NIARCHOS COLLECTION

ODILON REDON — VASE OF FLOWERS. PASTEL (20 × 17 3/4 ") — PRIVATE COLLECTION, PARIS

162

from it. This picture does not stink of the model, technique and the so-called rules —from which I have always broken away, but sometimes with some apprehension... " Mystery and perpetual renewal of birth, love, mystique and death—such appears to be the deep meaning of this painting which can take its place alongside the decorative compositions of the greatest masters. The artist then left for the Marquesas Islands, and noteworthy among paintings from a stay at Dominica (August 1901 to May 1903) are *And the Gold of their Body* (Jeu de Paume), *A Barbaric Idyll* (Folkwang Museum, Essen) and the *Horsemen on the Beach* (Niarchos Collection).

Gauguin also practiced engraving, ceramics and sculpture (his wood carvings, the best known of which is *Be amorous, you will be happy*, are powerfully archaic). He also left some illustrated manuscripts; the two most famous, preserved in the Print Room in the Louvre, sum up their author's ideas and tendencies : *The ancient Maori Worship* and above all *Noa-Noa*, the text of which, written in collaboration with Charles Morice during the winter 1893-1894 from memories of his first voyage to Tahiti and divided into eleven chapters, is of the greatest interest for the understanding of Gauguin's work. This precious manuscript is enhanced by photographs, engravings and innumerable drawings and water colors of remarkable brilliance.

One recalls that Mallarmé saw " the supreme primitive man " in every artist. Now, Gauguin strove continually—and the choice of Brittany and Tahiti are the proof—to link up with the art of the most primitive schools, to go back beyond the Renaissance and even beyond Greek art. " I have gone a very long way back " he said, " beyond the horses of the Parthenon, back to the pet of my childhood, the good wooden horse. " And he exclaims : " For me Barbarism is a rejuvenation ! " He generally lends his figures ritual gestures and thus achieves the hieraticism of the ancient Egyptians. His conception of color is very different from Van Gogh's; this is how he defines it to Fontainas : " Color, which is vibration like music, has the power to achieve the most general and yet the most indeterminate element in nature : its inner force. "

Anxious about the merit of his art, he writes to Daniel de Monfreid : " If my works do not endure, there will always be the memory of an artist who liberated painting from many of its ancient academic failings, its Symbolist weaknesses (another kind of sentimentalism)... "

This anxiety, now stripped of any false literary element, is expressed in that inimitable and mysterious message : *Whence do we come ? What are we ? Whither are we going ?*

ODILON REDON

IN his book *To oneself*, Odilon Redon analyzes his own pictorial conception : " My concern, as I made them [his monsters] was to organize their structure... the whole of my originality consists in the fact that I make improbable beings live humanly according to the laws of the probable, by putting, as far as I can, *the logic of the visible at the service of the invisible.* " He strives in this way to extract the naturalness from the supernatural. A vigorous analyst, he scrutinizes the appearance of people and things down to the minutest details; then he transposes it in terms of his dreams and confers on it a mysterious, wholly imaginery poetry : at this point he is a visionary.

" The object of art is not the imitation of nature, " he thinks, " but the expression of the soul of the painter and the apprehension of the Being to whom the artist gets closer than either the scientist or the philosopher. Any liberty with nature is therefore permissible, provided that it is expressive. " This imaginative man is a rational being : he is unable to create without starting from scrupulously analyzed reality : but in him fiction always outdoes reality. And we could apply to him Shakespeare's : " We are such stuff as dreams are made on... "

Until quite recently Odilon Redon's work had been far too neglected. Mlle Roseline Bacou's writings have thrown light on this sensitive and highly cultured

ODILON REDON — MADNESS. DRAWING. 1877 (14 1/4 × 12 1/4 ”) — PRIVATE COLLECTION, PARIS

artist. Charcoal drawings and lithographs, entitled *Noirs* by Redon himself, compose his essential production up to the year 1890 and are, in my opinion, the best part. The multiplicity of the sources of light, the density of the blacks, the strange arrangement of the page put their author among the direct precursors of Surrealism.

Does he not himself explain : " Suggestive art cannot provide anything unless it has recourse to the mysterious play of the shadows and rhythms of mentally conceived lines " ? One of his masterpieces, the study entitled *Madness* (Private Coll., Paris) foreshadows the tragic element in Picasso. We should also mention *The Smiling Spider* (Louvre), *Armor* (Metropolitan Museum, New York), *Profile of Light* (Private Coll., Paris), *Pegasus captive* (lithograph, Bibliothèque nationale, Paris).

But Redon also wanted to express himself in color, and from 1895 his pastels assume an important place in his work. Among the finest we should mention the *Portrait of Madame Redon embroidering* (Ari Redon Coll.), *Portrait of Madame Arthur Fontaine* (Jean-Arthur Fontaine Coll.), *Buddha* (Marcel Kapferer Coll., Paris), *The Birth of Venus* (Petit-Palais, Paris) and admirable flower pieces conceived with all the care of a botanist or transmuted into phantasmagoria (Petit-Palais, Jeu de Paume, Private Collections, etc.).

Redon practiced oil painting all his life. " The oil substance contains an evil spell, " he writes to André Bonger in April 1906. " It subjugates you, holds you fast before the easel, every day with some new torment, some new excitement. " In *The Closed Eyes* (Jeu de Paume) we find the strange presence of those heads surging out of the nothingness, a theme that constantly recurs in his work. Redon often returns to the subject of *Apollo's Chariot*, a reminiscence doubtless of Delacroix, for whom he professed great admiration.

IN conclusion, how are we to define the contribution of this Impressionism which aimed at renewing the art of painting ? Essentially, it represents the triumph of color and light; a contribution which successors of the movement, whatever their divergencies or differences, would hardly dispute. The whole of contemporary art has in fact its origins in Impressionism, and perhaps even more in the reaction it produced : the Nabis stem from Gauguin and Symbolism, the Fauves from Van Gogh and the Cubists from Cézanne.

NOTES

1 – Edmond RENOIR, *Souvenirs inédits. Le tableau de Monet.*

2 – M. GUILLEMOT, " Claude Monet, " *La Revue illustrée*, March 15, 1898.

3 – *Bulletin de la Société de l'Histoire de l'Art français*, 1928, first section, p. 40.

4 – Notebooks, circa 1855. MOREAU-NÉLATON, *Histoire de Corot et de ses œuvres*, vol. I, p. 105.

5 – Notebooks, circa 1855-1860. MOREAU-NÉLATON, *op. cit.* vol. I, p. 126.

6 – MOREAU-NÉLATON, *op. cit.* vol. II, p. 66.

7 – BOSSUET, *Connaissances*, III, p. 3.

8 – BUFFON, *Dictionnaire naturel :* animaux. Œuvres, vol. V, p. 276.

9 – Paul SIGNAC, *D'Eugène Delacroix au Néo-Impressionnisme*, 1939, p. 62.

10 – *Ibid.*, p. 68.

11 – *Ibid.*, p. 70.

12 – *L'Amour de l'Art*, February 1939, n° 1, p. 11.

13 – Musical glossary. *Revue Musica*, n° 41, August, 1957.

14 – International days of art studies, June 25-27, 1953, in the context of the exhibition *Le Greco, de la Crête à Tolède par Venise*, Bordeaux, p. 21.

15 – *Obras*, III, p. 317.

16 – Maurice SÉRULLAZ, " L'Impressionnisme de Velasquez, " *Cahiers de Bordeaux*, 1955, pp. 61-63.

17 – E. DELACROIX, *Journal*, new edition by André JOUBIN, Paris, 1932, vol. III, p. 380 (supplement to the *Journal*).

18 – *Ibid.*, p. 147.

19 – *Ibid.*, pp. 451-452.

20 – *Correspondance générale d'E. Delacroix*, published by André JOUBIN, Paris, 1938, vol. IV, p. 60.

21 – DELACROIX, *Journal*, vol. II, April 29, 1854, p. 175.

22 – *Ibid.*, April 29, 1854, p. 176.

23 – *Ibid.*, 1852, vol. I, p. 500.

24 – *Ibid.*, September 29, 1850.

25 – *Ibid.*, September 29, 1850.

26 – Posthumous notes. *La Revue Blanche*, May 15, 1896.

27 – Quoted by Théophile SILVESTRE, *Les Artistes français, études d'après nature*, Paris, 1862, ...Corot, p. 220.

28 – *L'art du paysage en France*, 1925, p. 191.

29 – Th. SILVESTRE, *Les Artistes français, études d'après nature*, Paris, 1862, Courbet, p. 65.

30 – Georges RIAT, *Gustave Courbet, peintre*, Paris, 1906.

31 – André FONTAINAS, *Courbet*, Paris, 1921, p. 58.

32 – Charles BAUDELAIRE, *Curiosités esthétiques*, pp. 340-341.

33 – Jean AUBRY, *Eugène Boudin*, Paris, 1922, p. 39.

34 – *Ibid.*, p. 36.

35 – SIGNAC, *op. cit.*, p. 60.

36 – CASTAGNARY, Salons 1857-1870, vol. I, 1892, p. 170.

37 – *Ibid.*, Salon of 1873, vol. II, p. 68.

38 – Théodore DURET, " Un grand peintre de la Provence, Paul Guigou, " in *L'Art et les Artistes*, p. 98.

39 – John REWALD, *History of Impressionism*, pp. 61-62, Museum of Modern Art, New York, 1946.

40 – *Ibid.*, p. 62.

40b – *Translator's note :* " Among so many beauties to be seen everywhere, I understand, my friends, how much your choice wawers. But in Lola de Valence you see the glow of the unexpected charm of a pink and black jewel. "

41 – Z. ASTRUC, Article in *Le Salon de* 1863, May 20, 1863.

42 – " Courbet, " Conversations reported by Albert WOLFF, in *Le Figaro*, May 1, 1883.

43 – E. CHESNEAU, " Le Japon à Paris, " *Gazette des Beaux-Arts*, 1878.

43b – *Translator's note :* The allusion is to Boileau's famous half-line " Enfin Malherbe vint... " inferring that Daguerre had a similarly revolutionary effect in the twentieth century.

44 – Charles BAUDELAIRE, *Curiosités esthétiques. Le Salon de 1859; le public moderne et la photographie*, reissued 1923, pp. 264-272.

45 – Charles BAUDELAIRE, *L'Art romantique; le peintre de la vie moderne*, IV : *La modernité*, new edition 1885, pp. 68-73.

46 – Lionello VENTURI, *Les Archives de l'Impressionnisme*, 1939, vol. II, pp. 255-256.

47 – J. CLARETIE, *Le Salon de 1874*, reprinted in *L'Art et les Artistes français contemporains*, Paris, 1876.

48 – Lionello VENTURI, *op. cit.*, pp. 257-259.

49 – Reference is to Berthe Morisot.

50 – Lionello VENTURI, *op. cit.*, pp. 259-261.

51 – *Ibid.*, pp. 262-264.

52 – *Ibid.*, pp. 264-265.

53 – *Ibid.*, pp. 265-267.

54 – *Ibid.*, pp. 267-269.

55 – *Ibid.*, pp. 269-271.

56 – Octave MIRBEAU, *Des Artistes*, 1st series, *Claude Monet*, p. 91.

57 – Catalog of the Berthe Morisot Exhibition, Paris, Orangerie (1941). Preface by Paul VALÉRY, p. IV.

58 – *Ibid.*, pp. V and VI.

59 – Property of Mme Ernest Rouart. Cf. JAMOT, WILDENSTEIN, BATAILLE, *Manet*, Paris, 1932, n° 249.

60 – Paul COLIN, *Manet*, Paris, 1937, p. 139.

61 – E. MOREAU-NÉLATON, *Manet raconté par lui-même*, 2 vols., Paris, 1906, vol. II, p. 85.

62 – Paul VALÉRY, *Degas, Danse, Dessin*, Paris, 1938, p. 97.

63 – Paul SIGNAC, *D'Eugène Delacroix au Néo-Impressionnisme*, 4th ed. Paris, 1939, p. 13.

64 – Paul SIGNAC, *op. cit.*, p. 94.

65 – Matila C. GHYKA, *Le Nombre d'Or*, 2 vols. 3rd ed., 1931.

66 – Elisa MAILLARD, *Du Nombre d'Or*, Paris, 1943.

67 – Letters from Vincent Van Gogh to his brother Theo. Paris, 1937, pp. 95-96.

68 – Letters..., *op. cit.*, p. 123.

69 – Maurice SÉRULLAZ, Van Gogh and Millet, in *Etudes d'Art*, published by the Musée national des Beaux-Arts d'Alger, no. 5, 1950, pp. 85-92.

70 – *Le Mercure de France*, November 1, 1932.

71 – A. AURIER, *Mercure de France*, February 9, 1891, p. 155.

72 – We remind the reader that the works of the Impressionists which belong to the Louvre are on permanent exhibition in the Musée du Jeu de Paume, Paris.

ANGRAND, *Charles*.

Born at Criquetot-sur-Ouville (Seine-Maritime), April 29, 1854, he began as an assistant master at Rouen, then at Paris, but his meetings with Seurat and Signac caused him to turn his attention to painting, and he exhibited at the first Salon des Indépendants in 1884. Subsequently he became a member of the Neo-Impressionist group and adopted Pointillism. After taking part in numerous exhibitions, he withdrew into solitude, painting landscapes, rustic compositions or genre scenes. He died in Rouen on April 1, 1926.

ANQUETIN, *Louis*.

Born at Etrépagny in Eure, January 26, 1861, he entered Cormon's studio where he made the acquaintance of Van Gogh and Lautrec, but disdaining academic teaching, he became interested in the works of the Impressionists, then practiced Divisionism. His influence on the friends with whom he exhibited was considerable but of short duration. He participated in the exhibition of the " Impressionist and Synthetist group " organized by Gauguin at the Café Volpini in 1889. Eclectic by temperament, he took an interest in all schools and was fascinated by technical problems. His work shows in particular the influence of Flemish painters of the seventeenth century, especially Rubens. He exhibited at the Salon des Indépendants, then at the National des Beaux-Arts, at the Salon and the Salon d'Automne. His vigorous realism can be seen in his large mural compositions, ceilings and tapestries. He also painted numerous portraits. A writer, he studied the principles of pictorial technique and published a work on Rubens. He died in Paris in 1932.

BAZILLE, *Jean-Frédéric*.

Born December 6, 1841, at Montpellier into a family of the Protestant upper middle-class which had as a neighbor the collector Bruyas, a friend of Courbet's, whose collection he often visited. In 1859 he began his studies at the Faculty of Medicine at Montpellier; at the same time he was drawing under the guidance of the sculptors of Montpellier, the Baussans, father and son. In 1862 he obtained his father's permission to continue his medical studies at Paris and also his painting. On the advice of a friend of the family, he entered the studio of a Swiss painter Gleyre. There he made the acquaintance of Claude Monet with whom he formed a friendship and who gave him useful advice. Thanks to a private income which enabled him to lead a comfortable existence free from financial worries, he helped artist friends who were less fortunate than himself. In June 1864 he was in Normandy with Monet where he painted landscapes; shortly afterwards he abandoned medicine for painting once and for all. At Méric, his parents' estate near Montpellier, he painted his first portrait in the open air, *The Pink Dress* (Louvre[72]). With Renoir, Sisley and Monet, Bazille left Gleyre's studio and at the beginning of 1865, jointly with Monet, rented a studio at 6, rue de Furstenberg where he lived until February, 1866. Several months later his work was rejected by the Salon, and out of pique, he omitted to withdraw his canvas *Girl at the Piano*. During the winter of 1866-1867 he contemplated holding a joint exhibition with Courbet, Corot, Diaz, Daubigny and Monet, but this project was never fulfilled. In June 1867 he painted landscapes at Aigues-Mortes, and at Méric painted *La Réunion de Famille* (Louvre) exhibited at the Salon of 1868. Back in Paris he frequented the Café Guerbois, boulevard des Batignolles, where among others Manet, Zola, Fantin-Latour, Monet and Cézanne were to be found. In 1868 he painted *La Toilette* (Montpellier Museum). In the spring of 1870 he was at Méric but on July 15, after the declaration of war, left to enlist. Sent first to Algeria, he later returned to France and took part in the fighting with the army of the Loire; he was killed at Beaune-la-Rolande November 28, 1870 at the age of twenty-nine.

BERNARD, *Emile*.

Born at Lille April 28, 1868, he entered Cormon's studio, where he met Lautrec and most important to him, Van Gogh, whose first Paris exhibition he organized in 1893. He was also associated with Gauguin whom he himself influenced before being, in turn, influenced by him. He developed very different genres and idioms — all marked by a symbolism which seems to be the basis of his inspiration. His best period was his Pont-Aven period of Cloisonnism. Later Bernard claimed to have forestalled Gauguin in this discovery. He traveled a great deal, particularly in Spain and Italy, and spent a long time in Cairo where he did some painting. At the same time he published a collection of French and

Arabian poems *Le Parnasse Oriental*, a book of his own verses *Le Voyage de l'Etre* and a monthly review, *La Rénovation Artistique*. The influence of the masters of the Renaissance perceptibly affected his second phase of work. In 1911 Vollard published the *Lettres de Van Gogh à Emile Bernard* with comment by the latter. Emile Bernard also illustrated *Les Fleurs du Mal*, *The Odyssey*, *Les Amours de Ronsard*, the poems of Villon and *Fioretti*. He died in Paris April 16, 1941.

BOUDIN, *Eugène*.

Born July 13, 1824 at Honfleur, Boudin was the son of a former naval gunner. Apart from this he himself sailed as a cabin boy between Le Havre and the Antilles before abandoning the sea for the trade of paper maker and picture framer at Le Havre. He exhibited in his shop pictures by artists staying in the region. Amongst them were Troyon and Millet who encouraged him to paint. In 1848-1849 he began to paint still lifes in the spirit of Chardin and portraits. In 1850, thanks to a grant from the town council, he went to work in Paris, often leaving it in order to paint in his native Normandy. Finally he settled once more in Le Havre, where he had a struggle to live. In 1858 he made the acquaintance of Monet, who was then seventeen and worked with him. The following year he met Courbet and exhibited *The Pardon of Sainte-Anne-la-Palud* at the Salon, which was praised by Baudelaire. In 1861 Corot who encouraged him nicknamed him " the king of skies. " He subsequently became associated with Jongkind. Although his seascapes were beginning to be appreciated, Boudin was still leading a hard life. From 1871 onwards he shared his time between the Normandy coast, Brittany, Belgium and Paris. In 1874 he worked in Holland; finally, in 1881, Durand-Ruel opened the gates of success to him by taking an interest in his work. The Salon approved the succession of medallions which he submitted, but the death of his wife in 1889 left him in despair. Three years after, reasons of health forced him to settle on the Côte d'Azur, where he continued to work with regularity. In 1895 he left for Venice, in order to seek fresh subjects but illness slowed down his production. He died at Deauville, August 8, 1898, facing his great source of inspiration, the sea. He exhibited with the Impressionists at their first exhibition in 1874.

BRACQUEMOND, *Félix*.

Born in Paris, May 22, 1833, he worked as a lithographer's apprentice before devoting himself to painting and exhibiting at the Salons of 1852 and 1853. He taught himself etching while continuing to paint and executed many portraits; he associated with Baudelaire, the Goncourt brothers, Manet, Gavarni, Barbey d'Aurevilly, Théodore de Banville, etc. Success and recognition came slowly and Bracquemond received the *Grand Prix de Gravure* at the Exhibition of 1900. Appointed director of arts at the Sèvres Workshop after the war of 1870, he subsequently became artistic director of the Haviland ceramic workshops from 1872 to 1880. During his retirement near Paris, he worked alone, now engraving copies of old masters, now rustic landscapes, book illustrations and portraits. He died in Paris on October 23, 1914. He took part in the Impressionist Exhibitions of 1874, 1879 and 1880.

BRACQUEMOND, *Marie*.

A pupil of Ingres, she married Félix Bracquemond in 1869 and first exhibited at the Salon of 1874. She took part in the Impressionist Exhibitions of 1879, 1880 and 1886.

CAILLEBOTTE, *Gustave*.

Born in Paris, August 19, 1848 into an upper middle-class family. His father, a judge on the Seine Tribunal, died in 1873, leaving him, at barely twenty-five years of age, in possession of a substantial fortune which allowed him to indulge his taste for painting and to work at the École des Beaux-Arts. The first Impressionist Exhibition revolutionized his art; he then became associated with Renoir, Monet and Pissarro. In 1875 he painted *The Parquet Planers* (Louvre) in the naturalist spirit and took part in the second Impressionist Exhibition in 1876. He also painted open air subjects and in their company at La Grenouillère, at Bougival and at Chatou he executed scenes of " rowers. " He then became interested in the spectacle of the Paris streets, conveying the same feeling of " modern life " as Degas. He helped his friends generously and through his many purchases, built up an important collection of their canvases. Towards 1880 he abandoned the representation of scenes of contemporary life for still lifes, to which he attempted to apply the Impressionist technique. Then he went to work on the coast of Normandy (1880-1882). Finally in 1887 he settled at Petit-Gennevilliers where he again took up the themes of rowers and regattas. Suddenly stricken by a congestion of the brain, he died on February 21, 1894. His collection, which was bequeathed to the state, became the subject of a major lawsuit between the administration of the École des Beaux-Arts and his heirs. Thirty-eight canvases were finally selected by the state for the Musée du Luxembourg to which they were taken in 1897. Caillebotte took part in the Impressionist Exhibitions of 1876, 1877, 1879, 1880 and 1882.

CALS, Adolphe-Félix.

Born in Paris, October 19, 1810, he began engraving before he entered the studio of Léon Coignet at the École des Beaux-Arts. He exhibited for the first time at the Salon in 1835 and from then onwards, but without any success. About 1860 he was working at the Saint-Siméon Inn near Honfleur, nicknamed " the Normandy Barbizon, " where he came under the influence of Jongkind. He died at Honfleur on October 3, 1880. He took part in the Impressionist Exhibitions of 1874, 1876, 1877 and 1879 and homage was paid to him at that of 1881.

CARRIÈRE, Eugène.

Born at Gournay (Seine-et-Marne) in 1849. He was first a lithographer's assistant at Saint-Quentin. He entered Cabanel's studio at the École des Beaux-Arts but soon liberated himself from the academic influence. He first exhibited at the Salon of 1876, and in 1879 *The Young Mother* brought him much lively encouragement. Although living in conditions of extreme poverty, he continued to work, performing obscure tasks for printers and lithographers to keep alive. He became associated with Gustave Geffroy, Roger Marx, Victor-Émile Michelet and Frantz Jourdain who encouraged and defended him. His true style emerged slowly from his tentative experiments, while his *Maternités* assured his reputation. He also painted numerous portraits of Alphonse Daudet, Verlaine, Edmond de Goncourt, Anatole France, Rochefort, Rodin, etc., and executed lithographs and decorative murals, notably *The Four Ages* for the town hall of the *XIIe* arrondissement in Paris. He died in Paris, March 27, 1906.

CASSATT, Mary.

Born in Pittsburgh (U.S.A.) in 1845; of French origin on her father's side, a rich banker, she spent her childhood in France before returning to the United States where she studied painting at the Academy School in Philadelphia. She returned to Paris in 1868, entered Chaplin's studio and copied paintings in museums. She exhibited at the Salon of 1872. The art of Rubens attracted her and she went to Antwerp and the Prado to study his work and received the advice of Degas, with whom she became closely associated. The revelation of Japanese prints gave direction to her processes of composition. Her relations with rich American collectors, the Havemeyers in particular, were responsible for the numerous purchases of Impressionist canvases by collectors and museums of the United States. A painter of the family and of maternal love, Mary Cassatt is equally the artist of *At the Opera* (Boston Museum of Fine Arts) and *La Loge*. She died, almost blind, on June 14, 1927 at her property of Mesnil-Theribus (Oise). She took part in the Impressionist Exhibitions of 1879, 1880, 1881 and 1886.

CÉZANNE, Paul.

Born January 19, 1839 at Aix-en-Provence, he was the son of a hat manufacturer who later became a banker. At the Collège Bourbon he associated with Émile Zola whose best friend he was to remain until their quarrel in 1886. At nineteen a second prize for drawing at the École des Beaux-Arts decided his vocation : he would be a painter. His father was reluctant and insisted that he enroll at the Faculty of Law. At the end of April 1861 he obtained permission to go and paint in Paris for several months where he found Zola again and joined the *Académie Suisse*. Refused by the École des Beaux-Arts, Cézanne returned to Aix, a disappointed man. He came to Paris a few months later where he met Monet, Degas, Renoir and then Manet, but their respective temperaments and their different conceptions of painting clashed. In 1886 he was rejected by the Salon. His violent impasto canvases aroused storms of abuse. A truant from conscription, he hid away at l'Estaque, near Marseilles, with his friend Hortense Fiquet during the war of 1870. He returned to Paris during the summer of 1871 and began to work in the open air under the influence of Pissarro and settled at Auvers-sur-Oise where he painted *La Maison du Pendu, Auvers*, (Jeu de Paume, Louvre), which marks the transition between his first and his second manner. Cézanne showed his canvases for the first time at the Impressionist Exhibition of 1874 where they provoked sarcasm and laughter. Wounded by this setback, he returned to Aix and refused to exhibit in 1876 but in 1877 he occupied a complete panel with his seventeen canvases. That same year he worked at Pontoise, at Auvers and at Chailly on the banks of the Marne. Then in 1874 he returned to paint at l'Estaque. After staying in Paris, the Ile-de-France or Provence, where he fitted up a studio near Aix in the family property, " Le Jas de Bouffan, " in 1885 he went to seek out Renoir at La Roche-Guyon in Seine-et-Oise and then, until 1888, he did not leave the South of France again. He painted numerous landscapes, the principal subject of which is the Montagne Sainte-Victoire and in which he sought to "do Poussin again from nature." His style emerged slowly. *The Card Players*, of which five variants existed between 1890 and 1895, is the first attempt at balanced composition with people, which was to culminate in the series of *Baigneuses*. In 1899 he exhibited at the Salon des Indépendants and, in the following year, three of his canvases were accepted for the Centennial of the 1900 Exhibition. The Salon d'Automne of 1904 gave its blessing to work to which the public remained hostile, but which was striking more and more sympathetic chords in the young painters. On September 21, 1906 he wrote to Émile Bernard : " I am still working from nature and it seems to me that I am making slow progress. " A few weeks later on October 15th, he was caught in a storm when he was working out of doors : he was carried home unconscious and died on the 22nd. Cézanne took part in the Impressionist Exhibitions of 1874 and 1877.

CORDEY, *Frédéric*.

Born in Paris, July 9, 1854. He exhibited at the Salon des Indépendants from 1887. He mostly painted landscapes in the Ile-de-France and scenes of country life. He died in Paris, February 18, 1911. He took part in the Impressionist Exhibition of 1877.

COUSTURIER, *Lucie*.

Born in Paris, December 19, 1876, she first exhibited at the Salon des Indépendants in 1901. She painted luminous landscapes, flowers and still lifes with a Pointillist technique. A visit to West Africa influenced her work considerably. She brought back numerous canvases as well as studies on the customs and the psychology of the natives. She died in Paris on June 16th 1925.

CROSS, *Henri-Edmond*.

Born in Douai, May 20, 1856, he began his studies at the School of Fine Arts in Lille before entering François Bonvin's studio in Paris in 1876. He exhibited at the Salon in 1881. He quickly abandoned an academic style for the Neo-Impressionist technique of Seurat. Between 1904 and 1908 he made many trips to Italy, to Venice, Tuscany and Umbria. He was amongst the founders of the Salon des Indépendants in 1884. He died at Saint-Clair, near Le Lavandou (Var) on May 16, 1910. Cross's real name was Delacroix, and it was thanks to his friend Bonvin's advice that he had exchanged his surname – extremely challenging for a painter – for its English equivalent.

DEGAS, *Edgar*.

Born in Paris, July 19, 1834 into a rich and cultivated family, he found no obstacle to his artistic tastes; on the contrary, his father, a banker, took him to visit museums and private collections. At nineteen he entered the studio of Barrias and later that of Lamothe, a disciple of Ingres. He made many journeys to Italy where his grandfather and some members of his family lived. Under the influence of the master of the Renaissance, he was attracted to historical painting and painted great compositions which he swiftly abandoned in order to express " the feeling of modern life, " the taste for which he revealed as early as the *Family Portrait* (1858). In 1861 he became interested in horse racing. He made Manet's acquaintance and frequented the Café Guerbois. In 1865 he painted the *Woman with Chrysanthemums*, his first asymmetric composition. After the war he embarked for New Orleans in 1872 where his brothers and some of his mother's family lived. He brought back the *Cotton Office* (Pau Museum). On returning to Paris, Degas became a regular visitor to the Opera; he took a very active part in preparing the First Impressionist Exhibition. After 1870 a great part of his work was to revolve round the successive or alternate themes of horses, dancers, dressmakers or laundresses and finally women at their toilet. Technical problems fascinated Degas. Apart from painting he practiced pastel, engraving and monotype and even produced many statuettes of dancers and horses in which he breaks down their movements. About 1878-1880 he sensibly modified his technique and made an increasing use of pastel for big compositions in which his plastic researches on the theme of nudes at their toilet took on an ever increasing scale. In 1893 he exhibited some small landscapes at Durand-Ruel's gallery which he called his " states of the eyes. " Affected by bad sight, Degas worked with increasing difficulty and progressively abandoned painting for sculpture; entrenched in his solitude, he only visited a few friends. His flat and his studio were filled with masterpieces patiently assembled throughout his life. He died almost completely blind on September 27, 1917 aged eighty-three. He took part in the Impressionist Exhibitions of 1874, 1876, 1877, 1879, 1880, 1881 and 1886.

DUBOIS-PILLET, *Albert*.

Born, Paris on October 28, 1845. A lover of painting, he associated with many Impressionist artists. In 1884 he was amongst the founders of the Salon des Indépendants. Chiefly in a Pointillist style he painted landscapes of Paris and the Haute-Loire where he was appointed a commander of the *Gendarmerie*. He died at Le Puy in 1890.

FANTIN-LATOUR, Henri.

Born in Grenoble, January 14, 1836, the son of the painter, Théodore Fantin-Latour, he worked in Paris in the studio of Lecoq de Boisbaudran, then in that of Courbet. He copied many paintings at the Louvre and from 1861 he exhibited at the Salon. In 1864 he showed his *Homage to Delacroix* and in 1870 *The Batignolles Studio* where he grouped around Manet the regulars of the Café Guerbois : Renoir, Zola, Bazille, Monet, Zacharie Astruc, etc. Similarly in *Un Coin de table* in 1872 he gathered his poet and writer friends : Verlaine, Rimbaud, Léon Valade, Emile Blémont, Jean Aicard, Camille Pelletan, etc. He painted portraits, flowers and compositions inspired by his musical admirations. Attracted by Whistler, he made three successive stays in England in 1859, 1861 and 1864 and enjoyed a great success there chiefly as a flower painter. He died at Bure (Orne) on August 25, 1904.

GAUGUIN, Paul.

Born in Paris, June 7, 1848, of Hispano-Parisian descent on his mother's side, he spent his childhood in Peru from 1851 to 1855. At the age of seventeen he joined the navy in which he stayed until 1871. In the same year, he went to work for a stockbroker and two years later married a young Danish woman, Mette Gad. He began painting as an amateur under the influence of Pissarro and exhibited at the Salon. The encouragement which he received induced him to abandon his job in 1883 and devote himself to painting, despite the reproaches of his wife. Then he went to Denmark with his family and subsequently returned to Paris. In 1886 he settled at Pont-Aven, where Émile Bernard gave him advice and where he abandoned Impressionist composition. In 1887, attracted by life in the colonies, Gauguin set sail for Martinique whence he returned a year later to work once more at Pont-Aven. There with Bernard and Sérusier he worked out the theory of Cloisonnism and Synthetism. In the autumn of 1888 he joined Van Gogh at Arles, where the two of them formed the project of establishing the " Atelier du Midi, " but an attack of madness in the latter broke up their friendship and Gauguin returned to Paris. After a first exhibition by the Pont-Aven group, he left for Le Pouldu where he spent the year 1890 in the company of his friends Bernard, Sérusier, Seguin, Meyer de Haan and Charles Laval. The receipts from the sale of thirty of his canvases for nine thousand eight hundred francs permitted him to take the boat to Tahiti. Two years later he returned, in August 1893. His first exhibition, at Durand-Ruel's gallery, was a failure. He went back to Pont-Aven and then in 1895 returned to Tahiti. While in Paris his friends were trying to sell his pictures, he was leading the same kind of life as that of the natives there, but illness slowly undermined him and he experienced terrible periods of suffering, following weeks of calm and of work. His art became more and more symbolic and he expressed his philosophico-religious preoccupations in a great composition : *D'où venons-nous ? Que sommes-nous ? Où allons-nous ? (Whence do we come ? What are we ? Where are we going ?* Museum of Fine Arts, Boston, Mass.). He produced many carvings and also wood engravings with which he illustrated a satirical journal, *Le Sourire*, which he founded. In 1901 he left Tahiti for Fatu-Iva, one of the Marquesas Islands, where he found himself subjected to the importunities of the administration. He died there on May 8, 1903. Gauguin took part in the Impressionist Exhibitions of 1879, 1880, 1881, 1882 and 1886.

VAN GOGH, Vincent.

Born in Groot-Zundert (Holland), March 30, 1853, the son of a pastor. He first worked as a clerk in the local branches of Goupil, the art dealer, in the Hague, Brussels and London. After disappointments in love, he went back to Holland in July 1874. Then he returned to London; finally he was transferred to Paris. His job became an increasing burden to him. In April, 1876 he decided to become a missionary in le Borinage where he spent his energy without counting the cost and began to draw and paint. Dismissed by the evangelical Consistory for excess of zeal, he led a life of adventure and wretchedness. In the Hague he received advice from the painter Mauve and painted realistic subjects, among them *The Potato Eaters* (V.W. Van Gogh Collection, Laren), still lifes and very gloomy landscapes. In 1885 he left for Antwerp and then in the following year for Paris where he entered Cormon's studio. He discovered the clear painting of the Impressionists and met Lautrec, Gauguin, Cézanne, Seurat, etc. His palette lightened; he painted *The Gardens Plots on the Hill at Montmartre* (Amsterdam Municipal Museum), *The Portrait of Père Tanguy* (Musée Rodin, Paris), *The Restaurant " la Sirène "* (Louvre). On the advice of Lautrec he left for the South of France in February 1888, where at Arles the intense light plunged him into an extraordinary exaltation. He painted unceasingly despite his bad health and an excessive expenditure of nervous energy. In October 1888, Gauguin went to visit him, but frequent quarrels broke out between the two men. On December 25th Vincent cut his ear off and was interned first in a hospital at Arles and then in the asylum of Saint-Paul-de-Mausole, near Saint-Rémy. In May 1889 new attacks of madness laid him low, but nonetheless he continued to paint; his canvases became more and more exalted : *The Cypresses by Moonlight* (Kunsthalle, Bremen), *The Olive Trees* (John Hay Whitney Collection, New York). He begged his brother to bring him back to the North; he left the asylum on May 16, 1890 and settled on May 21, at Auvers-sur-Oise under the supervision of Doctor Gachet. On July 27 he shot himself with a revolver and died on the 29th.

GONZALÈS, *Eva.*

Born in Paris, April 19, 1849, the daughter of the novelist, Emmanuel Gonzalès. She was initiated into the art of painting by Chaplin. She became associated with Manet who had a great influence on her and painted her portrait (Salon, 1872). Eva Gonzalès exhibited for the first time in London in 1869; then at the Salon. In 1872 Zola defined her talent and her limits with wit : " *Indolence...,* a virgin fallen from a stained glass window who has been painted by a naturalist artist of our time. " She painted chiefly scenes of feminine intimacy and after 1880 many small pictures, landscapes or seascapes. She worked in pastel. In 1879 she married the painter Henri Guérard. She died of an embolism on May 5, 1883, a few days before Manet.

GUIGOU, *Paul.*

Born February 15, 1834 at Villars, near Apt (Vaucluse), he began as a notary's clerk, but also took up painting on the advice of the Marseilles painter Loubon. He painted many landscapes and took part in exhibitions organized in Marseilles. In 1860 he settled in Paris where he exhibited at the Salon from 1863 onwards. He shared his time and his work between the Ile-de-France and the country of his birth, over which he traveled, his bag on his back, in the company of Monticelli. After the war his situation seemed to be improving when he suddenly died of a congestion of the brain, December 21, 1871 in Paris.

GUILLAUMIN, *Armand.*

Born in Paris, February 15, 1841, he studied drawing while earning his living as an employee at a hat factory. From 1860 onwards he spent his leisure from work as a railway official painting in the open air. In 1863 he worked at the *Académie Suisse* where he met Cézanne and Pissarro. He took part in the gatherings at the Café Guerbois and exhibited at the Salon des Refusés. After leaving his job, he painted window-blinds in the company of Pissarro in order to earn a living. Then he entered the service of the Roads and Bridges department of the City of Paris. Closely associated with the majority of the Impressionists he was none the less unacceptable to some of them, like Degas and Monet, who had little admiration for his art. He chiefly painted landscapes on the outskirts of Paris. In 1892 he had the luck to win a sum of a hundred thousand francs on the lottery of the Crédit Foncier and left his job in order to devote himself entirely to painting. He stayed at Saint-Palais-sur-Mer, on the Côte d'Azur, in the Auvergne and in the Haute-Loire. In 1904 he went to paint in Holland, near Saardam, then he settled at Crozant in the Creuse. He died on June 26, 1927 at the Château de Grignon at Orly (Seine). He took part in the Impressionist Exhibitions of 1874, 1877, 1880, 1881, 1882 and 1886.

JONGKIND, *Johann-Barthold.*

Born at Latrop in Holland, June 3, 1819, he followed the lectures at the Academy of the Hague where the landscapist Schelfhout was his first master. Pensioned by the king of Holland, he left in 1843 for Paris where the painter Isabey gave him advice and sought to get him away from the bohemian existence he was leading. He took him to Normandy where the young man painted many landscapes which won him appreciable successes at the Salon but his taste for debauchery often interfered with his work. From 1854 onwards he painted a series of " Views " of Paris; then in order to break away from a life of wretchedness he returned to Holland. He worked there a great deal before coming back to France in 1857. In August 1861, after a fresh stay in Rotterdam he settled in Nivernais, then in Normandy where he painted chiefly at Honfleur. From 1873 onwards, Jongkind decided to seek new subjects for his inspiration and went to work in the Dauphiné where he established himself at the Côte Saint-André in 1878. There he spent the last years of his life, interrupted by several journeys; but his health was undermined by alcoholism and slowly degenerated. Crises of madness caused him to be put away in a Grenoble asylum, where he died on February 9, 1891. Though he never adhered to the Impressionist group and did not exhibit with them, Jongkind nonetheless had a decisive influence on several of them, and on Boudin and Monet in particular.

HAAN, *Isaac MEYER de.*

Born in Amsterdam, April 14, 1852, he started work painting in an academic manner but was captivated by Impressionism. In London he got to know Pissarro who put him in contact with Gauguin. After this, he followed the latter to Pont-Aven, to le Pouldu and painted under his influence, but his family prevented him from accompanying him to Oceania. He died in Holland on October 24, 1895.

LEBOURG, Albert.

Born at Montfort-sur-Risle (Eure), February 2, 1849, he began as an architect's clerk in Rouen, while studying drawing with the painter Victor Delamare. In October 1872 the Algiers collector Laperlier brought him to Algiers as a teacher at the municipal school of drawing. On his return to France in 1877, he discovered Impressionism. He associated chiefly with Monet, Pissarro and Degas and painted in Paris, in Rouen, in Eure and from 1884 onwards in Auvergne at Pont-du-Château (Allier). Two years later he painted many landscapes of the outskirts of Paris. He traveled to Holland (1895-1897), to London (1900) and to Switzerland. During the war he worked in la Manche and later in Auvergne. He died in Rouen on January 6th 1928. He took part in the Impressionist Exhibitions of 1879 and 1880.

LÉPINE, Stanislas.

Born, October 3, 1835 in Caen; despite his industry he was impoverished in youth. A pupil of Corot, he succeeded in exploiting his deep feeling for nature. The chief theme of his work is Paris, its quays and most picturesque corners. He exhibited at the Salon from 1859 onwards. With the help of Count Doria, at whose home in the Château d'Orrouy he went to paint, he led a solitary life until his death in Paris on September 28, 1892. He took part in the first Impressionist Exhibition of 1874.

LOISEAU, Gustave.

Born in Paris, October 3, 1865, he worked at Pont-Aven beside Gauguin and then adopted the Post-Impressionist technique to which he adapted a so-called " trellis-work " style. He exhibited at the Salon de la Nationale and the Salon des Indépendants. A great traveler, he painted chiefly in Normandy, at Mortain, at Dieppe, at Marly-le-Roi and in the Dordogne and left behind him many views of Paris. He died in 1935.

LUCE, Maximilien.

Born in Paris, March 13, 1858. A pupil of Carolus Duran, he also entered the Gobelins school of drawing, but was largely self-taught, working from nature. His friendship with Pissarro gave his art a very definite direction. He painted not only landscapes but compositions in which he exalts men at work : navvies, dockers, quarrymen, masons, etc., which won him the nickname of " the Steinlen of Impressionism." With Signac, he is one of the founders of the Neo-Impressionist school. From 1888 onwards he exhibited at the Salon des Indépendants. A vigorous lithographer, he illustrated Mazas by Jules Vallès and collaborated with radical newspapers in which he supported the struggle of the working classes with his lithographic chalk. He worked a great deal in Holland, in Brittany and at Rolleboise in the Ile-de-France. For a long time he was solitary and lived remote from the world of art but enjoyed a sudden popularity between 1927-1930. He died in Paris, February 6, 1941.

MAILLAUD, Fernand.

Born at Mouhet (Indre), December 12, 1862, a pupil of Humbert and Wallet, he exhibited at the Salon from 1896 onwards and there won many awards. He also exhibited at the Salon des Indépendants and at the Salon d'Automne. He painted chiefly rural scenes, landscapes of Berry or Limousin, he executed mural decorations (Paris Hôtel de Ville, Préfecture de Police; Église du Sacré-Cœur, Issoudun) and produced cartoons for tapestry. He died in Paris in September 1948.

MANET, Édouard.

Born in Paris, January 23, 1832 into a prominent upper middle-class family of magistrates. He decided first of all to become a sailor and then, in 1850, renounced his vocation in order to enter the studio of the painter Couture where he remained for more than six years. But his real education took place in the galleries of Italy, Germany and Holland and at the Louvre where he copied numerous paintings. Although he had not yet been to Spain, he was greatly influenced in his early years by the masters of the Peninsular, notably Velazquez and Goya. In 1863, Le Déjeuner sur l'herbe (Louvre) caused a scandal at the Salon des Refusés. In 1864 he painted at Boulogne-sur-Mer; his works, of a realism which was considered outrageous, shocked the public and Olympia (Louvre) caused a fresh scandal at the Salon of 1865. Manet was the subject of passionate controversies which split the press and public opinion; he was defended by Théodore Duret and Zola and the young painters considered him to be the uncontested leader of the " innovators." He stayed in Spain in 1865. The Fifer (Louvre) having been refused at the Salon of 1866, he decided to exhibit his canvases the following year in a hut in the rue de l'Alma, opposite Courbet's. The Salon of 1868 welcomed his *Young Woman with a Parrot* and the *Portrait of Émile Zola* (Louvre), and that of 1869 *The Balcony*, inspired, as usual, by Spain. At the Salon of 1870 a canvas by Fantin-Latour, *The Studio in Batignolles* (Louvre) shows Manet surrounded by his friends and disciples; his ascendancy over the founders of Impressionism was always greater than his influence, which remained limited. A staff officer of the Garde Nationale in 1870, he rejoined his family at Oloron-Sainte-Marie after the war and then painted landscapes in Bordeaux and Arcachon. In 1874 he spent several weeks in Argenteuil with Monet, under whose influence he came; his palette grew brighter but he refused to take part in the Impressionist Exhibitions. He then worked in Venice. His canvases, sometimes accepted and sometimes rejected by the Salon, emanated more and more from the atmosphere and the spirit of naturalist literature; following the example of Degas, Manet deliberately turned his attention towards street scenes and scenes of Parisian life. At the Salon of 1879 he exhibited a portrait entitled *In the Hothouse*, and *Boating*, a scene of rowers painted five years earlier. Stricken with ataxy in 1880, he stayed at Bellevue, Versailles and then Rueil, where he painted gardens and pastel-portraits which alternate with compositions of contemporary inspiration. Still faithful to the Salon he exhibited *Le Bar des Folies-Bergère* (Courtauld Collection, London) there in 1882. He fell seriously ill in the following year and died on April 30, 1883.

MARTIN, Henri.

Born in Toulouse, August 5, 1860 he entered the studio of J.-P. Laurens in 1879 and exhibited at the Salon in the following year. His first success was a large composition, *Francesca di Rimini* (Carcassonne Museum). In 1895 he received a traveling scholarship to Italy which had a happy influence upon his development. He adopted the Pointillist technique which he applied to important mural decorations at the Sorbonne, the Conseil d'État, the Paris Hôtel de Ville, the Toulouse Capitol, etc. He received many official rewards and was elected to the Academy in 1918. He retired to Labastide-du-Vert in the Tarn and died there in November 1943, aged eighty-three.

MAUFRA, Maxime.

Born in Nantes, May 17, 1861, he began to paint about 1880. His father put him in a Liverpool business house, and he continued to work from nature, chiefly in Scotland. On his return to France in 1883, he associated with the painter from Nantes, Flornoy, with Charles Le Roux and the sculptor, Le Bourg, who persuaded his father to let him follow his inclination and paint. He sent *Deep Sea fishing Boat* and *Flood at Nantes* to the Salon of 1886, which inspired an article in praise of them by Octave Mirbeau. In 1890 Maufra made the acquaintance of Gauguin and Sérusier at Pont-Aven. They had little influence on him but became his friends. Being of an independent character and desiring to give himself neither to Impressionism nor to Synthetism, he settled in Montmartre, but continued to work in Brittany and Normandy. He held an important exhibition in 1895 at Le Barc de Boutteville's gallery then Durand-Ruel developed an active interest in him. He painted many landscapes and views of Paris. In 1900 he dedicated a series of paintings to the church of Saint-Séverin. From 1912 onwards he painted in the south of France before returning to Brittany during the war. He died at Ponce in Sarthe on May 23, 1918.

MIGNON, Lucien.

Born at Château-Gontier, September 13, 1865, he began his art studies in Angers before entering Gérôme's studio at the École des Beaux-Arts. The friendship of Renoir, whose companion he was to become at Cagnes, influenced the direction his work took. His principal achievements are the great mural decorations, chiefly at the ministry of Public Works. He exhibited at the Salon des Indépendants and the Nationale. He died in Paris, March 13, 1944.

MONET, Claude.

Born in Paris, November 14, 1840, he spent his childhood in Le Havre, where at the age of seventeen he was receiving advice from Boudin. In 1857 he came to Paris where he worked at the *Académie Suisse* in the company of Pissarro. After performing his military service in Algeria, he returned to France and made the acquaintance of Renoir, Bazille and Sisley at Gleyre's studio. Not long after, he left it in their company in order to work in the open air. In 1862 the Manet exhibition came as a revelation to the young painter. His first success was at the Salon in 1865. From 1864 to 1870 he painted on the coast of Normandy where he tried to render the vibrations of the atmosphere in a series of little rapid touches. The influence of Manet led him to work on outdoor compositions with figures, like *Le Déjeuner sur l'herbe* (Louvre), painted in 1865 at Chailly-en-Bière and strongly criticized by Courbet. In the same vein of inspiration Monet painted *Camille* or the *Lady with the green Dress* (Bremen Museum), exhibited at the Salon of 1866 and *Women in a Garden* (Louvre). At that time his life was extremely squalid and he even contemplated suicide. In 1869 he set himself up near Bougival, then at Argenteuil, but he left France on the declaration of war and took refuge in London where he made the acquaintance of Durand-Ruel who helped him and took an interest in his work. From 1872 to 1878 he painted river subjects or landscapes at Argenteuil and took part in the first Impressionist Exhibition to which his picture, *Impression, Sunrise* (Musée Marmottan) gave its title. Concerned with capturing the incidence of light, he scarcely left the banks of the Seine up to 1881 : then he went to paint in Normandy. In April 1883 he settled at Giverny in Eure where he was to remain until the end of his life and where his garden was to serve as the setting for his *Water Lilies*. In December he followed Renoir to the shores of the Mediterranean where he was to return in 1888. In 1886 he made a short stay in the Hague and in 1889 he painted in the Creuse where he found different subjects to inspire him. His reputation began to be established and the exhibition he held with Rodin in 1889 confirmed the place which he held amongst the innovators. At this point he began to embark upon his various " series " : *The Haystacks* (1890-1891), *The Poplars on the Banks of the Epte* (1891-1892), *Rouen Cathedral* (1892-1894). In 1895 he went to Norway, then after a stay in Normandy, he went to paint in London and finally in Venice in 1904, always in search of " effects " of light whose transparency and variety he tried to capture. After the war of 1914 his sight grew weaker and he devoted himself almost entirely to the subject of the *Water Lilies*. He died at Giverny on December 6, 1926. Monet took part in the Impressionist Exhibitions of 1874, 1876, 1877, 1879 and 1882.

MONTICELLI, Adolphe.

Born in Marseilles, October 14, 1824, of an unknown father and mother. His parents were in reality Thomas Monticelli and Clarisse Bertrand who after their marriage on September 29, 1835 acknowledged him. He spent his childhood with some peasants at Ganagobie in Haute-Durance, then went to school at the Pensionnat Rey in Marseilles and at the lycée in the same town. In 1842 apprenticed to a pharmacist, he attended drawing classes at the School of Fine Arts under the direction of Augustin Aubert and copied paintings in the Marseilles Museum. In 1846 he entered the studio of Paul Delaroche in Paris. From 1849 to 1856 he traveled in Auvergne and Languedoc, selling his canvases to earn a living. On his return to Paris he made the acquaintance of Diaz who influenced him. From 1862 to 1870 he live at Batignolles and was commissioned in 1865 to paint a mural for the Tuileries. Exploited by the dealers, he lived in poverty. In 1868 Lille Museum bought two pictures from him. After the war he returned to Provence on foot, earning his living by painting. He used to visit Cézanne there. In Marseilles where he went regularly to the Opera, he painted many canvases inspired by Gounod's *Faust* or by the Italian comedy, portraits (*The Fortune Teller*, Lyons Museum), landscapes and flower paintings, among them *Still life with the white Jug* (Louvre). Stricken with hemiplegia in 1885, he died in Marseilles, June 29, 1886.

MORET, Henry.

Born in Cherbourg, December 21, 1856, he first worked with Jean-Paul Laurens and exhibited at the Salon of 1880 before turning to open air painting. He met Gauguin at Pont-Aven and became associated with him. Very much in love with Britanny he was inspired by the most diverse sites there. One can discern the influence of Monet in his interpretation of the sea. He exhibited chiefly at the Salon des Indépendants. He died in Paris May 5, 1913.

MORISOT, Berthe.

Born January 14, 1841 in Bourges where her father was the Prefect. In 1856 she received her first art lessons from the Lyons painter, Guichard and, with her sister, copied many paintings at the Louvre, where they met Fantin-Latour and later Manet. Guichard introduced them to Corot who became one of their friends. In 1863 Berthe Morisot painted her first landscapes at Auvers-sur-Oise and in the following year exhibited at the Salon. In 1868 she posed for *The Balcony* (Louvre) by Manet, who influenced her a great deal. In 1872 she made a journey to Spain. Drawn towards the Impressionist movement by Manet and Degas she took part in its exhibitions in 1874, 1876, 1877, 1880, 1881, 1882 and 1886. On December 12, 1874, she married Eugène Manet, the brother of the painter and in the following year joined Renoir, Monet and Sisley for the sale of their paintings at the Hôtel Drouot on May 24th. Her daughter was born in 1868. Berthe Morisot made several journeys : to Italy in 1882, to Belgium and Holland in 1885, to Jersey in 1886. She spent the winter at Nice and the summer at Bougival or at Mézy near Meulan, where Renoir, who had a very definite influence over her often came to paint. Eugène Manet died in 1892. The following year she went to stay with Mallarmé at Valvins. In 1894 she was in Brussels where she exhibited at "La Libre Esthétique", and then traveled to Brittany. She died in Paris, March 2, 1895.

MUGUET, Antoine.

Born at Thizy (Rhône) on August 1873. A chemist by profession, he painted and came to Paris where he was captivated by Impressionism and by Signac, with whom he became associated and who induced him to exhibit at the Salon des Indépendants. He died in Paris on May 19, 1954.

NITTIS, Giuseppe de.

Born at Barletta in Italy in 1846, he joined the Academy of Fine Arts in Naples and was expelled for indiscipline. He then came to Paris in 1868 where he joined the École des Beaux-Arts in Gérome's studio. The following year he exhibited two canvases at the Salon and from then continued on to take part in the artistic manifestations of Paris. He was closely associated with Degas who invited him to take part in the first of the Impressionists' Exhibitions to counterbalance, with other realist painters like himself, the contribution of the "pleinairistes." His canvases mostly represent street scenes painted in London or in Paris and portraits whose elegance was greatly prized by fashionable society. He died at Saint-Germain-en-Laye in 1884. He only took part in the first Impressionist Exhibition in 1874.

OTTIN, Auguste.

Born in Paris, November 11, 1811, a sculptor, the pupil of David d'Angers, he took his place beside his son, Léon-Auguste, a pupil of Delaroche, at the first Impressionist Exhibition with one canvas : La Butte Montmartre. He died in 1890. Léon-Auguste Ottin, a genre and portrait painter and glass painter, exhibited at the Salon from 1861 to 1880 and featured at the Impressionist Exhibitions of 1874 and 1876.

PETITJEAN, Hippolyte.

Born at Mâcon in 1854, he entered Cabanel's studio in 1872 but underwent the influence of Puvis de Chavannes and then worked for the architect-decorator, Motte. In 1884 he met Seurat and became associated with him and adopted the Divisionist technique. He exhibited at the Salon des Indépendants in 1891. Some years later he was appointed drawing master in a Paris École communale. He died in Paris on September 18, 1929.

PIETTE, Ludovic.

Born at Niort, May 11, 1826, a pupil of Couture and Pils, he met Manet at Couture's studio and came under his influence. In 1875 he exhibited at the Salon. His work consists of landscapes, scenes of country life and genre paintings. The Kaiser Wilhelm I bought from him The Appearance of the Witches before Macbeth which was kept in Berlin at the castle of Sans-Souci. He frequently signed his works with his name allied to that of his country house, Montfoucault, where he frequently received Pissarro. His canvases featured in the Impressionist Exhibitions of 1877, the same year as his death, and 1879.

PISSARRO, Camille.

Born on Saint-Thomas, a Danish island of the Antilles, July 10, 1830, he went to school in Paris. In 1847 he returned to Saint-Thomas and entered a business house, but wanted above all to give himself up to painting. His father agreed and he returned to France and entered the studio of Anton Melbye in 1855, at the same time as he was receiving the advice of Corot. In 1857 he met Monet at the Académie Suisse. The pictures he submitted to the Salon were accepted from 1859 to 1870, except in 1861 and 1863. He exhibited at the Salon des Refusés in 1863 and worked at Montfoucault (Mayenne) at the house of his friend, Piette, then at Pontoise where he lived. In 1870 he joined Monet who had fled to London. On his return to France he took part in the Impressionist movement, the technique of which he propagated amongst his friends, Cézanne in particular. He painted chiefly landscapes or scenes of country life. Pissarro had a hard struggle and was obliged to take various jobs to earn a living. About 1881 he evolved towards a constructive representation of nature; his art became more synthetic. From 1884 onwards, he exhibited at the Salon des Indépendants and took his stand amongst the Neo-Impressionists, but his Divisionist period did not last long and he returned to the Impressionist technique. Reputation came to him with the retrospective exhibition which Durand-Ruel devoted to him in 1892. He settled at Éragny near Gisors in Eure, then traveled to London before returning to Paris and undertaking his series of bird's-eye views of streets which was followed by several series based on the bridges of Rouen. Little by little he substituted townscapes for landscapes. In 1901 he was at Moret, in Dieppe where he painted a series of canvases on the theme of the Church of

178

Saint-Jacques, next at Le Havre, interrupting his journeys with stays in Paris and Éragny. His sight was weakened by illness and he died on November 13, 1903. Pissarro participated in all the Impressionist Exhibitions.

PISSARRO, Lucien.

Born in Paris, February 20, 1863, the son of Camille Pissaro, he exhibited very young with the Impressionists at their final manifestation of 1886 and then from 1888 to 1894 at the Salon des Indépendants. In 1893 he settled in England and took part in numerous exhibitions in London, Birmingham, Bradford and Manchester and in the United States. A publisher and printer in a house in Éragny, he illustrated with colored engravings the thirty-two volumes of the *Eragny Press* which he had founded. His landscapes spring from the " earthy " vein of his father. He became a naturalized British subject in 1916 and was shown at the Venice Biennale of 1928. He died at Hewood, South Chard, Som. in 1944.

PUVIS DE CHAVANNES, Pierre.

Born in Lyon, December 14, 1824, he was studying to enter the École Polytechnique when a serious illness obliged him to withdraw from the competition. It was during his stay in Italy where he had gone to convalesce that he first realized his vocation. The example of the masters of the Renaissance guided his first works. On his return to France he entered the studio of Delacroix; then, when the latter gave up teaching, he joined that of Couture, where he only remained a year. He then set up in the Place Pigalle and worked alone. In 1856 at Chassériau's he met the woman who was his principal inspiration, the Princess Cantacuzène, whom he was to marry in 1897. His early works, influenced by his first admirations, are of literary or religious inspiration. They led him on to the great mural which he began in 1867 and which brought him success, whereas he had previously experienced many rebuffs at the Salon. From then on he did not cease work in response to the innumerable commissions which he was given : Musée de Picardie in Amiens, Palais de Longchamp in Marseilles, Poitiers *mairie*, the Panthéon, the Palais des Beaux-Arts in Lyons, the great amphitheatre of the Sorbonne, Rouen Museum, the Paris Hôtel de Ville, the Boston Museum of Art, etc. Greatly affected by the death of his wife in 1898, he died two months after her on October 24th, in Paris.

RAFFAELLI, Jean-François.

Born in Paris, April 20 1850, he began life as an actor and lyric singer, then entered Gérôme's studio and first exhibited at the Salon of 1870. He painted genre pictures before devoting himself to compositions inspired by the sights of the Paris streets and then to scenes of middle-class life. He made many etchings on the same subjects and illustrated books among them, in collaboration with Forain, the *Croquis Parisiens* of Huysmans. He received the Gold Medal at the Salon in 1889. Raffaëlli took part in the Impressionist Exhibitions of 1880 and 1881.

REDON, Odilon.

Born in Bordeaux, April 22, 1840, where he spent his childhood and later produced his first works of art. In 1863-1865 he met the engraver, Rodolphe Bresdin and came under his influence before entering Gérôme's studio at the École des Beaux-Arts. Shortly after this, he became associated with Corot, Chintreuil and Fromentin. After the war he settled in Paris for good and in 1875 he worked on landscapes in the Forest of Fontainebleau and in Brittany. He traveled in Holland in 1878 and in the following year he published his first album of lithographs, *Dans le Rêve*. In 1881 he exhibited his charcoal drawings at the *Vie Moderne* and in 1882 at the *Gaulois*. In 1883 Redon published the album, *Les Origines* and in 1884 took part in the first Salon des Indépendants. Successive albums were published : *Hommage à Goya* (1885), *La Nuit* (1886), *La Tentation de Saint Antoine*, first series (1888), *A Gustave Flaubert* (1889), *Les Fleurs du Mal* (1890), *Songes* (1891), *La Maison Hantée* and *La Tentation de Saint Antoine*, second series (1896), and finally *L'Apocalypse* (1899). He became associated with Mallarmé, Huysmans, Valéry, Gide, etc. In 1891 *L'Œuvre lithographique d'Odilon Redon* appeared in Brussels. He traveled to London in 1895, to Italy in 1900 and 1908, to Switzerland and to Holland. Redon's work is Symbolist in inspiration and has many aspects; he was a painter, a draftsman, a pastel artist (there is an important series of " bouquets " in this medium). In 1899 Durand-Ruel organized an exhibition of young painters as a homage to Redon. In 1901-1902 Redon painted murals at the house of Ernest Chausson, in Paris, at the Château de Domecy and in 1910 at the Abbey of Fontfroide (Aude). In 1913 he took part in the International Exhibition in New York. He died in Paris on July 16, 1916. He took part in the Impressionist Exhibition of 1886. Odilon left his " diary " under the title of " A Soi-Même. "

RENOIR, Auguste.

Born on February 25, 1841 at Limoges. His family left there for Paris soon after his birth. He entered a porcelain factory while still very young and often visited the Louvre. He then worked in Gleyre's studio before attending the drawing classes at the École des Beaux-Arts from 1862 to 1864. He became associated with Cézanne, Pissarro, Monet and Sisley. He exhibited at the Salon from 1864 onwards but frequently had pictures refused there. After the war he settled in Argenteuil where his development towards clear painting and light under the influence of Monet became more defined. He took an active part in the preparation of the Impressionist Exhibitions. In 1876 he painted *Le Moulin de la Galette* (Louvre). He was a regular attender at the salon of the publisher Charpentier, who commissioned him to paint the portrait of his wife and children which was hung at the Salon of 1879. He stayed at Wargemont in Normandy with his friend, the collector Paul Bérard, then traveled in Algeria in March and April 1881. In the autumn he was in Italy where the Raphaels filled him with enthusiasm. He painted *Luncheon of the Boating Party* (Philips Collection Washington). In February 1882 he was with Cézanne at l'Estaque. 1883 marks the start of the " severe period " which contrasts with the feathery style of the preceding years. Renoir was after a style that was more linear and more " compact. " From 1885 until 1887 he painted his series of *Grandes Baigneuses*. In 1888 he began to suffer from attacks of rheumatism. He stayed with Cézanne on several occasions and decided to paint as much as possible in the south of France. In 1892 he made a journey to Spain; then in 1895 to London and Holland. He set himself up in Montmartre at the " Château des Brouillards "; in 1898 he bought a house at Essoyes (Aube), the country his wife came from, where he was to go every summer. His health obliged him to spend the winter on the Côte d'Azur. He worked there a great deal and painted many pictures inspired by his youngest son, Claude, nicknamed " Coco. " Increasing pain hampered his work. He bought " Les Collettes " at Cagnes. In 1910 he went to Munich to the house of his friends, the Thurneyssens. In 1913 forty-two of his canvases were assembled at an important exhibition at Bernheim's gallery. Almost completely paralyzed, he continued painting, despite everything, until his last breath. He died at Cagnes on December 3, 1919. He took part in the Impressionist Exhibitions of 1874, 1876, 1877 and 1882.

ROPS, Félicien.

Born in Namur (Belgium), July 7, 1833, he began drawing and engraving on his own and enjoyed considerable success while still quite young. With his friends Constantin Meunier Charles de Groux, Louis Dubois and Charles de Coster he founded a group called the " Atelier Saint-Luc, " and worked now at his property of Thorée in Wallonia (Belgium), now at Campine or in the Ardennes. He collaborated as a humorist artist on the satirical magazine *Crocodile* before founding his own sheet, *Uylenspiegel* (the Imp) in which he published many landscapes and scenes of Brussels life. In 1861 he made the acquaintance of Courbet who encouraged him. In the following year he found himself in Paris where he perfected his etching technique. From now on he shared his life between this city and Brussels, where he met Baudelaire in 1868. His etchings, romantic in inspiration at first, are surprising for their erotic or macabre inspiration which accentuates their evolution towards the naturalism which was then fashionable. Rops did not abandon painting and produced many landscapes and genre scenes influenced by Corot and Boudin. He was closely associated with numerous writers : Péladan, Huysmans, Camille Lemonnier, Mirbeau, Demolder, etc. He died at Essonnes, near Corbeil, on August 22, 1898.

ROUART, Henri.

Born in Paris in October 1833 into a family of wealthy industrialists, he studied for the École Polytechnique while taking an interest in painting both as a collector and as a painter. He received advice from Corot and Millet. Closely associated with Degas, he collected an important number of his oils and pastels and exhibited at the first Impressionist Exhibition after appearing at the Salon from 1868 to 1872. His collection included works by Brueghel, Poussin, Fragonard, Goya, Tiepolo, Delacroix, Courbet, Daumier, Manet, Renoir, Toulouse-Lautrec, Gauguin, etc. He died in Paris on January 2, 1912. He took part in the Impressionist Exhibitions of 1874, 1876, 1877, 1879, 1880, 1881 and 1886.

VAN RYSSELBERGHE, Théo.

Born in Ghent, November 23, 1862 into a family of architects, he had his art training in his native town and then in Brussels. His meeting with Seurat helped him to evolve from the Impressionism of his youth towards the Neo-Impressionist technique, softening its dogmatism in street scenes, nudes and landscapes. Associated with the Belgian and French Symbolist circles, he mixed with Maeterlinck, Viélé-Griffin, Félix Fénéon, Verhaeren, Gide, etc., whom he grouped together in a large composition called *The Reading* (Ghent Museum). He exhibited with the " Vie et Lumière " group. Captivated by the light of the Mediterranean, he settled in the south of France where he died at Saint-Clair (Var), December 13, 1926.

SCHUFFENECKER, Claude-Émile.

Born at Fresne-Saint-Mamès (Haute-Saône), December 8, 1851, he exhibited at the Salon from 1874 onwards; he was one of the founders of the Salon des Indépendants in 1884. He was at first a pupil of Paul Baudry and Carolus Duran but abandoned academic technique when he met Gauguin whose friend he became. He also became associated with Pissarro and Seurat. He died in Paris in August 1934. He took part in the Impressionist Exhibition of 1886.

SÉRUSIER, Paul.

Born in Paris in 1865 and intended for a career in commerce he was accepted for the *Académie Jullian* when he left school. He exhibited at the Salon of 1887 but in 1888 Gauguin, whom he met at Pont-Aven at the Pension Gloanec, converted him to " Symbolist and Synthetist " painting. He then created the group of the " Nabis " (the " prophets " in Hebrew) which included Ranson, Maurice Denis, Bonnard, Ibels, Piot, Roussel, Vuillard. He himself was the " Nabi with the bright red beard. " He took part in the first exhibition of the Nabis at the Galerie Le Barc de Boutteville in 1891 and worked at Pont-Aven. An extremely cultivated man who studied philosophy and theology, Sérusier was the theoretician of the group. His art was as much influenced by Gauguin as by Symbolist literature. He was closely associated with Maeterlinck and Claudel. His journeys to Italy in 1893 and 1899 and his visits to the convent of Beuron, where the painter Jean Verkade lived, who had become a monk, led him towards a more severe art, founded on the " sacred proportions " and the golden section. He set out his theories in a book : *L'A.B.C. de la peinture*, which appeared in 1921. He died at Morlaix, October 6, 1927.

SEURAT, Georges.

Born in Paris, December 2, 1859 he first worked at the municipal school of drawing before entering the studio of Henri Lehmann, a pupil of Ingres at the École des Beaux-Arts. After twelve months of voluntary service at Brest he returned to Paris in 1880 and studied Ingres, Delacroix and Veronese. At the same time he became intoxicated with the theories of color and light of Chevreul, Edouard Rood and Charles Henry. Up to 1884 he devoted himself almost exclusively to drawing and exhibited *Bathing at Asnières*, (Tate Gallery, London), which was rejected by the Salon, at the first

exhibition of the Salon des Indépendants, December 10, 1884. He painted his first seascapes at Grandcamp, near Le Havre, where he was to work often as well as at Crotoy and Gravelines. From 1885 onwards Seurat, whom Signac had introduced to Pissarro and the Impressionists, practiced Divisionism and Pointillism, and the term of Neo-Impressionism was invented to describe him and his disciples in 1886. *La Grande Jatte* (Art Institute, Chicago) painted in 1886, is the illustration of this new aesthetic which met with little public approval. From 1889 onwards his art became more and more cerebral. Seurat painted landscapes, notably sea scenes on the Channel coast and then the *Woman powdering herself* (Courtauld Institute, London) and *Le Chahut*, exhibited at the Salon des Indépendants in 1890. Undermined by hard work, he was unable to resist an infectious quinsy which killed him on March 29, 1891 at the age of thirty-one, leaving unfinished his painting, *The Circus* (Louvre, Paris). He took part in the Impressionist Exhibition of 1886.

SIGNAC, Paul.

Born in Paris on November 11, 1863, he exhibited for the first time at the Salon des Indépendants of 1884 of which he was one of the founders. He began as a portrait painter but subsequently devoted himself almost exclusively to landscape to which he applied the Pointillist technique derived from the Divisionism of Seurat. He set out his theories in a book entitled *D'Eugène Delacroix au Néo-Impressionnisme*. He traveled a great deal and painted numerous series some in oils, some in water color : La Rochelle, Saint-Raphaël, Antibes, Venice, Constantinople. He painted a large mural composition at the Maison du Peuple in Brussels : *In the days of Harmony*. A fine man of letters he published studies on Jongkind, Stendhal, etc. He took part in the *Salon des Indépendants* (of which he was to remain president until his death), in the Brussels *Salons des XX* (1890-1893) and that of *La Libre Esthétique* (1894-1913). He died in Paris on August 15, 1935. He took part in the Impressionist Exhibition of 1886.

SISLEY, Alfred.

Born in Paris, October 30, 1839 of English parents, he spent a part of his youth in Great Britain; then in 1862 he entered Gleyre's studio where he met Monet, Bazille and Renoir. He worked in the open air in their company in the tradition of Corot and Courbet. In 1866 he exhibited two canvases at the Salon, one of them being *The Chestnut Avenue at La Celle-Saint-Cloud* (Musée des Beaux-Arts de la Ville de Paris). In 1867 he painted at Honfleur and subsequently after the war, during which he took refuge in London, at Argenteuil, Louveciennes, Argenteuil, Marly-le-Roi, Bougival. With a change in his financial situation, he led a life of recurrent poverty, selling his works with difficulty at trifling prices. Nevertheless he did not tire of painting the scenes of the Ile-de-France which were particularly close to his heart. From 1883-1884 onwards Sisley worked at Moret-sur-Loing. He exhibited quite regularly at the Salon de la Nationale. The influence of Monet guided him towards a greater and greater systematization. Alone of all his Impressionist friends he achieved neither fortune nor success. He contracted a cancer of the throat and died at Moret on January 29, 1899. He took part in the Impressionist Exhibitions of 1874, 1876, 1877 and 1882.

SOMM, Henry.

His real name was François-Clément Sommier; he was born in Rouen in 1844. He enjoyed a great reputation above all as a satirical draftsman, and illustrating damaged his career as a painter. His water colors, executed swiftly, are the best of his work. He died in Paris on March 15, 1907. He took part in the Impressionist Exhibition of 1879.

TILLOT, Charles-Victor.

Born in Rouen in 1825, he worked first of all under the direction of Ary Scheffer and Théodore Rousseau and first exhibited at the Salon in 1846. He became associated with Degas who introduced him to the Impressionist group. He took part in the exhibitions of 1876, 1877, 1879, 1880, 1881 and 1886.

TOULOUSE-LAUTREC, Henri de.

Born at Albi, November 24, 1864, his poor physical constitution was aggravated by two successive accidents. In 1878 and 1879 he broke both hips. His growth was arrested and he was to remain deformed. During the periods of immobility resulting from his falls he devoted himself to painting. He stayed at the Château du Bosc, near Albi, at Nice, at Barèges, at the Château de Malromé in Médoc. In 1882 he entered first Bonnat's studio, then Cormon's. In his first paintings — of horses, equestrian or military scenes and portraits — the influence of Bastien-Lepage and John Lewis-Brown can be felt. From 1884 onwards he frequented the dance halls and cabarets of Montmartre. He did mural decorations at the Auberge Ancelin in Villiers-sur-Morin and painted figures inspired by Suzanne Valadon who was then a model and also numerous por-

traits. From 1888 to 1892 he executed numerous compositions on the themes of Montmartre life, of which the principal types are Jane Avril, La Goulue and, 'Valentine the Boneless.' He painted *At the Moulin Rouge* (Chicago Art Institute) and in 1891 he composed his first poster destined for this establishment. From 1892 onwards the painter worked in brothels and executed his first lithographs in color. He collaborated on the *Revue Blanche* and in 1893 held his first exhibition at Boussod-Valadon's gallery. In 1895 he met Oscar Wilde whose portrait he painted. He painted two large compositions for La Goulue's booth at the Foire du Trône and finished *The Salon* (Albi Museum). In January 1896 he held an exhibition at the house of Manzi and Joyant and published an album of lithographs, *Elles*. His health began to deteriorate. In 1898 Lautrec illustrated *Les Histoires Naturelles* by Jules Renard and exhibited in London. At the end of February 1899 he was taken to a nursing home at Neuilly after a fit of delirium tremens. There he composed the thirty-nine drawings of *Le Cirque*. His health restored, he went to Le Crotoy and then Le Havre and stayed at Taussat near Arcachon. In September he was at the Château de Malromé, his mother's home. In the first months of 1901 he painted numerous portraits. He died at Malromé on September 9th, at the age of thirty-seven.

VIDAL, Eugène.

Born in Paris he first exhibited at the Salon of 1873. He received the bronze medal at the Exhibition of 1900 and died at Cagnes.

VIGNON, Victor.

Born at Villers-Cotterets (Aisne), December 25, 1847, he first received advice from Corot before painting from nature. His meeting with Pissarro and Cézanne drew him into the wake of the Impressionists and he painted many landscapes round Pontoise, Auvers-sur-Oise and Nesles-la-Vallée, his favorite places. An exhibition of his works in 1884 achieved a great success. He died at Meulan (Seine-et-Oise) in March 1909. He took part in the Impressionist Exhibitions of 1880, 1881, 1882 and 1886.

ZANDOMENEGHI, Frederigo.

Born in Venice, June 2, 1841. A pupil of his father, he arrived in Paris in 1874 and at once took part in the Impressionist movement. He was closely associated with Degas and chiefly painted landscapes and portraits. He died in Paris, December 30, 1917. He took part in the Impressionist Exhibitions of 1879, 1880, 1881 and 1886.

182

LIST OF ILLUSTRATIONS

183

BIBLIOGRAPHICAL NOTE

In *Les Archives de l'Impressionnisme* (2 vols, pub. Durand-Ruel, Paris, 1939) Signor Lionello Venturi has collected together the essential documents which consist of exhibition catalogs, artists' correspondence with Durand-Ruel, the Memoirs of Paul Durand-Ruel and contemporary criticism.

There is no lack of historical and critical studies on the Impressionists and their times, still less of monographs on individual artists.

The following is a selection : Germain BAZIN, *L'Epoque Impressionniste* (Tisné, Paris, 1947) which provides extremely full accounts and (second edition, 1953) a bibliography; John REWALD, *History of Impressionism* (Museum of Modern Art, New York, 1946; French edition, Albin Michel, Paris, 1950) and *Post-Impressionism : From Van Gogh to Gauguin* (Museum of Modern Art, New York, 1956); Jean LEYMARIE, *Impressionism* (2 vols, Skira, Geneva, 1955); Hélène ADHÉMAR, Maurice SÉRULLAZ, Michèle BEAULIEU, *Catalogue des peintures, pastels, sculptures impressionnistes du Musée du Louvre (Jeu de Paume)*, with a preface by Germain Bazin (Musées nationaux, Paris, 1958).

INDEX

186

CONTENTS